SCHLEIERMACHER: LIFE AND THOUGHT

by

MARTIN REDEKER

Translated by

JOHN WALLHAUSSER

Don Haynes
8/26/80

FORTRESS PRESS

Philadelphia

Translated from the German *Friedrich Schleiermacher, Leben und Werk*, published by Walter de Gruyter & Co., Berlin, 1968.

Library of Congress Catalog Card Number 72-91526
ISBN 0–8006–0149–1

CONTENTS

ABBREVIATIONS

S. W.   *Friedrich Schleiermachers sämmtliche Werke.* 31 vols. in
           three divisions: theological, homiletical,
           philosophical. Berlin: Reimer, 1835–1864.

Briefe   *Aus Schleiermachers Leben in Briefen.* 4 vols. Edited
           by Wilhelm Dilthey. Berlin: Reimer, 1858–1863.

Letters   *The Life of Schleiermacher as Unfolded in His Auto-
           biography and Letters.* English translation of the
           first two volumes of Dilthey's *Briefe* by Frederica
           Rowan. London: Smith, Elder and Co., 1860.

Reden   *Über die Religion: Reden an die Gebildeten unter ihren
           Verächtern.* Critical edition by G. C. B. Pünjer.
           Braunschweig: C. A. Schwetschke, 1879.

Speeches   *On Religion: Speeches to Its Cultured Despisers.* English
           translation of *Reden* by John Oman. London,
           1893. The Harper Torchbook edition (New York:
           Harper & Row, 1958) is based on Oman's trans-
           lation of the third edition; the pagination is the
           same in both books.

Monologen *Monologen nebst den Vorarbeiten.* Critical edition by
           F. M. Schiele. Leipzig: Dürr, 1902. Expanded
           by H. Mulert. Leipzig: Meiner, 1914.

Soliloquies *Schleiermacher's Soliloquies.* English translation of
           Monologen by H. L. Friess. Chicago: Open
           Court, 1926.

Denkmale   "Denkmale der inneren Entwicklung Schleiermachers."
           In Wilhelm Dilthey, *Leben Schleiermachers.*
           Berlin: Reimer, 1870. This appendix to Dilthey's
           Leben Schleiermachers consists of Schleiermacher's
           early essays and journals, and is found in the
           first edition only.

INTRODUCTION

"The philosophy of Kant can be understood fully without a further
concern for his life and character. Schleiermacher's significance,
outlook, and works require a biographical presentation in order to
be fully understood. Therefore, the desire for a biography of this
man, who is so significant and yet so difficult to interpret, has been
frequently expressed and repeated."[1] With these words, Wilhelm
Dilthey began the introduction to his biography of Schleiermacher.
Dilthey projected a comprehensive study of Schleiermacher's life
which would set him within the cultural and intellectual history of
the nineteenth century; but at the same time it would analyze and
illumine the development of Schleiermacher's own thought forms,
and allow his ideas and life to explain one another. However,
Dilthey's undertaking was not completed; it remained an extensive
but unfinished fragment.[2] The second volume, dealing with
Schleiermacher's system, was published posthumously. It is extremely regrettable that Dilthey could not complete the work himself
for he was in a unique position; he had at his disposal Schleiermacher's
entire literary remains, including his extensive correspondence, and
valuable information from friends of Schleiermacher who were still
alive.

Besides this large-scale undertaking by Dilthey, which has become
a model for attempting biography from the perspective of intellectual
history, only one other biography of Schleiermacher has appeared.
Written by D. Schenkel in a more popular vein, it was published in
1868 on the one hundredth anniversary of Schleiermacher's birth.
Hermann Mulert also wrote a brief sketch of the life of Schleiermacher
as a result of his study of Dilthey's literary remains; it was published
in 1918 in the *Religionsgeschichtliche Volksbücher*. It is astonishing
that until now no further more extensive biography of Schleiermacher
has appeared. Apparently Dilthey's vast undertaking and the

---

1. W. Dilthey, *Leben Schleiermachers*, vol. I, 1st ed. (Berlin, 1870); 2d ed., ed.
H. Mulert (Berlin, 1922).

2. Dilthey himself published a condensed version of Schleiermacher's entire
life in *Deutsche Biographie*, vol. 31, pp. 422–57. It was republished in
Dilthey, *Gesammelte Schriften*, vol. IV, pp. 454–89.

difficulty in obtaining the numerous sources have sapped Schleiermacher scholars of the courage to undertake a comprehensive interpretation.

It is no longer possible to write a biography of Schleiermacher in the manner of Dilthey or even Schenkel. We are separated from Dilthey by a criticism of Schleiermacher which was part of a rejection of liberal Protestantism. According to this critical view, the liberal Protestantism of the nineteenth century was the great "fall" of Protestant Christianity. In the condemnation of the three major streams flowing into liberal Protestantism — pietism, the Enlightenment, and idealism — Schleiermacher was included as chief offender. Furthermore, after decades of estrangement from German Idealistic philosophy, Schleiermacher's language is either misunderstood or else falsely interpreted, because for a long time we would not or could not listen to him.

In the meantime, this criticism of liberal Protestantism has itself run into difficulties. The great problems that arose with the advent of the so-called modern world, particularly those resulting from the reorientation of Western thought in transcendental philosophy, have again become acute with new force and in a new manner. This is especially so since the attempted solutions of transcendental philosophical thinkers can no longer help us today; we cannot again adopt them uncritically.

Schleiermacher's image as projected in the theology that was critical of liberal Protestantism is no longer sufficient; Schleiermacher is "different" and just for that reason he is relevant. He experienced the shock to Christian proclamation and certainty of faith resulting from the collapse of traditional notions of God and of the biblical mythology, and the erosion of traditional biblical and dogmatic authority. He was particularly concerned with the changes brought on by the devastation of supernaturalistic metaphysics in the wake of modern science and Kant's critical philosophy. Even so, he did not join the chorus of those who complained about the collapse of the older dogmatic, biblical-mythological outlook with its values and ideals. He was confident that the gospel would be rediscovered and authenticated in a new way. The outmoded philosophy of supernaturalist metaphysics as well as the moral philosophy of the Enlightenment must be "exchanged." However, a simple change is not enough. Philosophy itself can never prove or substantiate the gospel; it can only act as a resource for restating its meaning and truth. A change of vocabulary, however, is of only secondary importance, even if not every philosophy is an appropriate resource for Christian confession and witness. God and his revelation in Christ need to become newly experienced in faith. The destruction of the older religious concepts of a metaphysical and mythological kind is itself a unique challenge, a "right moment," a *kairos* for experiencing God's reality in Christ. In this way Schleiermacher is convinced one can rediscover the genuinely "religious" in religion and the genuinely "Christian" in Christendom.

A new Schleiermacher emerges from this perspective. He wanted to witness in a new way to the living relation with the Christ who is present in His community, and to relate this witness to the reality of God as he experienced it in its omnipotence and glory in the creaturely feeling of absolute dependence and in the positing of human existence through God.

The conceptual world of objective idealism, modified by both Schleiermacher's study of Kant and the Christian understanding of revelation, became his vehicle for expressing his praise of the glory of God in Christ. He reinterpreted the relationship between God and world and between God and the human self with the help of the idealistic conceptual world; in so doing he was faithful to the needs of his own day. He grasped the challenge set for him by his historical situation and saw it through successfully, insofar as one can claim this for any spokesman for the pilgrim character of all theology. At the same time, however, he moved beyond the bounds fixed in the world view of idealism.

His mastery of the conceptual modes of expression and thought during his own time should spur us on to seek with new courage and intrepidness an encounter between the Christian gospel and the prevailing conception of truth expressed in contemporary philosophy. Schleiermacher can give us the courage and show us the ways to witness to the truth of the gospel in our own day of major reorientation and to persevere in seeking dialogue with contemporary thought and understanding (*Weltweisheit*).

In the area of ethics, however, Schleiermacher did not leave behind such comprehensive and definitive statements as we find in the field of dogmatics, for example in his *The Christian Faith*. Nevertheless, even here the following should be noted. Schleiermacher sought to master the questions posed by modern culture from the point of view of the philosophical system of objective idealism as well as from the point of view of his theology of redemption. The philosophy of culture based on an idealistic, humanistic ethos and the theological presentation of the ethos of the kingdom of God complement and complete one another. The cultural ethics receives its refinement and completion in Schleiermacher's theology of redemption.

This development can be understood from the perspective of the intellectual history of that day. Dilthey's philosophy of culture is of great help for clarifying this philosophical achievement of Schleiermacher.

It is difficult for us today to think in terms of this philosophical ethics of culture and "humanity." Since Nietzsche, our own cultural consciousness has been shaken by the destruction which skepticism has worked on the ideal of humanity and by the danger of dehumanization that has appeared in the wake of the thoughtless "rationality" of modern technocracy. Theological ethics lacks precisely what Schleiermacher thought could be assumed, a humanistic ethics as a partner in dialogue. Consequently, we cannot be content with Schleiermacher's attempted solutions, bound as they are to the understanding of a previous cultural situation. The atheistic and thoughtless rationality of the contemporary life-style is simply not an authentic partner for dialogue with theological ethics. Lutheran theology and ethics are based on the dialectical tension between law and gospel. Accordingly, the difficulty for any real dialogue between Lutheran ethics and modern ethical thinking is compounded by contemporary skepticism. The Christian ethics of love and redemption needs a complementary ethic, for it claims to apply not only to believing Christians but universally to all men. On this issue Schleiermacher's achievement in ethics gains new relevance. To be sure, we cannot simply adopt and repeat his answer. But here as well as in the area of theology, Schleiermacher's conviction is applicable. There is no reason for Christians to join the alarmed cries of those who in the present historical and cultural upheaval announce the demise of the Christian faith, the Christian ethos, and humanity.

This biography will try to present a cultural and historical analysis of Schleiermacher's thinking with a view to illuminating the fundamental problems which reach beyond his day and still afflict us in new and different ways. In this light we shall see that Schleiermacher belongs not to the prophets of doom but to the proclaimers of Christian hope, faith, and love.

Even beyond the concern for interpreting the historical Schleiermacher with a view toward the present relevance of his ideas, it is also of interest to see his life and work on a broader canvas, reaching far beyond the sphere of theology as such. Schleiermacher was a professor, a founder, and an organizer of the University of Berlin, a prominent member and secretary of the Berlin Academy of Sciences, one of the most distinguished classical philologists and Plato interpreters of his time, a political figure, briefly a cabinet advisor, and a philosopher of culture who had an intellectual mastery of almost every area of culture.

Theology, however, remained his major concern. He created the classic theological statement of liberal Protestantism in *The Christian Faith* and ushered in a new period of systematic theology by applying to theology the method of transcendental philosophy. He was an untiring academician and teacher, lecturing almost every morning from 7:00 to 10:00. Nearly every Sunday for forty years he devoted himself to the service of the Christian community as a preacher of the gospel.

Our understanding of Schleiermacher's theological achievement is sharpened when his deliberate concentration on the theological center is seen against the background of the universality of his intellectual interests and activities.

I.

CHILDHOOD, YOUTH, STUDENT YEARS

Schleiermacher's development is clarified when we discern the various impulses and intentions of his life and thought and at the same time observe how these forces influence and shape his life and work at different stages of his career. A synoptic view of his life and work suggests two major divisions: (1) the intuitive-creative period during his first stay in Berlin from 1796 to 1802, and (2) the systematic period of his thought which already begins in Stolp after leaving Berlin, shows itself clearly for the first time at Halle, and finally culminates with continued clarification and refinement in Berlin from 1811 to 1834. These major periods of his life also contain two subdivisions. In the years 1803 to 1811 Schleiermacher, then under the influence of Schelling, was preoccupied with the development of a comprehensive theological-philosophical system. This system has two foci, faith and reason, theology and philosophy, bound together by overlapping ellipses into a comprehensive whole. After 1811 — particularly during the years 1811 to 1814 — he moved to a stronger christological interest and a greater concern for historical Christianity. Influenced by Kant and separated from the identity philosophy of objective idealism, he continued the further development and restructuring of his system toward a new view of the relation between faith and reason.

The main themes in both these periods of his life, however, are apparent already in Schleiermacher's childhood, youth, and student years.

Schleiermacher, like his parents before him, grew up in the home of Reformed pastors. In fact, Schleiermacher represented the third or fourth generation of pastors in his family. His grandfather, Daniel Schleiermacher (b. 1695), to his own misfortune — even tragedy — became involved as a Reformed clergyman in Elberfield with the current turmoil and disorders of the Rhenish sectarians. He lived to experience the deepest disillusionment. A charge of sorcery and witchcraft was even brought against him to the Palatinate of Mannheim by his fellow believers. Today we are astonished that such a proceeding against witchcraft was still possible in 1749. A lasting impression was made on the son (Schleiermacher's father), for in the criminal proceeding he and his mother were required to testify against the father and husband. Daniel Schleiermacher escaped imprisonment only by flight to his sister in Arnheim, Holland. There he died without ever again receiving a pastoral office.

Schleiermacher's father was the oldest child, born May 5, 1727, at Oberkassel. He appears to have been quite gifted and precocious. When only fourteen (1741) he matriculated as a theological student at the University of Duisburg, completing his studies at nineteen. Following the collapse of the fateful sect to which his father had belonged he became a teacher in Magdeburg (1758). After 1760 he was active as a chaplain in the king of Prussia's army while the Seven Years' War was still going on.

With the war's end he moved to Breslau and at thirty-seven married the twenty-eight-year-old Katharina-Maria Stubenrauch. She had been born in Berlin on July 27, 1736. Her father and grandfather were both court chaplains at the Reformed cathedral in Berlin. A daughter, Charlotte, was born in 1765; she was her brother Friedrich's lifelong confidante, encouraging and supporting his religious and theological views at every stage of his life. November 21, 1768, a second child, Friedrich Ernst Daniel, was born to the Schleiermachers. On November 27, 1768, just six days later, the infant was baptized in the Reformed Church in Breslau. The godfather was his grandfather now exiled in Holland. "Daniel" was a name in the Schleiermacher family tradition. The Christian name "Ernst" he took from his second godfather, Samuel Ernst Timotheus Stubenrauch, a professor of theology at Halle. "Friedrich" was taken from the Prussian king, Friedrich II, in whose army his father served as a chaplain. Somewhat later he was followed by a younger brother, Carl. His mother died on November 17, 1783, while she was still a young woman. Gottlieb, his father, entered the following memorial into the church register: "The Lord be praised for the love and devotion she has shown me and my children; may she be rewarded for this in God's most blessed eternal fellowship."

As chaplain, Gottlieb Schleiermacher was required to make long trips to the garrisons in Silesia. He was the only Reformed chaplain in Silesia; his three colleagues were Lutheran. According to his own estimates, every year he covered about nineteen hundred miles in a coach. During these journeys he would visit the garrison at Pless where a Reformed congregation had developed composed of the families of civil servants of the prince of Anhalt-Pless. The congregation was later strengthened by Reformed Polish immigrants whom the Prussian king had brought to Anhalt under the protection of his Hussars. In addition to his duties as chaplain, Gottlieb also took care of this congregation. Consequently the Schleiermacher family settled in Pless in 1778 where the father joined the troops in the field during the Bavarian war of succession. With the war's end they shifted their residence to neighboring Anhalt. Young Friedrich's earliest childhood memories are associated with the parsonage in Anhalt; later in 1806, while at Halle, he wrote: "There is a house in Anhalt that my father first occupied, a garden he first worked and which I helped create; there my religious sentiment stirred for the first time. It is the earliest memory I have of my own inner life."[1]

Gottlieb Schleiermacher, owing to the tragic experiences of his youth, had disassociated himself from the pietism of his parents and had become an Enlightenment theologian. He was somewhat divided in his character. According to his own admission, when he was not persuaded by the traditional doctrines of Reformed orthodoxy, he would make a so-called accommodation in his sermons. He later recommended to his son, "Consider that you speak to people who believe in a revelation and that it is your duty to reach them at their level."[2] His first obligation, as he saw it, was to preach in a way that complied with what the congregation expected by way of traditional Christian truth, adjusting it to their level of understanding. His real interest, however, was in his studies. By great personal sacrifice he regularly managed to obtain theological and philosophical literature. When he was sixty years old he still studied Kant and Spinoza and even requested that his son provide him with an explanation of the Platonic system. This tension between the thought of the Enlightenment and orthodox preaching gave his personality some contradictory traits.

A complete change occurred in his religious life and theology through an encounter with the Moravian community at Gnadenfrei. In 1778 Prussian troops were quartered in Gnadenfrei for the period of April to June. Gottlieb Schleiermacher as well as many of the Prussian soldiers experienced a pietistic reawakening upon contact with the life and worship of this congregation. Inwardly he became a Moravian, without, however, actually becoming a member of the

---

1. Heinrich Meisner, ed., *Schleiermacher als Mensch: Familien- und Freundesbriefe*, vol. II (Gotha, 1922, 1923), p. 60.
2. *Briefe*, I, p. 102. *Letters*, I, p. 104.

community; this was not possible for a Reformed chaplain at that time. Christ's expiatory sacrifice on the cross became the basis of his certainty of salvation and fountain of a new life. He now lived with his Savior in intimate communion and converted his wife and children to the Brethren's faithfulness in Christ.

Together the parents resolved to entrust the education and instruction of their children to the schools of the Moravian Brethren. On April 5, 1783, the parents traveled to Gnadenfrei with their children. They remained there about eleven weeks awaiting a decision by the Brethren on the acceptance of their children which was still dependent upon the drawing of lots. Friedrich Schleiermacher's first conscious religious experience occurred during the weeks he and his parents shared in the common life of the Brethren; he later would refer to this as the birth date of his "higher life." The Moravians would have referred to these religious experiences as "the breakthrough of grace" or "conversion." Years later Schleiermacher would remember exactly the time and the place. In a letter to Eleanore, August 19, 1802, he dated the experience at Gnadenfrei in his mid-fourteenth year. When later in the *Speeches* he defends those who can state the birthday of their spiritual life, he spoke from personal experience. While visiting Gnadenfrei twenty years later, he explained the experience in a letter to Georg Reimer, April 30, 1802: "Here my awareness of our relation to a higher world began. . . . Here first developed that basic mystical tendency that saved me and supported me during all the storms of doubt. Then it only germinated, now it is full grown and I have again become a Moravian, only of a higher order."[3]

After Schleiermacher entered the Moravian school in Niesky (June 14, 1783) he became a Moravian outwardly and inwardly. He made himself thoroughly at home in the language and feelings of the Moravians. His life as a student at Niesky (June 14, 1783 to September 17, 1785) involved three underlying motifs important for his later development: the intense, almost enraptured, sharing in the devotion to Jesus characteristic of the Moravians, the happy experience of sharing in common studies with youthful comrades, and the current humanistic education which made the pietistic educational efforts at Niesky superior to those of Halle pietism. The study of Latin and particularly Greek was the basis of the humanistic education at Niesky. Next came mathematics and botany, studies Schleiermacher often and happily renewed throughout his life, and an intensive

---

3. *Briefe*, I, pp. 294–95. *Letters*, I, p. 284.

study of English through close association with his English schoolmates and teachers. The school had a large percentage of English teachers and pupils since all the theologians of the English Brethren were instructed at Niesky and Barby.

E. R. Meyer's *Schleiermachers und C. G. von Brinkmanns Gang durch die Brüdergemeinde* gives a most informative look at the life of this school by its use of the voluminous original sources about the Moravians.[4] On the one hand, it was a kind of monastic school with a pietistic curriculum. The students were separated from their parental home. Many did not even spend their vacations at home with their parents but at Niesky. Schleiermacher himself did not see his parents again after he entered the school at the age of fifteen; they kept in touch with each other in a moving exchange of letters. His mother died on November 17, 1783, shortly after he entered the school; his father died on September 2, 1794, at the age of sixty-seven without ever seeing his son again. Intensive and strict pastoral care was exercised in relation to each student. Its aim was to keep the student away from the "evil world." This effort, to turn the student's attention away from the external world to the inner life and to concentrate their energies on their religious life and scholarly pursuits, involved extensive regimentation. Swimming and skating were prohibited, as were not only card games but also such harmless games as chess and checkers.

On the other hand, the principles and methods of this school had some quite modern features. Religious education, in compliance with Moravian piety, did not consist primarily in the transmission of dogmatic teachings. Schleiermacher's later and well-known thesis that religion could not be taught but only awakened bears the stamp of the Moravian Brethren. The Brethren not only wanted the students to learn about the Christian teaching of sin and grace but to experience these for themselves. This was a distinctive feature of Moravian piety. Zinzendorf and his followers rejected the penitential agonies typical of Halle. The breakthrough of grace rests only upon the work of the Spirit and not on human effort. Moravian piety uncovered anew the essence of Christian faith which transcends morality. Joy in the assurance of salvation and the vividly experienced communion with the Savior were the decisive factors which filled all areas of their daily life. The immediate presence of God was experienced within the most inner recesses of the self. But among

---

4. E. R. Meyer, *Schleiermachers und C. G. von Brinkmanns Gang durch die Brüdergemeinde* (Leipzig, 1905).

the Moravians this immediacy of individual religious life had a powerful counterweight in the communal life of worship. Four daily services, monthly confession, and monthly communion were included in the rules of the community.

In contrast with the strict control over the student's personal life, the academic work of the school included many freedoms. There were no final examinations, no comprehensive examinations. Every student was judged individually according to his own development. Consequently there was no need for a rigid system of classes. The students were given a great deal of time for private study. The extensive free hours were used for individual study of languages, literary efforts, and letter writing. Schleiermacher and his friend Albertini, to whom he was so close that they were called Orestes and Pylades, translated classical Greek authors and even the Hebrew Bible with the help only of a lexicon and grammar. In his autobiography he mentioned reading Homer, Sophocles, Euripides, Plutarch, and Lucian; of the Romans he cites Virgil, Tacitus, and Cicero, whom he disliked and criticized as a prattler. As yet, Plato had made no impression on him. His love for Plato first awoke at Halle, although his extensive acquaintance with the Greek language and literature had already taken root in his private studies at Niesky. Consequently, in his later life, he always studied the Greek poets with great pleasure. Thus in 1809, for instance, he read Homer and Sophocles to his stepsister during evening tea.

The focus of his life was the Brethren devotion to Jesus, which he fervently accepted, although in his own unique way. This devotion is seen, for example, in the poem he dedicated to his sister, Lotte, on her birthday, March 25, 1785. The sixteen-year-old secondary school student composed his birthday wishes on the basis of the assigned text for the day (Romans 4:25). He wrote a somewhat uneven, proselike verse in which the language and even the customary rhyming of the Brethren dominate:

> Behold him there upon the cross,
> and thus be blessed with satisfying hours,
> the martyred one beloved by us,
> the sacred Lord now wounded.
> Beloved, that is blessedness,
> the highest good in all the earth.
> And even in eternity,
> none greater could be given.
> He washed me there in his blood,
> from each and every sin,

> and gave forgiveness with his death,
> and showed me peace and rest.
> He led me also to his fold,
> that I might be secure,
> from all the evil of this world,
> with his own people sure.

Of a better quality are the verses from Klopstock's *Messias* which
he wrote in his friend Brinkmann's album at their farewell in 1785:

> Mortals, if you know the honor which
> glorifies your race, then sing to the
> eternal Son by a godly life.

He would later respond to this summons, but in a totally different
manner from that taught by his pietistic father and Moravian teachers.

On September 17, 1785, Schleiermacher left the school in Niesky
with ten other graduates to journey by foot to Barby, the seat of
the Brethren's theological school. They arrived there September 22,
1785, after a five-day walking tour. The town of Barby, housing
a small Brethren community of around 225 members, was situated
on the left bank of the Elbe not far from where it meets the Saal.
This theological academy, called a seminary, served to prepare the
theologians and teachers of the community and was dominated by
the typical pietistic approach to theological study. Religious education
meant above all the intensification of personal piety; the theoretical
side of the discipline was brought in only secondarily. Training in
the pietistic relation to the world was also part of its religious education.
This relationship demanded of education near monastic seclusion
from the external world. The dormitory regulations, detailed by
Meyer, were marked by a renunciation of the world and submission
to authority. The reading of modern belles lettres and philosophy,
for instance, was forbidden by strict censorship. However, the
Enlightenment spirit which had come to dominate the neighboring
University of Halle, and the humanistic movement of German poetry
also affected the monastic seclusion of Barby. Awakened to critical
thinking and calling themselves "independent thinkers," the circle of
friends around Schleiermacher read the *Jenaer Literaturzeitung*.
They smuggled in contemporary works such as Goethe's *Werther*
and Wieland's writings. Enlightenment theology such as Semler's
biblical criticism was, however, unavailable to them except in the
one-sided and unsatisfactory polemical expositions of their instructors.

Inevitably, pietistic religiosity and its world view came into conflict with Enlightenment theology and above all with the humanistic, cultural influence of the early idealistic poets. The humanistic "high spirits" of the poets and their totally different attitude toward life was in complete opposition to the pietistic derogation of man to the experience of sinfulness which required Christ's redemption. Schleiermacher's circle of friends found this new feeling for life in Goethe's *Werther*; but they also found it in Hölty, a young poet whose lyrics Schleiermacher quoted time and again in later life. Hölty (1748–1776) was a theology student in Göttingen who together with Stolberg and Bürger belonged to a league of poets known as the *Hainbund*. His poems were the expression of a pious, serene, partly melancholy spirit absorbed in the contemplation of nature and its beauty. The friends combined this ardor for nature with a faith in divine providence and human nature or "humanity" which was progressing toward perfection. It is self-evident that this totally different attitude toward life was incompatible with the pietistic devotion to Jesus and its consciousness of sin and grace. The awakening criticism was directed at the very center of Brethren piety, against the doctrines of Christ's divinity and the atonement of the crucified Lord.

In the manner of Enlightenment theology, Schleiermacher rejected the necessity of Christ's vicarious sacrifice. God has given men the power to strive for perfection; this was the accepted opinion of enlighteners as well as cultured humanists. Since God must take into account this striving for perfection, it would be unjust for him to damn men eternally for their sins. But if no eternal damnation threatens men, then Christ's expiatory sacrifice is also unnecessary. Schleiermacher even doubted whether this sacrifice by Christ could be a substitution for the punishment that man would have to take upon himself for his sins. Vicarious suffering for another's sins, according to his moral awareness, appeared quite impossible. Christ's divine sonship is not to be affirmed in any supernatural way but only symbolically and humanistically in analogy to our all being children of God. With such a religious attitude, the nineteen-year-old student had to come into conflict with the Moravian community and its theological teachers as well as with his pietistic father.

His theological teachers in Barby had little understanding for the struggles of an honest doubter; for them all doubt was the expression of a sinfull will. Severe disciplinary measures were taken. In 1786 the circle of friends was prohibited from pursuing independent philosophical studies. Okely, his English friend, was barred from the community. In the long run, Schleiermacher refused to play the hypocrite and hide his criticism. After some hesitation he revealed his situation to his father and also to his Uncle Samuel [Professor Stubenrauch]. The original correspondence between father and son, still available to Dilthey one hundred years ago, is regrettably lost now. We must rely on the incomplete publication of the letters by Dilthey, and hence it is no longer possible to follow clearly the course of the argument between father and son. The father's own strict pietism afforded him no basis for understanding his son's struggles. Like the theological teachers, he too saw in his son's doubt only pride, a defective love for Jesus, and a worldly longing. "Go then into the world whose approval you desire. See whether your soul can feed itself on the world's husks now that you spurn the divine refreshment Jesus bestows on every thirsting heart. Have you ever tasted a drop of balm from his wounds? And is all that you have written and so often professed to feel only deception and hypocrisy? If it was the truth, it will convict you mightily on that last Day, if you do not return again to your eternal and merciful God."[5] In his answers the son fought to save the bond of trust between father and son. But he rejected any attempt to dismiss his unanswered doubts and boldly stuck with his plan to study theology at Halle.

It was particularly painful for him that his theology teachers and advisors at Barby — he called them "the plodders" — sought to put him under considerable pressure with the threat that his father would withdraw completely and would separate himself from his son. In a letter of February 12, 1787, he wrote: "My blood boiled when I heard that they so misunderstood you, so lovelessly judged you, but I suppressed it. . . . I commend myself to divine protection, to your prayers and your paternal care as your obedient son, Fritz."[6]

The father relented. If the complete correspondence were still available we might know the grounds for the reconciliation. He was now ready to provide three or four semesters of study for his son to prepare for a teaching position. His Uncle Samuel was a consolation, a man who knew how to use a gentle hand. He wrote to his nephew that honest doubting must be given time and dealt with gently, but then admonished him, "Trust in God, in your good cause and genuine love of truth, and seek to be master over your sorrow." The uncle was also willing to have Schleiermacher live with him at Halle for the time being.

---

5. *Briefe*, I, p. 46. *Letters*, I, p. 50.
6. *Briefe*, I, p. 52. *Letters*, I, p. 50.

Schleiermacher matriculated at Halle University during Easter, 1787. The blossoming of Halle University, brought on by the philosophy of Christian Wolff and Semler's theology, was now past. But Halle still had a large enrollment of 1156 students, 800 of whom were theology students. Schleiermacher was a diligent student, working on his own study projects late into the night. He had already learned to pursue independent work at Niesky and Barby. He attended theological lectures only infrequently. It is not even certain that he heard his Uncle Samuel, an Enlightenment theologian with a bent toward a moderate form of supernaturalism, lecture. Semler was by this time old and the other members of the theological faculty — Niemeyer, Nösselt, and Knapp — were not very significant. Schleiermacher does not even mention Professor Samuel Mursinna, to whom he was distantly related, although Mursinna wrote a glowing report for Schleiermacher when he left the university, a report later found among Schleiermacher's documents.

Through the encouragement of his friend Brinkmann he attached himself to the philosopher Johann August Eberhard, at that time the most important teacher of philosophy at Halle. Eberhard was a student of Christian Wolff and lectured on that system with finesse. Above all he conveyed to the young students a thorough knowledge of Kant's philosophical system. *The Critique of Pure Reason* had just appeared in 1781; Schleiermacher had already read the *Prolegomena* (1783) at Barby. In 1785 the *Foundations for a Metaphysics of Morals* was published and in 1788 *The Critique of Practical Reason*. The young student devoted himself for many years to the intensive study of Kantian philosophy, "because it returns Reason from the metaphysical wasteland back to the fields that properly belong to it."[7] Eberhard was a critic of Kant and acquainted his students with the objections that could be directed against Kant. By this time, however, Schleiermacher was much too independent a thinker not to work his way into Kant's writings, particularly *The Critique of Pure Reason*, on his own.

In addition, Eberhard gave his students insight into the various philosophical disciplines, acquainted them with the history of philosophy, and above all provided access to Plato and Aristotle. Schleiermacher's literary remains still contain his translations of Aristotle, particularly the eighth and ninth books of the *Nicomachean Ethics*. At that time, too, the study of the Greek philosophers was being promoted in the lectures of the young philologist, Friedrich August

---

7. *Briefe*, I, p. 66. *Letters*, I, p. 68.

Wolf. At his father's wish he pursued studies in English and French to prepare himself as a private tutor. His aunt, Judith Stubenrauch (née Chabanon), came from a French Huguenot family and was a sympathetic helper in his language studies.

After a scant two years, Schleiermacher cut short his time of study at Halle. His Uncle Samuel, who had meanwhile accepted a pastorate in the country town of Drossen, not far from Frankfort on the Oder, offered him accommodations so that he would have the leisure time to continue and complete his education. Both uncle and father urged him to conclude his studies by taking the theology examinations. However, Schleiermacher appears to have spent little time drilling for the examination. Instead, he devoted himself to far-ranging philosophical studies, to first attempts at his own writing, and to lively correspondence with his friends.

His studies *On the Highest Good* and *On the Freedom of Man*, composed while at Drossen and Schlobitten, are examples of these first attempts at writing which can be found in his literary remains.[8] These decidedly ethical writings show how religious feelings and theological interests receded while he was at Drossen. Following Kant, whom he studied even more intensely at Drossen, the young candidate now gave ethics preeminence over religion. He evaluated the Christian faith from the standpoint of Kantian ethics. Originally the essence of the Christian faith was a collection of moral laws easily understood by everyone.[9] "Only after some superstitious sophists became Christians did the heathens begin to view Christianity as another philosophical sect. . . . Now the philosophical Christians . . . also had to ascertain the relation of the Bible to reason . . . and thus emerged full-blown dogmatics, which will always adapt itself to the philosophy of the time."[10] Without the philosophical Christians and their additions to original Christianity perhaps Christianity would have remained primarily beneficial and in no way detrimental. What today goes as Christianity should be discarded and a theory of virtue, as found in Kantian ethics, should be offered in its place. Surely this Kantian teaching is in complete accord with the teachings of Jesus in the Gospels. Schleiermacher, however, rejected Kant's moral proof for God and Kant's conclusion on moral grounds about the reality of immortality. Man's only task is present obedience to duty and in this alone does the highest good consist. The hope in

---

8. See *Denkmale*, pp. 6 ff. and 21 ff.

9. *Briefe*, IV, p. 29.

10. Ibid.

a hereafter only brings a false eudaemonistic motive into Christian ethics.

The winter of 1789/90 in Drossen was by far the lowest point in Schleiermacher's personal history. He was filled with skepticism and resignation. In addition, the state of his health was poor. His eyes were inflamed from too much reading (he was nearsighted all his life), and chronic stomach pains, which also followed him throughout his entire life, troubled him particularly.

Only reluctantly did he prepare for the theology examination, for he despised the theological subtleties and conceptual juggling. He lists as books that he read during this time such dissimilar works as August Sack's *Christian Belief Defended* and Johann David Michaelis's *Introduction to Holy Scripture*.

Under pressure from his father and uncle, he traveled to Berlin in 1790 to take the first theology examination before the Directorate of the Reformed Church. The court preacher and church officer, Samuel Gottfried Sack, who had been a friend of Schleiermacher's Uncle Samuel since his student days, was a prominent member of the examination committee. The examinee was given six weeks to submit examination papers in Latin and German. The examination dealt with the following items: (1) "Exposition of the fifth chapter of Galatians with particular attention to the doctrine of Christian freedom" (in Latin); (2) "For what purpose does a future Christian teacher study polemics?"[11] Over and above these he had to prepare the following examination papers under supervision: "What is the essence of Hebraic poetry? What issues in ancient and modern times concerning man's natural powers have been most beneficial? What are the chief translations of the Old Testament? What kind of books should the beginning theologian have read in order to pursue successfully his academic program?" The examination sermon on the pericope about Jesus and the tax collector (Luke 5) was held in the Cathedral Church on July 15, 1790, before the Council of Court Preachers. In the examiner's report the sermon was judged quite favorably, although the objection was raised that it was not a popular sermon for the people but more a philosophical discourse.

The grades for Schleiermacher's written work were recorded as "very good" and "excellent" on his diploma. In most disciplines he received the marks "very good" or "good." Only his work in dogmatics was judged "satisfactory," which is without doubt unex-

---

11. See H. Meisner, *Schleiermachers Lehrjahre* (Berlin, 1934).

pected for the future author of *The Christian Faith* and perhaps may be a consolation for many candidates taking their examinations.

His fatherly friend, Sack, found a position for him as a private tutor in the home of Count Dohna in Schlobitten in distant East Prussia. Originally, Schleiermacher was to have accompanied young Count Wilhelm Dohna, who studied political science in Königsberg, as a tutor and companion. But upon presenting himself to the family in Schlobitten, it was agreed that the young candidate would instead remain in Schlobitten as the tutor for the younger sons.

His stay in Schlobitten from October, 1790, until May, 1793, brought about a major change in his mood and attitude toward life. Drossen had been a time of most profound depression and skepticism, whereas in Schlobitten a strong intellectual and spiritual recovery took place. The transformation came about for many reasons. First of all it was a change of social milieu. The student, who constantly had to contend with financial difficulties, left the confined conditions of the Drossen parsonage and now entered into the life of a well-to-do East Prussian family belonging to the oldest line of Prussian nobility. Even more significant was the change in the spiritual climate. The solitary studies in Drossen and the joyless exam preparations were past, and the twenty-two-year-old candidate was offered for the first time a meaningful educational task which he happily accepted. But he was especially taken by the cordial and open atmosphere of the Dohna family. After Schlobitten, Schleiermacher became a virtuoso in friendship and in the deeper sharing of human fellowship. Schleiermacher himself referred to this experience in the *Soliloquies*: "In a stranger's home my sense for beautiful shared experiences was first opened; I saw how freedom first ennobles and rightly orders the delicate mysteries of humanity, whereas they remain forever obscure to the uninitiated who respects these only as the bonds of nature."[12]

The master of the house, Count Dohna, had taken part in the Seven Years' War as an officer of the Prussian army. In all his convictions he remained a conservative Prussian. As a patron [*Patronatsherr*] he was responsible for filling four Reformed pastorates. As a monarchist he repudiated all the political ideas of the French Revolution that now pressed upon Germany and filled the minds of many young Germans. Eventually, clear differences along these lines would develop with the private tutor. The wife was a born countess (Finckenstein), grew up at the Prussian court, and represented

---

12. *Monologen*, p. 108. *Soliloquies*, p. 74.

the tradition of the refined social life of the educated Prussian nobility. She was a warmhearted and intelligent mother for her twelve children; she also kept a vigilant eye on their young tutor and did not refrain from criticizing him on occasion.

Schleiermacher had to instruct the younger sons in French, mathematics, history, and geography. In addition he gave general lectures on ethical, philosophical, and religious questions for the cultivation of the intellectually alert and talented young countesses: the oldest was Caroline at twenty, then seventeen-year-old Friederike, and sixteen-year-old Auguste. In young, attractive, charming, and sensitive Friederike he met for the first time a gracious and gentle girl growing into womanhood. Schleiermacher developed a strong secret affection for her. Following her early death — she died of tuberculosis — he retained this secret affection for her; he never could or would even hint at it while at Schlobitten owing to the social disparity between the countess and the young tutor and to the strict forms required in social contacts. Perhaps the memory of Countess Friederike lies behind these words: "Not in vain have I seen various forms of feminine character and become acquainted with the beauty of their quiet inner life."[13]

In his literary remains there is a page which he apparently kept as a "relic" out of respect for his young student. It contains a copy of a prayer by Countess Friederike to God justifying her decision to oppose the wishes of her parents that she marry a man she did not love. "Before Thee, omniscient God, will I examine myself. . . . I come to Thee, Heavenly Father, Protector of my innocence and Guide for my youth. My Father, I know there are no more beautiful duties to be fulfilled than those of a virtuous wife. But these are also the most difficult if one has not a friend but only a man."[14]

In these surroundings such a profound change took place in young Schleiermacher's life that the religious depths of his spirit were stirred. The skepticism and the philosophical-theological brooding which had buried his piety gradually dissolved and he awoke to a new life. On August 6, 1791, he wrote his father and told him about the change. "Here my heart is properly nurtured and need not wither under the weeds of cold erudition and my religious feelings do not die under theological speculation. Here I enjoy the family life for which man is made and this warms my heart; . . . I am coming to know both myself and others, I have models to imitate and feel

---

13. *Monologen*, p. 117. *Soliloquies*, p. 80.
14. W. Dilthey, *Leben Schleiermachers*, vol. I, 1st ed. (1870), p. 71.

that I am becoming a better man. . . . You surely must thank God
with me for his gracious providence and send me your blessings
that I may wisely profit by them."[15]

The young candidate, who had felt such a strong aversion against
preaching while in Drossen, now gladly stepped into the pulpit in
Schlobitten. Nevertheless, in youthful self-irony he continued to
refer to preaching as "thundering down,"[16] but he was now gripped
by the challenge of preaching and worked intensively to develop his
own preaching style. Important for him was stimulating correspondence with his uncle and father to whom he submitted copies of his
sermons. The first sermon, for instance, "On Prayer in the Name
of Jesus," immediately makes evident his singular rhetorical skill
and the ingenious construction of his sermon ideas.

In content and language these sermons are still representative of
the devout and morally earnest Enlightenment religion like that of
Schleiermacher's Uncle Samuel. The biblical testimony was often
willfully changed. Ethical questions were placed in the center of his
exposition and his Christology had not yet grown beyond the Enlightenment. Christ is an original prophet, an ethical ideal, and a bene-
factor of mankind. The level of his sermons was more attuned to
the count's family than to the townspeople. The countess found
these sermons much too modern, since she strictly adhered to the
saving truths of the Bible, and she did not hesitate to tell him so.
The New Year's sermon of 1792, for instance, was a philosophical
discourse on the false belief that happiness and unhappiness define
the value of life. The same ethical-philosophical tendency also
shows itself in many other sermons that he preached at Schlobitten.
Thus on Easter Monday he preached on the duties which the certainty of the resurrection imposes on us; on the second Sunday in
Advent he preached on "The Necessary Limitation of One's Attachment
to Worldly Happiness"; on another occasion he preached on the
theme "How the Human Race Has Come of Age through Christ."

Although the dogmatic content and the form of speech still remained
grounded in the Enlightenment and although Schleiermacher was
seeking to follow the model of the Enlightenment preacher — he
studied published German and English sermons — the sermons
nonetheless contain a deeper tone which suggests that the author
was inwardly at the point of going beyond the Enlightenment. At
first glance the sermons appear to be rationalistic moral homilies.

15. Meisner, *Schleiermacher als Mensch*, vol. I, pp. 64–65.
16. Ibid., p. 68.

But behind them one recognizes that piety is the deeper source and spring of morality. The young preacher was filled with a vigorous sense for the moral ethos discovered in Kant's concept of duty. God satisfies men when they pray to him; he does not satisfy their idle wishes for worldly prosperity. The purpose of life is the growth of the good in men; the ultimate goal of this striving for moral perfection is for man to become more and more like God. This was for him the religious content of Kant's and Plato's ethics. At this point the young preacher only managed to express indirectly the fact that inwardly he was already growing out of Enlightenment piety.

These ethical observations led the young theologian first of all to an analysis of the human heart and life. If we look closely we will already be able to observe unique and deep religious currents emerging, currents which allow one to allude to him as a "Moravian of a higher order." For instance, in a very early Christmas sermon on the text from Galatians 4:4, which he probably preached at Schlobitten, Schleiermacher spoke on a theme he would continue to develop: "Unhappy man had lost his relation with God. Then God gave us Christ as a gift, for he returns to us all that we have lost." He continued to stress the edifying aspect of preaching and its application to the actual religious life. Through this his sermons gained an inner vivacity which filled the theological concepts of the Enlightenment with new content; only later in the *Speeches* was he successful in finding the new theological-dogmatic formulations themselves.

In addition to his preaching, to which he lovingly and joyfully devoted himself, he also continued working on his philosophical treatises. Already in 1791 while at Schlobitten he had begun an essay "On the Freedom of Man" and apparently continued to work on it until the end of 1792. On his birthday in 1792 he began to write down personal reflections which are a preparation for the later *Soliloquies*. Dilthey later published a summary of these reflections under the title, *On the Worth of Life*. The first conception of his ideas on individuality and humanity also came during the time at Schlobitten. Schleiermacher refers to these beginnings in the *Soliloquies*, "With a proud joy I remember the time when I first found the meaning of humanity and knew that I could never again lose it."[17] "I then came to what is now my highest intuition; it became clear to me that every man should represent humanity in his own unique way."[18]

---

17. *Monologen*, p. 36. *Soliloquies*, pp. 28–29.
18. *Monologen*, p. 40. *Soliloquies*, p. 31.

The first indication that he was occupied with the idea of individuality is found in the essay "On the Freedom of Man." This writing is an inquiry into the relation of freedom and necessity in men's moral action on the basis of Kant's ethics. The question about the origin and nature of *individuality* apparently emerged for the first time while he was still in Schlobitten. He asked whether the variety of souls and their diverse destinies might not best be explained by seeing each as "a distinct substance." However, he rejected such a quantitative distinction on the basis of substance and in opposition to such a view developed further the idea of individual existence. In the famous New Year's sermon of 1792 and in the essay "On the Worth of Life" he concluded that it was the individual diversity of powers within the self that make for the determination and destiny of human beings. Individuality is therefore that determination through divine providence by which each individual is assigned his proper place in the total world order. Schleiermacher asked: "I want to know what a man should be." He concluded: "Your obligation is to be what the consciousness of your being bids you to be and to become."[19]

Schleiermacher pursued the problem of individuality further, particularly in the time at Landsberg where he apparently became acquainted with Spinoza through Jacobi's publications. Therefore, the origin of his idea of individuality does not lie in romanticism or his meeting with Friedrich Schlegel; already in Schlobitten and Landsberg he had been occupied with the question, "What is the origin of the idea of an *individuum* and upon what does it depend?"[20] In fact, the real root of this idea is found in his Moravian period. The groundwork for this idea of individuality was laid when he experienced the piety of the Moravians and the consciousness of the immediacy and uniqueness of the individual's experience of faith practiced among them. Furthermore, he rethought the relationship between God and the individual in a wholly new way and strove to go beyond both the rationalistic and the supernaturalistic concepts of God and revelation.

Schleiermacher felt closely bound to the Dohna family. But the older generation, the count and the countess, also sensed much more vividly the difference between their own conservative religious and political views and those of the young theological candidate who

---

19. *Denkmale*, pp. 51–52. Compare P. Seifert, *Die Theologie des jungen Schleiermachers* (Gütersloh, 1960), p. 131.
20. *S. W.*, III/4, 1, p. 306.

strove to move beyond their world. As a result confrontations, mainly between the count and the tutor, were inevitable, arising from differences of opinion on educational matters. The ultimate causes, however, were deeper spiritual and political divergences. After a vehement dispute both sides decided it would be best for Schleiermacher to end his services as tutor. The departure, nevertheless, was cordial on both sides. The old count even shed tears at the farewell; Schleiermacher, too, was quite moved and in later years he continued to cultivate friendship with the Dohna family, particularly with the two older sons, Alexander and Wilhelm.

The young candidate returned to his Uncle Samuel at Drossen where he was warmly received. His uncle pressed him to complete the second theology examination. After working briefly in Friedrich Gedicke's pedagogical seminar in Berlin, Schleiermacher decided to accept the call at Landsberg as assistant pastor. For that reason he proceeded to complete the second theology examination on March 31, 1794, in Berlin. The examination required five research projects followed by an oral examination. The following written assignments were made: "What are the sources for church history during the first four centuries? What is the meaning of the word "faith" in Romans 14:13? What is the Talmud? Translate the thirtieth paragraph from Justin's first *Apology*. Which works are the most eminent in New Testament criticism?" The evaluation he received for the examination was glowing. His average mark was "very good"; only in dogmatics did he receive a mere "satisfactory."

After standing for the examination he assumed the post of assistant pastor in Landsberg from 1794 to 1796. In the Reformed Church at that time assistant pastors were called "Adjuncts," a designation that lasted at the Berlin Cathedral into the twentieth century. The death of his father in 1794 falls into the Landsberg period; he was deeply moved, particularly since the relationship with his father during this time had become very warm. At Landsberg, upon the suggestion of his patron, Sack, he also began to translate the sermons of the Scotsman, Hugo Blair, and the Englishman, Fawcett. The translation of Blair's sermons appeared in 1795 and was a continuation of the work Sack had initiated. The translation of Fawcett appeared in 1798 with a preface written by Sack. It was in Landsberg in 1794 that Schleiermacher's first known inquiry into Spinoza's ideas occurred, not on the basis of Spinoza's original texts, however, but through Jacobi's anti-Spinozistic writing.

In 1796 he obtained his first post as the pastor of the Charité Hospital in Berlin. With this move to Berlin his youth and time as a student ended. He was not quite twenty-eight years old when he delivered his inaugural sermon on September 18, 1796. Only now began the first intuitive and creative period in his activity as a theological and philosophical thinker and preacher.

II.

NEW INSIGHTS

A. BEGINNINGS IN BERLIN.
THE ROMANTIC FRIENDS.

Schleiermacher remained as Reformed preacher at the Charité for six years until he was thirty-four. At that time the Charité was very different both in reputation and appearance from today's large hospital that lies in the center of Berlin, within the sector that is now East Berlin. At the end of the eighteenth century, Berlin had approximately 140,000 inhabitants plus a garrison of 40,000 soldiers. Despite its rapid expansion from the middle of the eighteenth century the fast growing city had not yet reached the Charité, so the hospital still lay outside the city's core. The first floor of the building served as an old people's and nursing home, while the upper floors housed 250 patients. In Schleiermacher's first year (1796) about 3,000 patients were cared for there. The building was under the control of the public assistance administration of Berlin.

At that time the hygienic conditions and nursing care at the hospital were being sharply and publicly criticized. Gossips claimed that in a nearby veterinarian school dogs were treated like humans while at the Charité humans were treated like dogs. Prahm, Schleiermacher's Lutheran colleague, had complained to the Prussian king and achieved a reorganization of the hospital. In this conflict Schleiermacher apparently left the paper work to his Lutheran colleague. He was given lodging on the third floor. That he found this apartment "quite pleasant" is more a proof of Schleiermacher's modest needs than the quality of the lodging. In 1797, due to renovations at the Charité, he moved to a residence outside the Oranienburg Gate, apparently in what was later the *Chausseestrasse*.

Schleiermacher preached alternately with his Lutheran colleague in the Charité chapel. Besides the poor, the aged, and infirm from the hospital, people from neighboring districts also came to visit his worship services. These beginnings were relatively modest in comparison with his extensive involvement in preaching later at Trinity

Cathedral. He took great pains to adapt his sermons to the intellectual and spiritual level of his listeners. Consequently, in his first collection of sermons he included no sermons from Charité, since the congregation had different needs than the parishioners of Landsberg, Potsdam, or other Berlin churches. His inaugural sermon of 1796 is, however, preserved in the seventh volume of his sermons and it shows the great effort he made to identify with the real needs of his congregation.

> Do not let me ask you in vain for good will and brotherly love, which one should give to every Christian and which I require even more so as your companion; accept me in love as your friend. Here, where apparently so much undeserved suffering is brought together, and so many plaintive voices of distress are raised, and where by contrast the undeserved suffering is defied by such callous indifference, such impudent insolence — here one might easily begin to wonder whether it is in fact true that the Lord in Heaven looks down upon mankind and has established His throne for judgement. . . . Here the doubt could creep in whether the Law of the Most High is truly written in the hearts of all men.[1]

Schleiermacher first of all took steps toward establishing closer ties with those families of Reformed clergy in Berlin with whom his mother's family was on friendly terms, particularly the Spalding and Sack households. Sack, chaplain of the court, became a fatherly friend to him and later could remind him of the friendship in the following words: "The talents which God bestowed on you, the fine culture you have acquired, and the spiritual integrity I perceived in you earned my respect and affection."[2]

Provost Spalding was already well advanced in years. After the promulgation of the Wöllner edict on religion he had resigned all his offices as a protest against the reactionary orthodoxy. Schleiermacher's own attitude on the issues of church and civil politics of the time is revealed by an entry in his notebooks of 1796. It would be hard to outdo the sharp youthful criticism of the state of the church: "The church is a polyp; if a piece is torn away another complete polyp grows. It is of no use for men to separate themselves into still more churches according to their different opinions. The polyp must not be torn apart; it must be totally annihilated."[3] This critical

---

1. *S. W.*, II/7, p. 380.
2. *Briefe*, III, p. 276.
3. *Denkmale*.

observation can only be interpreted and understood in relation to the position on the state church that he took only a few years later in the *Speeches*, and also in relation to his positive comments about the nature of the true church.

Most significant for the creative intuitive years of his first period in Berlin were the friendships he found in circles beyond the families of Reformed clergy. Two circles, which were closely related, were most important for him: the circle of Berlin romantics and poets, among whom he found a place through his friendship with Friedrich Schlegel, and, second, the new Berlin society which had gathered there at the end of the eighteenth century.

This new society had been formed in opposition to the enlightened Berlin of Friedrich the Great. The prime mover for this society's new ideals and appreciation for art was Goethe, whose *Wilhelm Meister* enormously impressed cultured people of the time. This new society came together under Goethe's influence; already in 1795 Rachel Varnhagen could write that Goethe was the nexus for everything that man could be or would want to be.

Schleiermacher found Count Alexander Dohna in Berlin. Dohna, although three years Schleiermacher's junior, had already received an important position in the War Office. Through Dohna he was introduced into the home of the Jewish physician and student of Kant, Marcus Herz. The members of the Dohna family were among the patients of this famous physician. Alexander, the oldest son in the aristocratic Dohna family, became attached to the doctor's wife by an affection so deep and serious that he never later married. After Marcus Herz's death, disregarding all the prejudices of his aristocratic family, he proposed marriage to Henriette Herz. But she refused the proposal. Schleiermacher soon also developed a strong affection for this remarkable woman. Their relationship, however, was always that of friendship between two persons who were on a high intellectual and moral plane.

Henriette Herz was the daughter of a Jewish physician, De Lemos. In accordance with her parents' wishes she was engaged and married to the famed physician at a very early age, when she was scarcely more than a child. Her husband was seventeen years older than she and had relatively little understanding for his wife's cultural milieu. He was Kant's favorite student and was highly regarded in Berlin's philosophical community. The marriage was childless, yet it was a harmonious one, based on respect and friendship; Henriette was content to have made her husband happy. Despite all her sensitivity, cordiality, and deep feelings for others, the strict spirit of her parental home made her appear strongly disciplined. Even though she had inwardly outgrown her Jewish faith, she refused to be baptized as long as her mother still lived. Only very late in life did she convert to Christianity. She would not permit Schleiermacher to baptize her. (She was baptized by Pastor Wolf in 1817 in Zossen.)

In 1796 she was thirty-two, four years older than Schleiermacher. She attracted attention by her striking form, and her perfect beauty evoked many compliments with the social circle. The brothers Alexander and Wilhelm von Humboldt also adored her. Wilhelm von Humboldt learned Hebrew from her and even wrote love letters to her in Hebrew. She had a gift of intuitive understanding. Schleiermacher spoke of her "intellect which was scientific and passive at the same time." Already as a young woman she had mastered eight languages, to which she later added Sanskrit and Turkish.

The mutual attraction between this woman and Schleiermacher rested on their both being strong personalities, filled with a joyful self-awareness of their own individuality. Each supported the other in the certainty of their own moral view of life and in the certainty that there is a real moral substance to life. Mutual respect and understanding, free of erotic claims, was the basis for friendship. It was Henriette Herz who of all the Berlin friends could best understand Schleiermacher's commitment to his calling as a minister, while his other close friends in these Berlin years considered his theological calling incomprehensible. On the basis of this unique relationship Henriette Herz proved her loyalty to her friend Schleiermacher.[4]

Because of her understanding of the depth of Schleiermacher's Christian faith she vigorously defended her friend against his enemies and critics. On March 22, 1831, she wrote a letter to Count Alexander Dohna which stands as the most eloquent testimony of her loyalty in friendship and her deep understanding for Schleiermacher's personal Christianity.

> Schleiermacher is far removed from rationalism and genuinely believes in God and the Savior. The church newspaper (Hengstenberg's *Evangelische Kirchenzeitung*) called him a Jesuit; he kept silent and was right in doing so, for as much as I am for rational, quiet refutation I am against caustic irony. . . . What a divine sermon he gave yesterday. The text was, "The time is near when

---

4. When her husband died on January 20, 1803, she had been married to him for twenty-four years. After his death she lived in Rügen until 1809, and then returned to Berlin and lived in Charlottenburg. She received a pension from the Prussian king which protected her from poverty. By the time of her death, on October 22, 1847, she had outlived all of her friends.

the Son of Man shall be glorified.' How well he explained what kind of transfiguration the Savior meant; not the one the disciples saw on the mountain, but the one in his hour of death and how every good and faithful man is transfigured in this hour when everything worldly becomes as nothing. And this man is supposed to be a rationalist, a Jesuit! He does not adhere to the letter, not to the dead word — he believes rather in the living Spirit.[5]

At this earlier time Henriette Herz's home had become one of the centers for contemporary Berlin society. Jean Paul described her home in a letter: "Educated Jews, officers, and nobility, in short all those who elsewhere are at each others' throats, here have their arms around each others' necks and live together amiably, at least around the dining and tea table."[6]

Naturally there was a good deal of talk in Berlin about these two friends who were so different and yet intellectually so congenial. But this criticism had no effect on either Marcus Herz or Schleiermacher. Because of this criticism Schleiermacher wrote his sister Charlotte, who also did not understand the relationship between the two so utterly different friends:

It is a close and heart-felt friendship, having nothing to do with man and woman. . . . She has never affected me in a way that could disturb the serenity of my feelings. Whoever understands anything about how the inner soul expresses itself will recognize a dispassionate nature in her. And if I were to consider only the externals, then she is not all that attractive to me, although her face is incontestably very lovely and her full queenly form is so much stronger than my own. But I always find it so laughable and absurd to imagine us both free and in love and married that I can only get over my amusement with real effort.[7]

The romantic poets and authors were the second circle to which Schleiermacher belonged during this first period in Berlin. This circle was personally and intellectually linked with the new society of cultured Berliners that was coming together in the Berlin salons. Friedrich Schlegel was its leading exponent and most interesting member. It was Schlegel who arranged Schleiermacher's entry into this intellectual world. Friedrich Schlegel had come to Berlin in

---

5. Johann Bauer, *Ungedruckte Predigten Schleiermachers* (Leipzig, 1909), pp. 123–24.
6. Jean Paul, *Briefe*, vol. 4, ed. E. Berend (Weimar, 1952), p. 46.
7. *Briefe*, I, p. 261. *Letters*, I, p. 249.

the summer of 1797 when he was twenty-five years old; he was then
the best-known author and spokesman for the younger generation,
later called "romantic." Schlegel and Schleiermacher first met at
the Berlin "Wednesday Society" and afterwards came together in
the Herz home. Schleiermacher was at once attracted by Friedrich
Schlegel's interesting, versatile, and provocative personality. A very
close friendship and intellectual and literary collaboration began. At
the end of 1797 they even shared an apartment for a few months.
In a letter to his sister Charlotte, written December 31, 1797, Schleiermacher vividly sketched the life he shared with Friedrich Schlegel.
The arrangement ended in early July, 1798, when Friedrich Schlegel
moved for a time to Dresden with his brother.

Friedrich Schlegel was born on March 10, 1772 in Hannover,
where his father served as a general superintendent of the Lutheran
church. He first headed toward a business career but in 1790 chose
to study jurisprudence at Göttingen. From 1791 until 1794, however,
he devoted himself to the study of classical philology and art history
at Leipzig. He quickly became famous for his writings on the history
of Greek poetry. As with all the romantics he was greatly influenced
by Fichte, particularly by Fichte's *Theory of Knowledge* (*Wissenschaftslehre*), published in 1794. It is significant that Schlegel made
the comment that three great events had determined his times: the
French Revolution, Fichte's *Wissenschaftslehre*, and Goethe's *Wilhelm
Meister*. In Jena he came into contact with Fichte; then in 1797
he moved to Berlin, where he soon became the center of the romantic
circle.

What significance did this meeting with Schlegel and the romantic
movement have for Schleiermacher? What is the distinguishing
essence of this intellectual movement in which Schleiermacher participated in his own way and with which he had to come to grips?
The question whether Schleiermacher himself became a romantic
and whether, therefore, his first theological conception in the *Speeches*
should also be understood within a romantic point of view is a legitimate
question.

Since "romanticism" often has pejorative connotations, the use
of this term to describe the theology of the young Schleiermacher
usually implies severe disapproval and criticism. For many critics
romanticism is poetical subjectivism. Hence for them romanticism
means a poeticizing and sentimentalizing of the religious life.[8] They

8. Alfred von Martin, *Deutsche Vierteljahresschrift für Literaturwissenschaft
und Geistesgeschichte*, vol. III (1924), p. 416.

would see Schleiermacher as transforming the Christian faith, which must be personally accepted and made one's own, into intuition and feeling; this signifies a sentimentalizing of religion in general and of Protestant Christianity in particular. For such critics Schleiermacher represents a type of romantic religiosity. As a religious romantic he differs from Novalis who was the poetical-aesthetic type, as well as from Friedrich Schlegel and Adam Müller who respectively represent the intellectual and the political type of romantic life-style.

The concept of romanticism has been a point of special contention in German literature and cultural history. The very common view of romanticism as an irrational aesthetic subjectivism and artificial sentimentality remote from real life should be discarded. Such an attitude toward life and such an artistic style are also found outside of romanticism in other periods in the history of poetry and culture. It is advantageous, therefore, to limit the concept to the poetic and philosophical movement which in later literary and cultural history became known as romanticism, and played a decisive role from approximately 1797 to 1830 within the movement of German idealism. But even this movement is diverse and contains the widest variety of motifs within it. Generally the movement is divided into early romanticism, high romanticism, and late romanticism. Early romanticism is above all crucial for an interpretation of Schleiermacher's life. It began in 1797 with Wackenroder's *Heartfelt Effusions of an Art Loving Friar (Herzensergiessungen eines kunstliebenden Klosterbruders).* *Athenaeum*, the journal published in Jena by the Schlegel brothers together with their friends, became the movement's literary organ. August Wilhelm Schlegel's lectures in Berlin from 1802 until 1804 served as a provisional terminal point for early romanticism. Apart from the Schlegel brothers, the other leading representatives of the movement were Tieck, Novalis, and Wachenroder.

In an essay in the *Deutsche Vierteljahresschrift für Literaturwissenschaft und Geistesgeschichte* (1924), Franz Schultz emphasised that this circle of friends did, indeed, understand themselves as a literary and philosophical group, but that they did not yet use the noun "romanticism." Only later literary historians and critics have employed the name "romanticism" as a title. This should serve as a warning that the stereotyped notions of later literary historians should not hastily and uncritically be applied to the poetic movement itself. Nonetheless the concept "romantic" was used by them, particularly by the Schlegels. It was an adjective derived not from the noun "romanticism" but from the German *Roman* — novel or romance.

By the end of the eighteenth century this word had already become
quite fashionable. It signified the fictitious, i.e., the wondrous, the
fantastic, the remote in time. But it also referred to the sentimental
as that which alone has access to the primordial act of the human
spirit — feeling.

The Schlegel brothers used the term "romantic" to characterize
the contrast between ancient and modern. Romantic stands in
contrast to both antiquity and classical German art. As a result of
this contrast with classicism the Middle Ages were rediscovered and
the medieval romances and poems of chivalry were called "romantic."
Friedrich Schlegel sought to clarify the concept in his *Fragments*.
The result was his protean concept of "progressive universal poetry."
The term "universal" concerns form and style as well as content.
Universal poetry includes everything that can broadly be called poetic.
Even the naive art of children's songs can be romantic. Thus such
universal poetry is the mirror of the universe. "Progressive" is
meant to allude to the infinite striving after an unattainable ideal;
in a sense it is a feeling for the infinite. The infinite is a specific
romantic word for designating the divine and the absolute.

In Schlegel's *Letter on the Novel* we find a new definition of the
concept "romantic." Romantic "presents us with sentimental
content in fanciful form." The concept "sentimental" as used here
does not mean artificial sentimentality, but that which speaks to the
feelings of the human spirit. For Schlegel "sentimental" is not a
pejorative reference in the sense of a pseudo-sentimentality. The
"sentimental" speaks to feeling, to immediate self-consciousness.
Hence the romantic element is not a subdivision of poetry but the
essence of poetry itself.[9]

Two fundamental motifs in early romanticism stand out clearly.
The locus of feeling is the individual self, the inwardness of individuality. The stirrings of this inwardness find expression in the fantastic,
the magical. The second motif is the orientation of feeling to the
infinite; it is striving for the infinite that is found in the finite, the
view of the universe as the infinite in the finite.

These romantic motifs were directly stated by Novalis, whom
Schleiermacher never personally met and with whom he exchanged
ideas only after 1799. Novalis was the most powerful poetic genius
of early romanticism. He saw the essence of romanticism as "magical
idealism." For Novalis, romanticizing meant giving common things

---

9. Cf. Paul Kluckhohn, *Das Ideengut der Deutschen Romantik* (Tübingen,
1941), p. 176.

a higher meaning, finding the infinite in the finite, i.e., penetrating the deeper meaning and being of things. Hence poetry is the portal to the divine. "The path of mystery moves inward. Eternity is in us."[10] "God exists in the moment in which I believe in Him."[11] Such idealism he called magical because it had the power to transfigure finite reality and to consummate the meeting of the finite with the infinite in the world of poetry, the world of wonder.

1. WAS SCHLEIERMACHER A ROMANTIC?

Schleiermacher was a full-fledged member of the romantic poetic circle and yet retained his independence. That he was neither a poet nor an aesthete can be seen from his own unfinished poetic efforts undertaken at the prompting of his friends. But at that time he lived in the world of the romantics and spoke their language. Some have claimed that the basic original ideas of his creative Berlin period, for instance, the concepts of individuality and the universe, were derived from romanticism. Such a claim is untrue, for he had the idea of individuality earlier.

His *Speeches on Religion to Its Cultured Despisers* and the *Soliloquies* were the gifted writings of this time in Berlin. The *Speeches* especially made him famous overnight. They said what the young generation at that time felt about religion. It is difficult for today's generation to appreciate Schleiermacher's youthful works. We no longer have the same relation to them as did a great many of the educated youth of the nineteenth century; for them Schleiermacher's *Speeches* and *Soliloquies* became something like a religious and ethical devotional book. Between them and us stands an era of a critique of culture which found its radical expression in dialectical theology. The entire attitude toward life, the relation to the world of intellect and culture, has been altered. There has been a shift from confidence and optimistic certainty in the world of ideas and spirit to skepticism, criticism, and uncertainty bordering on nihilistic resignation. The mark of spirituality today is the refusal to accept and to work within a culture; criticism and skepticism are taken as the criteria for our outlook on life.

The only way that we can come to a genuine undertanding of Schleiermacher is by undertaking a cultural-historical analysis.

---

10. Novalis, *Schriften*, vol. 2 (*Blütenstaub*) (Stuttgart, 1965), p. 418.
11. Novalis, *Das allgemeine Brouillon*, in Novalis's *Gesammelte Werke*, vol. 4 (Zürich, 1946), p. 23.

Schleiermacher's theology and philosophy are among the most significant events within German, and especially Protestant, church history
since the days of the Reformation; but he must be understood in
terms of his own time and without cultural antipathy.

Around 1900 Friedrich Naumann pointed out with great regret
that German Protestantism has hardly known what to do with
Schleiermacher and has not really grappled with him. Protestantism
has not understood how to utilize the spiritual power that came to
expression in Schleiermacher's thought. This is much more than a
cultural-historical observation; historical observations always have
significance for contemporary life. But we can no longer directly
translate Schleiermacher's ideas into today's theological and philosophical discussion. We must proceed indirectly via precise historical
interpretation in order to evaluate the fundamental contemporary
relevance of his ideas for the totality of Protestant cultural history
as well as for present Christian proclamation and theology.

B. THE SPEECHES ON RELIGION

If there is to be a new inquiry into Schleiermacher's theological
significance it must recover one insight above all which recent
Schleiermacher criticism has either forgotten or overlooked, namely,
that a large number of his contemporaries, particularly the younger
generation of theologians around 1800, did not see Schleiermacher at all
the way we do. In the course of their lives many of them repeatedly
acknowledged his decisive influence on their faith and theology.
One need only mention such names as Twesten, Dorner, and De
Wette. Especially important in this connection is Claus Harms who, in
the course of his life, followed a very different road theologically and
ecclesiastically from Schleiermacher's. In his *Autobiography* Harms
acknowledged, "In my final academic years I read Schleiermacher's
Speeches; they killed rationalism for me. I cannot say it more clearly:
here began what I call the hour of birth for my higher life. I received
from this book (Schleiermacher's *Speeches*) an impetus toward an
unceasing momentum."

With his first work, composed when he was thirty, Schleiermacher
gave religion and theology a new importance for many young men.
We must therefore ask what the content of this work was that it could
have such an impact on the young.

The *Speeches* is not an academic book. It is addressed to non-
theologians, the "cultured despisers of religion." Stylistically the
book is neither a sermon nor a philosophical treatise, but rather a

typical literary performance in the spirit of the romantic age. Hence, such criticism of the literary form of the *Speeches* as Friedrich Gundolf's is unjustified. Gundolf claimed it was a mixture of an unctuous sermon and a dialectical tract, of edification and investigation. This judgment misses the point because the extant sermons from this same period have a markedly different style since they were addressed to the simple community of worshipers. The *Speeches* is thus a "confession" directed to the literary and philosophically oriented segment of society and, therefore, does not use the technical language of theology but that of romantic literature. Schleiermacher deliberately avoided the solemnity of theological preaching, the conceptual language of theology, and the typical theological polemic. He wanted to confront the cultured despisers on their own ground.

1. The Formulation and Method of the Speeches

(Divinatory Criticism)

People who try to read Schleiermacher's *Speeches* today are tempted to understand his discussion as a kind of psychological account of the religious life in terms of the psychological categories of that day. Religion is distinguished from knowing and doing because it is feeling. It is intuition and feeling for the universe, the sense and taste for the infinite. This first impression, however, is deceptive and false. Schleiermacher, in fact, rejected the "wretched empiricism" of the psychology of religion. In his opinion the psychology of the Enlightenment had exhausted itself and had virtually become dishonored by its excesses.[12] He wanted to find the spirit of religion,[13] to distinguish the essential from the borrowed and alien, the holy from the profane.[14] He can also frequently say that he wants to find the "idea" of religion.[15] However, he does not mean by "idea" a concept arrived at by abstraction but rather the essence, the center, that which makes religion religious.

Schleiermacher tried to employ the analytical-critical and cultural-historical method Kant had applied to pure and practical reason for the analysis of the unique content of religion. Schleiermacher wanted to reveal the profound depths out of which religion first arises in the soul. It is within this context that Schleiermacher's comment that

---

12. *Reden*, pp. 156 f. *Speeches*, p. 132.
13. *Reden*, p. 281. *Speeches*, p. 238.
14. *Reden*, p. 248. *Speeches*, p. 217.
15. *Reden*, pp. 23, 238, 248. *Speeches*, pp. 14, 211, 217.

religion necessarily springs from within the depths of every superior soul and has its own province in feeling, must be understood. This distinctive province in feeling, however, is not an empirically and psychologically identifiable locus of religion. Schleiermacher clearly states that religion "acts upon feeling in a unique way," dissolving all activity in an intuition of the infinite.

In this way Schleiermacher wanted to substantiate the independence, originality, and irreducibility of religion and contrast it with scientific thinking and moral behavior. He wanted religion to be critically aware of itself, of that which is religious in religion, of its sources and its manifestations. Friedrich Schlegel, in a different context, coined the term "divinatory criticism" for this method; religion should not be an object of investigation but the subject of self-examination. It should become certain of its own ground, its own truth; it should find the center of its own life.[16]

2. The Religious in Religion

What is the Center of Piety for Schleiermacher?

Today's reader does not immediately understand Schleiermacher's dated formulations: intuition and feeling of the universe, the sense and taste for the infinite, becoming one with the infinite in the midst of the finite. Even the simple term "universe" causes considerable difficulties for the reader of today. The Latin term *universum*, the Latin analog for the Greek *kosmos*, would be best translated as *Weltall* [literally, world-all]. But etymology is not much help at this point. And references to the use of this term by Shaftesbury and Hemsterhuis, whom Schleiermacher undoubtedly read, provide no unequivocal explanation for Schleiermacher's linguistic usage, for he had uniquely recast the meaning of the term.

In the *Speeches* Schleiermacher himself offers a variety of interpretations. Clearly the dogmatic and metaphysical-philosophical concepts are secondary for him and do not constitute the center of religion. They are but the means for expressing that which piety experiences in the mysterious event of the revelation of the universe. Of the many names Schleiermacher otherwise used to express more precisely the meaning of "universe," we will mention only the following now: the genius of humanity,[17] the sublime world spirit, eternal

16. *Reden*, p. 153. *Speeches*, p. 130.
17. *Reden*, p. 91. *Speeches*, p. 73.

love, retribution, destiny, deity. As difficult as it is to reduce these various concepts to a common denominator, it is nevertheless clearly understood that for Schleiermacher the universe cannot be the empirically identifiable, spatially and temporally perceptible, world *(Weltall)*. The universe is for him rather unity and wholeness in contrast to the multiplicity of natural and human events. "To accept trustingly every particular as a part of the whole, everything limited as a manifestation of the infinite, that is religion."[18] "To discover unity everywhere in all possible disguises and to rest nowhere except in the infinite and the one, [that is religion.]"[19] This wholeness and unity is not empirically perceived, nor is it the causal structure of nature in space and time; it is the ultimate, which acts upon men and things. Like the romantics Schleiermacher favors the concept of the infinite, but this infinite is not the infinity of space and time; it is rather the ultimate, the formative principle which encompasses finite multiplicity.

For us today, as it was for Schleiermacher's contemporaries, it is, to say the least, puzzling to some and quite offensive to many others, when a theologian like Schleiermacher adopts the concept "universe" for God and his revelation. This provocative use of words by the young Schleiermacher is understandable only when seen against the background of his times. The old traditional image of God, bound up with the mythology and world view of antiquity, had been destroyed for many thinking people by the advance of natural science. Heaven and the hereafter could no longer be represented in terms of a place "above" or "beyond" the earth; likewise eternity could no longer be a segment of time beginning after the end of earthly time.

The old world view and its metaphysical conception of God was no longer possible, particularly after Kant's critique of reason had redefined the meaning and the limits of scientific conceptualization. Supernaturalism had attempted to secure a realm beyond nature for God and his activity. But this brought Christian piety and theological thought into major difficulties: God's activity and revelation could only be understood as a miraculous event, as a violation of natural law, to which the concepts of natural science could not apply. This produced a conflict of ideas. More and more people found it impossible first of all to reject physics in order to believe that God acts in nature and history. Revelation and miracle could not be shoved

---

18. *Reden*, p. 56. *Speeches*, p. 277. (Notes on the first edition).
19. *Reden*, p. 172. *Speeches*, p. 142.

back into a realm not yet explored by natural science. If God is Lord of the world then even that sphere as studied in modern science must fall under his rule and governance. But how is it possible to experience God's living action as a reality within the causal mechanism of the scientific realm? The traditional supernaturalistic image of God made this impossible. God had to be "different" and a new conception of him had to be found.

On the basis of critical transcendental philosophy God cannot be the object of human knowledge, since human knowledge is bound to space and time and the categories of reason, i.e., the finite world. The solution of naturalistic pantheism, which equates God and nature, was likewise impossible since this identification undoubtedly meant the end of any faith in God. Hence, idealistic philosophy sought God not in the realm of what was boundless in empirical terms; it sought the infinite, that realm of the ultimate which was no longer accessible to objective knowledge. Some therefore thought that the essence of God could be characterized as "idea," representing itself as the absolute, totality, final unity to the intellectual intuition of philosophical speculation.

Most radical was the solution of Fichte's philosophy of the ego. Schleiermacher rejected this way and opposed it sharply in the *Speeches*.

> How will the triumph of your speculation, of your complete and fully rounded Idealism, fare if religion is not a counterpoise for it, opening to it an awareness of a higher realism than the one which it so resolutely and rightly subordinates to itself? It will negate the universe while appearing to form it, it will degrade it to a mere allegory, to an empty shadow-image of our own limitations.[20]

Fichte's speculations about God seemed to him much too forced. Such speculation is brash arrogance, impudent enmity against the gods. "Man has stolen only the feeling of infinity and God-likeness, and as an unjust good it cannot serve him well unless he is conscious of his limits, of the contingency of his entire form, of the soundless disappearance of his entire being into the infinite."[21] Idealist speculation does not reach the final core of reality, it does not lead to God as the reality of all realities. Schleiermacher strove for the certainty of God based on religion and not for the self-assurance of idealist speculation. He wanted to find a "higher realism"[22] which would

20. *Reden*, p. 54.   *Speeches*, p. 40.
21. *Reden*, p. 52.   *Speeches*, p. 279 (Notes on the first edition).
22. *Reden*, p. 54.   *Speeches*, p. 40.

overcome the conflict between supernaturalism, naturalistic pantheism, and the idealist idea of the absolute.

It is against this background that Schleiermacher's line of thought and conceptualization should be interpreted. He referred to God as the ultimate power active not simply in a supernatural realm but permeating the whole of reality. For this reason he described the process of revelation not as a supernatural miracle but as the much greater mystery of the infinite's self-manifestation in the finite. This divine infinite is for him the one and the whole. He meant by this what he later referred to as the absolute totality. It has been made clear that the one and the whole is not identical with the material world; the one and the whole encompasses the sensible-material world as a formative principle. But the infinite is also not to be identified with human history and the values of human life. It is "*outside of and beyond humanity*."[23] This absolute totality does not contain the contrasts that govern the human world (flesh and spirit, ignoble and noble, good and evil). The divine infinite is the one and the whole precisely because it does not include these opposites in itself and for this reason it is infinitely superior to the finite, the limited, the conflicting. The decisive point in all this is that the reality of this infinite totality is not accessible to philosophical speculation, nor is it a postulate of morality as in Kant. The universe creates its own admirers. "The universe is in an unbroken activity and reveals itself to us in every moment."[24]

The final decisive miracle is that man is gripped by this revelation. It is an activity of grace which Schleiermacher described in nearly the same manner that the pietists used to describe their conversion experience. Men can contribute nothing to it. Intuition and feeling are not activities of the human spirit by means of which reality is brought under control; rather they represent that primal act of the spirit in which reality is not yet divided into subject and object. Intuition does not mean sense perception or the knowledge and comprehension of a thing; rather it means allowing the activity of the infinite present in the finite to work upon it. Feeling is not a third psychological function besides knowing and doing; it is the original act of the human spirit itself. It is the experience of becoming established as a concrete individual existence in one's encounter with the universe.

23. *Reden*, pp. 125–26. *Speeches*, p. 282 (Notes on the first edition).
24. *Reden*, p. 56. *Speeches*, p. 278 (Notes on the first edition).

In the second edition of the *Speeches* and then definitely in *The Christian Faith* Schleiermacher dropped the concept of intuition, presumably because he wanted to separate himself clearly from the "intellectual intuition" of idealist speculation.   That is understandable, yet regrettable in a certain respect because the concept of feeling without the concept of intuition is too easily misunderstood as a simple internal process within the self, which in its pure inwardness is not open to the "higher reality."

Schleiermacher's recognition of the immediacy and inwardness of the experience of faith, which comes through revelation and which is directed to the very center of each individual, is linked with another insight which has methodological implications. Already pietistic theology had distinguished between doctrine and life; orthodox doctrines and the words of the Bible were complemented by the believer's experience of illumination and rebirth. Schleiermacher applied this pietistic distinction between doctrine and life to the distinction that transcendental philosophy was then making between reflection and event, thought and being, concept and experience, "expression" and "disposition."   Doctrine and reflection, therefore, are not themselves the foundation but that which has been founded. The certainty of salvation and of faith rests on the existential experience of revelation and not on correct theological understanding and formulation.   Christian faith is therefore never faith in correct doctrine and the dead letter but in the living relation between God and man. This basic insight of Schleiermacher which became decisive for *The Christian Faith* is already present in the *Speeches* as a fundamental tenet.

From the very start the theological presuppositions of the *Speeches* has been subjected to vehement criticism and charges of heresy. Three charges consistently recur: (1) Schleiermacher is a mystic, (2) he advocates pantheism, (3) he confuses art and religion, faith and aesthetic imagination and artistic intuition.   It is said that he brings to faith the enchanting display of artistic experience but not the truth of God's revelation.

There is some basis for the charge of mysticism since Schleiermacher applied the term to himself.   He himself referred to the center of his religion as mysticism.   In romanticism the concept "mysticism" still had a broad and, one might say, "pre-religious" meaning.   Mysticism seeks to exclude sense perceptions in order to partake of the more mysterious internal inspirations and intuitions.   It means above all the sphere of intuition in which the epistemological division of subject from object either has not yet occurred or has deliberately

been avoided. In a pre-religious sense it could mean participation
in the ultimate depths of life through existential encounter.

Schleiermacher applied this understanding of mysticism to the
primal religious experience itself without intending to dissolve the
line between God and man, God and the soul, into a complete unity.
Thus the expression "mysticism" also meant for Schleiermacher the
immediacy of the experience of God, that God-man relationship
which we today call existential. "Existential" means that revelation
is experienced only in one's own existence and is not acquired by
learning or adopting alien concepts. In its description of the experience of conversion, earlier pietistic theology meant precisely this
ultimate inwardness and illumination. The young Schleiermacher
humanized pietistic spirituality and inwardness.

The use of the terms "mysticism" and "mystical" by Schleiermacher
and the romantics is therefore not identical with their use in the
contemporary philosophy of religion and history of religion fields.
Our present concept is primarily influenced by Neoplatonic and
medieval mysticism and the spiritualistic developments of these
streams. Consequently, in our view today, mysticism is something
that appears in almost all great historical religions, transforming the
aspiration in every living religion for immediacy into the striving for
the unmediated, thus blurring the line between God and man and
God and the world. If we want to apply the term mysticism at all
to Schleiermacher's interpretation of religion, then the term itself
will need a more precise and clearer definition of its content.

Rudolf Otto successfully sought such precision for the interpretation
of Schleiermacher.[25] Research into the movement of so-called
German idealism by cultural historians has led to the recognition
that behind the basic metaphysical concept of idealism there is an
impulse which one might easily characterize as mysticism or "world
affirming" piety. Mystical conceptions stand behind the lofty
speculations of our idealistic poets and philosophers; in Schleiermacher
mysticism "on occasion exhibits a nearness to such romantic nature-
mysticism. In fact, however, it should be characterized as a mysticism
of the spirit that on occasion fights against the ecstatic nature-mysticism
of his own friends. In the strict sense this impulse in romanticism
is not mysticism."[26]

Apart from this general and figurative meaning of mysticism,
there are two elements in Schleiermacher's *Speeches*, analogous to the

25. Rudolf Otto, *West-östliche Mystik*, 2d ed. (Gotha, 1929).
26. Ibid., p. 325.

mystical state of the soul, that should be emphasized. The first element is the theme of awe which stands in opposition to Fichte's feeling of sovereign power. For Schleiermacher piety is just the opposite of the feeling of sovereignty described by Fichte. Piety is devotion and humility. With convincing clarity Otto has established that this element has nothing to do with mysticism. It is the specifically pious in piety. In this feeling of humility and creatureliness lies the antithesis to all the self-positing of the idealist philosophy of freedom. This religious motif was the most basic element in Schleiermacher's piety. And it was alive in him long before he came into touch with the romantics, specifically Schlegel and Novalis. In *The Christian Faith* he later called this religious motif the feeling of absolute dependence. "The feeling of absolute dependence is in and of itself God's co-presence in self-consciousness."[27]

A second element in the *Speeches*, closer and more akin to mysticism, is linked to this first motif of the devotion and awe that fills created beings: intuition and feeling of the universe. The universe is unity and wholeness, absolute totality. This is never merely the sum of particulars or the total number of the multiplicities of the finite world. The universe cannot be perceived by the senses. It opens itself only to religious intuition. But this is not mysticism in the strict sense either. In fact, Schleiermacher often seems to wonder whether finite men can really have this intuition of unity. It becomes accessible to men only in definite moments of revelation. In one way or another Schleiermacher is distrustful of such mystical intuition. Later in the second edition of the *Speeches* he dropped the term "intuition." He also eliminated it in *The Christian Faith*.

The concept of feeling moved into the foreground as the term for immediate self-consciousness. Never does a finite part become the whole, never does the temporal become the eternal, that is, the absolute totality which determines everything finite and temporal. God's reality is not revealed to mystical — and definitely not to metaphysical — speculation about unity. Finite men participating in the oppositions of finitude must first be redeemed through Christ before they can attain this religious intuition into the eternity and unity of the universe.

All the same, a certain speculative element remained in Schleiermacher's view of God. It has to do with the conception of God

---

27. Schleiermacher, *Der Christliche Glaube nach den Grundsätzen der evangelischen Kirche im Zusammenhange dargestellt*, 7th ed., 2 vols., ed. Martin Redeker (Berlin, 1960), p. 164. An English translation of the second edition is provided by *The Christian Faith*, trans. H. R. Mackintosh and J. S. Stewart (Edinburgh, 1948), p. 126.

which, simply as conception, can never be the basis for a relation with God. This understanding of unity also contributes to the definition of God's relationship to the world. God is the unity which upholds all particulars, the world is the diversity and multiplicity dependent upon this unity.

Hence the relation of mysticism to piety and also to the theological interpretation of religion and Christianity is not, for Schleiermacher, so unambiguous as many of his critics like to maintain. Schleiermacher indeed heard the ancient enticing melody of mysticism, but in the end he did not follow its song. He was prevented from doing so by the recognition of human finitude, the awe of the sacred, and the acknowledgment of the need for the redemption of man.[28]

The charge of pantheism was also raised very early. The argument between Schleiermacher and his solicitous older friend, Sack, comes to mind. All his life Schleiermacher vigorously defended himself and particularly the *Speeches* against this charge of heresy. To be sure he himself gave occasion to this opposition when he wrote that he wanted reverently to sacrifice a lock to the spirit of the departed holy, yet rejected, Spinoza.[29] Spinoza was for him a pious man filled with the Holy Spirit. Such a view had repercussions because until that time Protestant polemics had included Spinoza, as an alleged atheist, among the great seducers and corrupters of mankind.[30]

Apparently Schleiermacher had been occupied with Spinoza at least since 1794. His literary remains give evidence of this, although regrettably they are still not completely available. To the shock of his contemporaries Schleiermacher extolled Spinoza as a man of piety because he agreed with Spinoza's rejection of deistic and supernaturalistic interpretations of God. Since the essence of religion does not consist merely in accepting a dogmatic teaching, an idea of God cannot itself establish the living reality of religion. The experience of the infinite in the finite depends upon the activity of the universe and, therefore, upon the event of revelation. In the *Speeches* Schleiermacher makes the following provocative assertion in this connection: "God is not everything in religion but only one thing, and the universe is more; you cannot arbitrarily believe in Him or because you want to use Him for consolation and help; you believe in Him because you must."[31] In the second edition he formulated

---

28. Cf. Rudolf Otto, *West-östliche Mystik*, p. 338.
29. *Reden*, p. 55. *Speeches*, p. 40.
30. Cf. Christian Kortholt, *De tribus impostoribus magnis* (1680).
31. *Reden*, p. 133. *Speeches*, p. 282 (in condensed form in the Notes on the first edition).

it somewhat more carefully: "The usual conception of God as one particular being outside and behind the world is not everything in religion." The young Schleiermacher gave the superficial reader an impression of pantheism. But Schleiermacher shared with Spinoza's pantheism only the denial of the deistic and supernaturalistic Enlightenment idea of God.

Spinoza and his system can be interpreted in a twofold manner. Either God and nature are identical for Spinoza (in which case he is an atheist); or, and this is doubtless the profounder interpretation, Spinoza refuses to have God submerged in nature or the world but conversely lets the world be taken up into God. In this latter case Spinoza's metaphysics is an acosmic abstract pantheism built upon an untenable metaphysics of substance. Neither interpretation is found in Schleiermacher.

Already in his *Speeches* Schleiermacher stressed the distinction between God and human history. To religion also belongs "repentance for everything in us hostile to the genius of mankind, the humble wish to be reconciled with the Deity, the longing desire to return and to save ourselves and all that belongs to us in that holy region wherein alone there is assurance against death and destruction."[32] Only God is stronger than death.[33] Death and human insolence and man's betrayal of God stand between God and man. God is more than humanity. "But I have stated clearly enough that mankind is not everything for me, that my religion aspires to a universe of which mankind is only one infinitely small part, only a single passing form of the universe. Can therefore a God who is merely the genius of mankind be the highest in my religion?"[34] Another impassioned observation on this same point held that religion strives for an awareness of "something beyond and higher than mankind" and wants to be grasped by it.[35]

Schleiermacher is justified in repudiating the charge of pantheism, even as applied to his *Speeches*. In *The Christian Faith* he later argued even more precisely that a Christian theology must so emphatically differentiate between God and world and between good and evil that there can be no place for pantheism within it. Fundamentally this decision was already made in the *Speeches*. The seeming pantheistic outlook arose from his rejection of the traditional super-

---

32. *Reden*, p. 110. (Omitted in the third edition, English translation.)
33. *Reden*, p. 103. *Speeches*, p. 82.
34. *Reden*, p. 125. *Speeches*, p. 282 (Notes on the first edition).
35. *Reden*, p. 105. *Speeches*, p. 82 (This is a third edition modification).

naturalistic metaphysics, which Kant had already laid to rest, and his adoption of the new transcendental-philosophical, and to an extent romantic, interpretation of unity and wholeness for the relation between God and world, infinite and finite.

The final charge is that Schleiermacher's aestheticism confuses the boundaries between art and religion. This charge is readily bound up with the contention that Schleiermacher's religion, by virtue of its aestheticism, is a form of culture religion [*Bildungsreligion*]. Ostensibly the way to God, the way to salvation would lead from the intuition of aesthetic imagination to Goethe's artistically determined cultural ideal of a religion of humanity. It cannot be denied that in his formulations Schleiermacher freely availed himself of the aesthetic vocabulary of his romantic friends. He wanted to speak to the *cultured* among religion's despisers.

Of all areas of culture, however, the sphere of art and aesthetics was farthest from him. This can be seen in his later lectures on aesthetics. Since his youth he had been closely attached only to music. In the area of aesthetics he depended on his romantic friends. He first became engrossed in the whole area of the arts and aesthetics during his time in Berlin. The new artistic movement of the romantics impressed him so strongly because for him it was an ally in the battle against the Enlightenment. Hence he searched out the associations and affinities between art and religion. In his *Speeches* he prophesied that modern art would find its way to religion.[36] He himself admitted, however, that he did not yet know the way and considered this a deficiency in himself. He admitted he was not aware of any religion grounded in art which had dominated people and eras.[37] But appreciation of art has never approached religion without endowing it with a new beauty and holiness. The spirit of art in Plato was a prototype for Schleiermacher. He raised the holiest mysticism to the summit of divinity and humanity. Art and religion are intimate friends.[38] Later in his philosophy of culture he would coordinate both art and religion within the function of "symbolization." For him the most perfect symbol of God's rule in the world was the image of the creative artist, and the greatest work of art is that which has humanity itself as its object.[39]

---

36. *Reden*, pp. 166–67. *Speeches*, p. 283 (Notes on the first edition).

37. *Reden*, p. 168. *Speeches*, p. 140.

38. *Reden*, p. 169. *Speeches*, p. 140.

39. *Reden*, p. 173. *Speeches*, p. 142.

On the other hand, the young Schleiermacher was already critical of the development in romanticism which sought a way from art to religion and which (as is well known) led Friedrich Schlegel into the fold of the Roman Catholic church. Much of this romantic aestheticism was alien to Schleiermacher. A year later he commented on A. W. Schlegel: "It is noteworthy that such artistically affected enthusiasm for religion can never be original."[40] The young Schleiermacher already saw clearly the fantastic and unrealistic tendencies in the new religion of art.

> Imaginative temperaments fail in penetrating spirit, in the ability to master the essential. The light changing interplay of beautiful, often charming, yet always incidental and totally subjective combinations, satisfies them and is their highest goal; a deeper and more profound internal relationship presents itself to their eyes in vain. They are really only seeking the infinity and universality of enticing experiences.[41]

At this point already the young Schleiermacher posed the question about the reality and truth of the experience of God in the new aesthetic religiosity. He even predicted its collapse a few pages later in the *Speeches*. As far as he was concerned, its outcome would be "a vociferous yet misunderstood victim of the general contempt and maltreatment of all that is deepest in man."[42] Aesthetic religiosity, the "religion of art," was already declining for him during his romantic period. Art is religion's mode of expression but not its source. Art and religion are related as are thought and language.[43]

It is from this perspective that we should evaluate whether an aesthetic culture religion is advocated by Schleiermacher. Unlike most theologians he stands within the cultural movement of his time. Undoubtedly he ranks with Herder as one of the most important pedagogical thinkers of German idealism. He shares with the movement of humanistic culture a common struggle against the Enlightenment. Why, he asked, is the religious sense of our time so stunted? For the same reasons that the formation of a true humanity has been so hampered. It is not so much the doubters and scoffers who are detrimental as the sensible and practical people: "In the present state of the world these are the opponents of religion. Their pre-

---

40. *Briefe*, IV, p. 65.
41. *Reden*, pp. 157–58. *Speeches*, p. 133.
42. *Reden*, p. 160. *Speeches*, p. 134.
43. Cf. his ethics, *S. W.*, III, 5, proposition 255.

ponderance is why it plays such a meagre and insignificant role. From tender childhood they mistreat man, suppressing his higher aspirations."[44]

Therefore, one cannot teach religion by transmitting concepts and by demanding the memorization of quotations. But one can impart and awaken it. Under the personal impression of vivid experiences it awakens in the childlike soul. "The instant the sacred spark glows in a soul it leaps into a free and living flame, fed by its own atmosphere."[45] Throughout his life as a teacher of religion Schleiermacher, apparently from the experience of his own youth, had a very biased and one-sided point of view about memorizing catechetical articles and hymns. His own stepson, reporting later on Schleiermacher's confirmation classes, explained how a high regard for each child's individual development underlay his father's method of instruction. Consequently he himself never had to learn the catechism or a hymn.[46] Schleiermacher never wanted the children to memorize concepts, but sought always to awaken the "longing of young minds for the wondrous and supernatural" by presenting his own religious life.

It is something quite different if the young Schleiermacher is charged with teaching that the essence of religion is this formative process of the unfolding of the creative powers in the young, the creative projection of humanity as an ideal, and the striving toward this image of humanity — in short, if he is charged with teaching that the formative process is itself the way of salvation. However, an impartial reader of Schleiermacher's statements in the third speech will reject the above charge. The purpose of culture is to open up for the young the riches of this world and especially of humanity. In contrast, the religious in religion consists precisely in leading the young beyond the riches of this world.[47] One should lose the finite and find the universe.[48] As the absolute unity and whole, God is more than a *summum bonum* extracted from the humanistic ideals of culture. As absolute totality he is elevated above all antitheses of sensibility and understanding, flesh and spirit, death and life.

The charge, made particularly by Gundolf and others, that the content of Schleiermacher's religion is no more than humanistic

44. *Reden*, pp. 144–45. *Speeches*, p. 125.
45. *Reden*, p. 142. *Speeches*, p. 123.
46. Cf. E. von Willich, *Aus Schleiermachers Hause* (Berlin, 1909), p. 82.
47. *Reden*, p. 145. *Speeches*, p. 125.
48. *Reden*, p. 166. *Speeches*, p. 138.

culture is unjustified. Schleiermacher had called upon the cultured to struggle against the Enlightenment; he believed that he could show the cultured of his time how only a rediscovery of the Christian religion and its revelation would overcome the Enlightenment. He believed that art and religion were not merely friends and sisters, but that culture and religion must be allies. This awareness Schleiermacher communicated to many of the cultured in the nineteenth century.

3. THE CHRISTIAN IN CHRISTENDOM

The essence or, as Schleiermacher can also say, the "idea" of religion always manifests itself only in concrete historical form, i.e., intuition of the universe is always individual. Every individual form of religion is stamped by a specific basic intuition of the universe. The characteristic intuition of Christianity is the opposition or the conflict of the infinite and the finite in human history, and the over-coming of this conflict through Christ's redemption (Schleiermacher also speaks of this as reconciliation). "The original intuition of Christianity" is "simply the universal opposition of everything finite to the unity of the whole, and the way the Deity treats this opposition."[49] "Corruption and redemption, enmity and mediation are the two indissolubly united sides of this intuition."[50] Thus Christianity is "polemical" — i.e., it is critical of culture, of religion, but above all and with an ultimate radicalness it is self-critical. The moral world finds itself on the road from bad to worse and is incapable of liberating itself from the demonic cycle of self-destruction; philosophy undergoes the same fate and so too do the concrete historical religions. "Every revelation is in vain; everything is swallowed by the worldly sense."[51]

Because of its capacity for criticism, Christianity is the highest possibility of religion. Christianity shows up the irreligion and corruption in human religion; it can do this only because it also sees in the history of religion the universe's activity. This is how self-criticism operates in the Christian religion. "Never content with its achievements, even in its clearest intuitions and in its holiest feelings it is on the lookout for traces of irreligion and the tendency of every-thing finite to oppose and turn from the universe."[52] This self-

---

49. *Reden*, p. 291.   *Speeches*, p. 241.
50. *Reden*, p. 291.   *Speeches*, p. 241.
51. *Reden*, p. 293.   *Speeches*, p. 242.
52. *Reden*, p. 296.   *Speeches*, pp. 242–43 (modified in third edition).

judgment of Christianity is endless, and the basic feeling of this unending self-judgment Schleiermacher calls "holy melancholy."[53] The corruption of humanity is overcome only through reconciliation, through the mediation of Christ. Everything finite requires a higher mediation in order to be related to divinity. Jesus is the mediator of this salvation. The one who mediates does not himself require mediation and cannot be merely finite.[54] Hence he must "participate in the divine nature" in the same way "in which he shares in the finite."[55] The divine in Jesus is "the consciousness of the uniqueness of his relation to God, of the original way this awareness was in him, and of the power of the same to communicate itself and evoke religion in others."[56] His "yes" to the command of his Father in the prayer at Gethsemane, his freely given obedience on the cross was the "most glorious apotheosis"; "no Divinity can be more certain than the one who thus establishes himself."[57]

This understanding of the essence of the Christian in Christianity falls outside the classical humanistic interpretation of the world and life as well as the romantic apprehension of life. What is modern in Schleiermacher and what leads beyond classicism, beyond romanticism and idealist transcendental philosophy is expressed here. Goethe, who had read the first part of the *Speeches* with pleasure and approval, disgustedly put them aside when he reached this point of the work.

Above all Schleiermacher is polemicizing against the Enlightenment view of natural religion. Because its content is not that of a living and individual experience of revelation, natural religion — including that demanded by Kant in his philosophy of religion — is for Schleiermacher an abstract rational construction. In Schleiermacher's language, it is not immediate, it is not living, it lacks a true origin, uniqueness, and originality. Natural religion is "only an indefinite, meagre, and wretched idea incapable of real independent existence."[58] It is "the worthy product of an age which had as its fad pitiful generality and empty sobriety."[59] In contrast, living religion is infinite. But the infinite and immeasurable can become actual in history only in a multiplicity of individual forms. Religion must "have a prin-

---

53. *Reden*, p. 299.   *Speeches*, p. 245.
54. *Reden*, p. 302.   *Speeches*, p. 247.
55. *Reden*, p. 302.   *Speeches*, p. 247.
56. *Reden*, p. 302.   *Speeches*, p. 247.
57. *Reden*, p. 303.   *Speeches*, pp. 247–48.
58. *Reden*, p. 248.   *Speeches*, p. 217.
59. *Reden*, p. 277.   *Speeches*, pp. 233–34.

ciple for self-individualization without which it would not exist or be made known."[60]   Because religion is "a work of the world Spirit infinitely progressing, you must give up the rash and foolish wish that there should be only one religion."[61]

He apparently did not hold to Christianity's claim to absolute truth; he relativized this claim by the principle of individuality and the idea of historical evolution.   But, on the other hand, Christianity is the highest stage in the religious development of mankind up to the present time.   It "transcends others."   Nonetheless, he has to describe Christianity as a passing phenomenon.   He says of Christianity that even "in its glory" it is "more historical and humble" than the others.[62]   Therefore he believes that historical development would at least lead beyond the present form of Christianity.   But this new evolutionary era would again signify a palingenesis of Christianity, awakening its spirit in newer and finer forms.   The final goal of development lies "beyond all time."   Thus one finds in the young Schleiermacher a belief in mankind's infinite historical development combined with ideas from Pauline eschatology, according to which no further mediator is needed since the Father will be all in all.   But this stage of development lies "beyond all time."[63]   Christ is thus not the only mediator.   He never claimed to be the sole mediator and never confused his school with his religion.[64]   The Schleiermacher of *The Christian Faith* will correct this idea which arose out of his romantic philosophy of the infinite.

4. THE SOCIAL ELEMENT IN RELIGION

The line of argument in the fourth speech on the social element in religion (concerning the church and the priesthood) is less satisfactory than the others.   From the point of view of both the history of religions and theology this fourth speech is considered theologically one of the weaker efforts among Schleiermacher's youthful writings. It is filled with intense polemic against the existing church structure. He begins with the assertion that the protest against the church as the external social form is a clearer phenomenon than the dislike of religion.   "Hence your opposition to the church, to every organized effort to communicate religion, is always greater than your opposition

60. *Reden*, p. 241.   *Speeches*, p. 213.
61. *Reden*, p. 242.   *Speeches*, p. 214.
62. *Reden*, p. 308.   *Speeches*, p. 251.
63. *Reden*, p. 308.   *Speeches*, p. 251.
64. *Reden*, p. 304.   *Speeches*, p. 248.

to religion itself; and because the priests are the stays and the true active members of such structures they are for you the most hated of men."[65]

This censure does not touch the true church and the association of the genuinely pious; but then so much the more does he criticize the "teaching church." In this "teaching church" the free play of piety, uniqueness, and originality is suppressed. No matter how enlightened its teachings it still moves within the bounds of superstition and is attached to some mythology or other.[66] Its method of teaching is a dull mechanism, its activity a performance of empty conventions. However it is not the teaching church itself that is primarily to blame for these evils; it is rather the state that must be held accountable for the degeneration of the church. The state gave the church privilege, endowed it with property, and entrusted it with responsibility for the moral education of the people, which also included civil education. For these privileges the state exercised control over the church and kept it in bondage. All this inevitably corrupts the church.

But what then is the true church and why must there be churches at all? Here Schleiermacher introduces an important discovery which separates him in large part from the romantics. Religion is necessarily social. This term, which sounds strange to us, means: the church is not an institution, not a structure for salvation in the traditional sense; above all it is not a hierarchical institution with sacral-magical authority. The church is rather a community arising from within the religious life as a completely free spiritual communion of truly pious men. This is a significant complement to Schleiermacher's usual focus on the pious individual. What the *Soliloquies* later proclaimed as Schleiermacher's original discovery about the whole life of historical mankind the *Speeches* had already stated: one becomes a man when he discovers in his individuality his own origination, his own originality, and uniqueness. Schleiermacher demanded of his readers that they observe "how the Deity gradually builds up that part of the soul in which He specially dwells, in which He reveals and knows Himself in His immediate presence, making it into His own sanctuary, separating it from that which otherwise is developed and formed in man, and how He thus glorifies Himself in His full splendor through the inexhaustible variety of such forms."[67]

65. *Reden*, p. 175.   *Speeches*, p. 147.
66. *Reden*, p. 202.   *Speeches*, pp. 162–63.
67. *Reden*, p. 269.   *Speeches*, p. 229.

But this individuality is not a self-grounded subjectivity, not a titanism of the self which desires total self-sufficiency. By giving man his individuality God has opened the way to other individualities, bestowing upon man, in the sphere of religion, the gift of a spiritual community of understanding, of participation, of self-expression and mutual edification through language.

Beginning with this idea of a spiritual community he formed his concept of the true church. He did this in a dual manner. First of all he constructed the abstract idea of a universal church without consideration for the historical appearances of the church or of the historical religions, that is, "without regard for that which is actual up to now and that which experience teaches."[68] For him there are, of course, diverse religions but there is only one universal church which embraces all the truly devout. This is pure theory, proceeding from the romantic conviction that religion is infinite and everything human finite; consequently there is one universal church and various, historically conditioned, finite, imperfect religious communities. But then he apparently dropped this utopian idea and nonetheless sought to define the true church as a community where devout men concretely encounter each other in devotion and love of God. He wanted to begin not with what *should be* but with what already *is*. The true church he finds "in single, separate communities severed, as it were, from the church at large."[69]

There is no distinction between priests and laity in this true church. It is a perfect republic wherein each is alternately leader and people.[70] There is, also, in it no sectarian spirit or urge to proselytize; rather, the free spirit of understanding and communication of the self is dominant. It is a chorus of friends and brothers. "Everyone knows that he is also an aspect and a work of the universe, that in him its divine action and life are revealed."[71] "The closer each comes to the universe, the more each communicates with the other, the more perfectly do they become one. No one has a consciousness for himself alone, each has at the same time a consciousness of the other. They are no longer just men, but mankind also; going beyond and triumphing over themselves, they are on the way to true immortality and eternity."[72]

---

68. *Reden*, p. 176.   *Speeches*, p. 148.
69. *Reden*, p. 192.   *Speeches*, p. 157.
70. *Reden*, p. 184.   *Speeches*, p. 153.
71. *Reden*, p. 233.   *Speeches*, p. 180.
72. *Reden*, p. 234.   *Speeches*, p. 180.

With unrestrained enthusiasm Schleiermacher even ventured to apply the traditional concept of the church triumphant. This is consistent to the extent that eternal blessedness is even now experienced here on earth in the revelation of the universe. In this same sense he believed he could speak of the true church even now as the community of the blessed. There is no doubt but that Schleiermacher here expressed the idea of the Church of the Brethren which lived on in him through his youthful religious experiences and which he now rediscovered in a new form. These are the ideals of the church of his Moravian period. His ideal of the pietistic community of the converted and illuminated was applied to a spiritual community of elevated and inspired men created by the activity of the universe. The Moravian ideal of the Brethren community is transferred to the levels of the romantic–idealistic conception of humanity.

His proposals for reform of the church as the external society of his time are derived from this point of view. He first of all required the complete separation of state and church, including even the separation of the church marriage ceremony and the civil marriage contract. In this he found himself in opposition to the ecclesiastical practices of German Protestantism of that time. The old Protestant association of church and state within the confessionally unified states had been retained by pietism and the Enlightenment under the new conditions and structure of the absolute state. Spener's and Francke's form of Protestantism owed its great influence to the Prussian monarchy. The early phase of the Enlightenment even welcomed government control of the church as a better guarantor of tolerance and certain freedoms than the leadership of older Protestant orthodoxy. The later Enlightenment assigned the office of clergyman an important role in popular moral and religious education, and stressed the minister's concern for social welfare and his role in supporting the state. The Evangelical Church of Silesia was indebted to Friedrich the Great, the freethinking prince of Europe. After the oppression of the Hapsburg period he led the way to new reforms with government support and at the same time advocated tolerance toward the Catholics. All German Protestantism had come to expect that improvements in ecclesiastical affairs would be undertaken at the initiative of the state and of the state's ecclesiastical government.

The young Schleiermacher vigorously opposed this very powerful trend within German Protestantism. He desired the separation of state and church as a final goal for the sake of freedom of instruction and for the renewal of a vital religious community. Schleiermacher's main motive for separation certainly was not due to any misgiving about the increasing secularization of the modern state. He was concerned with the renewal of Christian piety, the reawakening of Christian community, the revival of a true priestly sense among the clergy. Clearly these ideas were directed toward the future. Hence the ideas of Schleiermacher's fourth speech, although theologically not the strongest of his youthful writings, have had significance for the further development of Protestant polity. The same is true of his other ideas for reform. He insisted upon personal communities. Through the activity of pietistic revival preachers such communities were actualized in the church's historical development during the nineteenth century. Above all he wanted the separation of preaching and the ministry from popular moral instruction as required by the state. These were all demands which prophetically anticipated the further development of the Protestant church in Germany. That, however, should not divert us from the fact that his theological definition of the nature of the church is quite unsatisfactory; his insights into the nature of Christianity go in quite different directions and make the christological center of Christian piety and of the Christian church much clearer. In his theological definition of the nature of the church he was too dependent on his romantically determined ethical ideas and on ideas growing out of his philosophy of history. On this question his Moravian heritage was adapted too much to his romantic ideas, while in his definition of religion and Christianity this Moravian heritage led him beyond himself.

The positive result in this transformation of the Moravian tradition is seen in Schleiermacher's refusal to describe the true church as a pietistic conventicle or sect with a restricted horizon. As a concrete unit of humanity the true church is also the true human community in which humanity works out and reflects the genius of mankind. This concrete community never has narrow horizons but the openness of religious universalism. Thus Christian and romantic universalism come together.

C. THE SOLILOQUIES

In the writings of the young Schleiermacher the *Soliloquies* is the companion piece to the *Speeches*. Just how closely both are linked and supplement each other in subject matter is indicated by a comment in Schleiermacher's first notes preparing for the *Soliloquies*: "Self-intuition and intuition of the universe are reciprocal concepts."[73] The event of the revelation of the infinite in the finite occurs in the

---

73. *Denkmale*, p. 118.

intuition of the universe; in self-intuition, on the other hand, the moral process itself, the origin of a new ethos occurs. In the *Soliloquies* Schleiermacher underscores the complete independence of religion from morality in a radical one-sidedness as a defense against Kant's and Fichte's postulates; at the same time he posits the continuity of religion and ethos in this internal bond between intuition of the universe and self-intuition.

What new ethos results from self-intuition? The formation of individual self-consciousness occurs in and through it. Individuality is the unique and original discovery of Schleiermacher's philosophy of life. But it is in the *Soliloquies* that the significance of this concept for Schleiermacher's understanding of ethos, life, and world comes to the fore. Individuality is not merely particular existence, limited, finite particularity. If it were that it would be determined and not really free. On the contrary, the *Soliloquies* is a song of praise to free individuality, to individuality as a higher inner life of men. In contrast to the *modes* in Spinoza's system which are limited, finite particulars, the individuality of Schleiermacher's self-intuition is the organ and symbol of the infinite; it is the place where the infinite as unity and totality encounters the final inner unity of the human self. Thus individuality cannot be classified within the causal network of natural and human life. It is not something accomplished, not something brought about, rather it is self-originating. Its formative process moves from within outward. It is original living; but it is not an absolutely autonomous subject. The universe posits an individual as its organ and reflection.

Here one of Schleiermacher's essential discoveries comes to light. The infinite is not a universal and abstract idea; rather the divine reveals itself by creating concrete structures that become organ and symbol for the Divinity. Accordingly it is impossible to attain the salvation of communion with God by way of metaphysical speculation. God is not a universal idea. One can only experience the reality of God through the manifestation of his reality in concrete life and to the individual. For this reason Schleiermacher asserts time and again that the universe creates its own admirers. This religious experience bestows on the individual his originality, his freedom and his participation in a higher infinite life. Individuality hence is not the biological self that asserts itself as a physical being. Nor is it the self that wants satisfaction of its earthly needs, striving for prosperity and good fortune. The self is unrestrained action and creative spirit. In the individual, multiplicity is brought together into a single living unity and in this wholeness and unity one sees

the reflection of the divine wholeness and unity. The creative freedom
of the spirit is also the positing, the organ, and the reflection of the
divine Spirit. This freedom and independence are demonstrated by
the fact that they are not products of a psychological necessity. On
the other hand, this freedom is not arbitrariness, for the self's freedom
and activity follow from its own being.

Despite his finitude and limitation the individual in his inner
life is free, having become organ and symbol for God. Here it becomes
clear that the most distinctive feature of Schleiermacher's interpretation
of individuality in the *Soliloquies* refers back to Moravian influences.
In a letter to Brinkmann, Schleiermacher himself attests that the
self-intuition of individuality goes back to his pietistic experiences in
the Moravian community.[74] It is the pietistic care for the soul's
salvation and the cultivation of inwardness which give the individual
his inner spiritual reality. His freedom and vitality have a religious
root.

Schleiermacher's encounter with the theory of education (*Bildung*)
in *Wilhelm Meister* enabled him to carry over his fundamental Christian
experience into the sphere of *humanité*. Because of this religious
root Schleiermacher's idea of individuality cannot be confused with
the aesthetic appreciation of individuality as propounded, for instance,
in Schiller's *Letters on Aesthetic Education.* Beginning with this
religious root Schleiermacher goes on to uncover the ethical-historical
meaning of individuality. It becomes the task and work of men,
the foundation stone for his own philosophical world view.

It has become customary in contemporary philosophy to use the
terms "existence" and the "existent" when speaking of the concrete
self. In much of existentialism "existence," the courageous act
of freedom, leaves behind that necessity which rules all objectified
beings and phenomena and faces ultimate solitude and responsibility
with courage. The existential self therefore can never be known
as an object. It can only be grasped in free self-actualization.
But Schleiermacher's "self" distinguishes itself sharply from the
self of modern "existence." As far as one segment of modern
existential philosophy is concerned, the self is characterized by its
being thrown into nothingness and by man's freely made "project" of
a possibility of human existence. Through this "projection" of his
own possibilities man becomes authentic. Thus the "existence" of
modern existential philosophy is not equivalent to existence (*Dasein*)
and actuality; it is rather man's capacity to be (*Sein-können*) based

---

74. *Briefe*, IV, p. 61.

on his own projects. Implicit in this is a radical renunciation of eternal truths. Man's "thrown-ness" is the meaningless facticity of existence (*Dasein*); the "project" originates from his own will. Being man thus comprises no more than finite historicity. For such a being there is nothing transhistorical and ultimate. The individual in Schleiermacher, however, is God's organ and symbol. Dilthey once even formulated it as follows: Individuality is the organ and symbol of God in the spirit of Jesus Christ. The pietistic roots of Schleiermacher's reflections on individuality point to this Christian spirit.

The individual is not only responsible for himself but because of this root in the Christian spirit he is "opened" and joined to other individuals. For the goal of this higher life is "awareness" (*Sinn*) and "love." "Awareness" is not sense perception; it is valuing the individuality of others, openness to the particularity and otherness of the other, acceptance of others. This attitude, in association with love, is reverence for the Thou of the other as an image of God. The obligation to acknowledge the other is deepened by devotion.

A further basic concept is important for Schleiermacher's evaluation of others: the concept of "mankind." It is perhaps difficult for us today to re-experience the meaning this concept had for Schleiermacher and his contemporaries. Mankind is not a universal abstract idea about the essence of men and the human race; mankind is for him rather the plenitude of free, concrete individualities which together form a whole. His vision for the future is such a formation of mankind. Schleiermacher gave his imagination free rein in expressing this vision. Mankind is something concretely living and comes to expression in the three forms of community — friendship, marriage, and fatherland. He did not consider it satisfactory simply to make advances in the domination of nature as advocated by the spirit of the age. Concern for the progressive well-being and perfection of human civilization is not the whole work of mankind. "Mankind" is rather the enhancement of the inner life, of love and of indestructible human concord. The national state, for instance, is not a necessary evil, not an external community of the material world for the increase of property and protection against misfortune and calamity.[75] The state is the finest work of human art by which man raises his being to the highest level.[76]

The state is for Schleiermacher the concretion of mankind as moral community and the higher life. The idea of individuality is

---

75. *Monologen*, p. 85. *Soliloquies*, pp. 59–60.
76. *Monologen*, p. 84. *Soliloquies*, p. 59.

here applied to the state as a social individual and tends to define the state as a moral and historical being.

The inner life of mankind is indestructible and infinite. It constantly strives beyond itself toward higher perfection. This striving is for Schleiermacher the true mark of youth. "I pledged myself to eternal youth"[77] was Schleiermacher's famous formulation. The mark of youth is not biological strength but freedom, the internal endless striving for moral perfection. "My will shall remain strong and my imagination vital, nothing shall wrest from me the magic key which opens the mysterious gates to the higher world, and never will I let love's fire be extinguished."[78] "The spirit which drives men forward and the constant craving for the new that can never be satisfied by what has been shall never yield. It is man's glory to know that his goal is infinite."[79]

Few of Schleiermacher's writings convey such one-sided and clear-cut signs of his ethical idealism which seeks to build within the finite itself a higher inner world of mankind as a kingdom of free spirits. The *Soliloquies* are a hymn of praise to the creative Spirit. There is considerable pride in this glorification and yet connected with it is an awe and humility which never forget that all higher life must be bestowed and comes as grace. The bounds and the limits of this romantically exaggerated moral idealism are only too clear. It is an idealism without the self-discipline of penitence, whereas the *Speeches* self-critically make conscious the opposition between the infinite and the finite Spirit.

The content and form of the *Soliloquies* correspond. The author strove for a rhythmical, nearly lyrical prose. In a letter to Brinkmann, Schleiermacher explained that he allowed the iambic, dactylic, and anapestic rhythms to flow into his prose. Presumably Goethe's *Egmont* soliloquy was the model for the use of iambs. As a result the style becomes artificial — something already criticized by Brinkmann. Schleiermacher began writing some time around his birthday (November 21, 1799), and by employing earlier material (e.g., *On the Worth of Life*) finished the work in four weeks; it could now be published almost simultaneously with Fichte's *The Destiny of Man* in the opening days of the new year. In his biography of Schleiermacher, Dilthey held that:

---

77. *Monologen*, p. 140.   *Soliloquies*, p. 94.
78. *Monologen*, p. 141.   (The passage is not in Friess's translation.)
79. *Monologen*, p. 141.   *Soliloquies*, p. 97.

As a literary work the *Soliloquies* displayed greater vigor than did [Fichte's] *Destiny*. They contain the results of a view of life and the world that is unrestricted by contentious philosophical assumptions; rather they truly free the heart because they form themselves in the same way in every noble soul that reflects. Therefore of all moral works by modern thinkers this one alone still exerts its influence on a large reading public today. It unfailingly exercises a definitive influence on deeper natures who come in contact with it during the decisive years of their development.[80]

We are today so remote from this time that it is difficult to soar to Dilthey's understanding, much less follow Schleiermacher's ideas. We are separated from this time by the criticism of culture and ethical skepticism which has gripped us since Nietzsche's *Zarathustra*, and by the shattering of German idealism as a spiritual and philosophical movement in the German cultural world.

D. SCHLEIERMACHER'S RELATION TO ROMANTICISM

The first steps toward a new theological outlook are to be found in both of Schleiermacher's early writings, the *Speeches* and the *Soliloquies*. During the course of his life the "speaker" acknowledged his return to these beginnings and interpreted the changes of his thought as a further elaboration and a deeper and clearer substantiation of them, more a change of concepts and modes of expression than of fundamental theological principles: "I have remained the same since the *Speeches*."[81]

There are only a few fundamental ideas in these works: first, there is his rejection of Enlightenment theology in its supernaturalistic as well as its modernistic form. Schleiermacher accomplished this by distinguishing areas; in its essence religion is something different from metaphysics and morality. He was not simply concerned with the distinctiveness of the religious sphere as distinct from metaphysical speculation and morality; rather he was concerned about the essence of religion. He wanted to find and newly define the distinctively religious in religion, the Christian in Christianity, and the theological in theology. God is not an idea of metaphysical speculation and not a postulate of the moral law, but the higher all-encompassing reality that opens itself through the action of revelation to the individual

---

80. Dilthey, *Leben Schleiermachers*, vol. I, pp. 449 f.; 2d ed., pp. 493 f.
81. *Briefe*, IV, p. 241.

believing heart of man.   An important methodological discovery is involved here.   It concerns the relation of revelation and theology, of faith and theological teaching, of the Christian's illumination by the spirit and the letter of dogmatic formulation.   The relation of God and man, brought forth in the faithful existence of men, is not grounded in metaphysical speculation.   Faith is not accepting ideas as true but the living relation of God and man.   Hence all theological concepts are not the foundation but that which is founded.

The Christian in Christianity is that which comes from Christ and establishes the living community between Christ and those in need of redemption.   However, the higher life of the human race which establishes the living communion with Christ is also "Christian." The distinctive mark of this higher life is the theological interpretation of individuality as organ and symbol for God.

It is now time to reconsider the question whether and to what extent these new theological perspectives are connected with the romantic spirit and thought.   Is the charge that Schleiermacher romanticized religion and Christianity accurate?

Without a doubt his language belonged to romanticism.   Both friends and opponents have taken considerable offense at this.   His friend Sack took the sharpest position against it.   In his letters to Schleiermacher, in which he gave furious expression to his anger over the *Speeches*, he asserted:

> The revolutionary new school appears to me extremely rebellious and destructive, wantonly toppling and tearing down everything. . . .   The revolutionary new language appears to me just as extreme; its first rule is to repay all rational speech and instruction with defiance, with counterfeit coin, to wrap itself in unintelligible darkness; and out of the fear of expressing itself in an accepted manner it becomes pompous exactly like a man who struts about on stilts in order to appear larger than other men.   A man like you, so knowledgeable in the noble simplicity of the Greeks, should at least disdain this pompous and tasteless style of writing and leave it to the visionaries and pseudo-poetic wisecrackers who satisfy themselves with adulation and praise from supersentimental culture-hungry ladies.[82]

Most critics, however, go beyond the complaint against stylistic affectation and charge that Schleiermacher has romanticized and sentimentalized religion and Christianity.   The very derivation and

---

82. *Briefe*, III, pp. 278–79.

origin of his ideas from romanticism is enough to bring discredit and reproach.

This contention contains an objection which has been made repeatedly by Schleiermacher researchers, most recently by both literary historians and theologians. This objection contains the usual basic criticism of romanticism. For these critics the romantic movement obliterated the boundaries between imagination and reality. Life, including the religious life, is for the romantics a beautiful dream and the assertions concerning the higher life with God and the contact of the infinite with the finite are a product of the imagination. Sentimentalizing is taken as a reduction of all spiritual life to an unclear, mysterious, subjective inwardness which evades the hard encounter with reality. Sentimentalizing of religion would then correspond to the dissolution of religion into a "religion without God," into an irrational, inward, infinite province of feeling in men.[83]

If one poses the question more precisely whether Schleiermacher was a romantic — as, for instance, Friedrich Schlegel was — then this can only be denied. Schleiermacher was no born romantic. He is done an injustice if one imputes to his theological understanding of religion a poetic-aesthetic subjectivism, and a desire for a religion without God. What he rejected were the representations of God within supernaturalistic dogmatics because they rested on the Enlightenment's supernaturalistic metaphysics which had been overcome by transcendental philosophy.

Schleiermacher's relation to romanticism, however, is not sufficiently depicted by this negative observation. The Berlin romanticism of his friends was an artistic movement. The circle which had come together was in no way homogenous. In a letter to Brinkmann, Schleiermacher clearly recognized precisely the same thing: "If one observes how totally different Friedrich Schlegel, Tieck, and A. W. Schlegel are and will continue to be in their productions and principles, then one can well understand that their inclination is not to form a sect as an offense — at most only as a defense; they could not possibly exist if the others who imagine themselves to be the old school were not taking the offensive against them."[84] Schleiermacher knew his own limits. He was no poet.

---

83. Cf. Friedrich Gundolf, "Schleiermachers Romantik," *Deutsche Vierteljahresschrift für Literaturwissenschaft und Geistesgeschichte*, Vol. III (1924), p. 451: "He wanted to establish religion without God and had to introduce poetically clothed allegories of the divine spirit and to personify activities of the soul as cosmic powers."
84. *Briefe*, IV, p. 83.

I have decisively shunned seeking that which makes an artist
... [who] in every work that comes to him ascertains the impression of all its parts, the composition and law of the whole, delighting
more in the artistic vessel than in the precious content which it
displays. ... But this only my sense discerned, for it is foreign
to my thinking. The humanity that radiates from every work
of art and is reflected in it is far clearer to me than the artist's
artistry. ... I do not seek to bring to perfection the material
upon which I impress my sense. ... Unlike the artist, therefore,
I cannot create in solitude.[85]

Schleiermacher sought to fathom the differentiation and the continuity
between artistic sense and religion. Language is to knowledge as
art is to religion. For him religion is fundamental and actual and
art is only the expression, the language, the word-event which may
express the truth of religious experience but not establish it. In
this sense the sermon is also a spoken work of art.

Schleiermacher had learned much from his romantic friends, even
to the point of appropriating too much. Only gradually did he
free himself from the bonds of romanticism and find his own center.
He not only borrowed his understanding of poetry and art from
romanticism, his hermeneutics, his interpretation of Plato and Plato's
philosophical development also received an impetus from the romantic
outlook. But he also contributed something substantial to romanticism.
He sought to convince his friends that the sense for art is still not
religion. Quite like metaphysical speculation, art and artistic intuition
are mostly a play of the spirit, imagination, and striving, of the search
for wholeness and unity in the midst of fleeting finite appearances.
The artistic cannot give the real answer to this quest. This occurs
only through the revelation of the universe in feeling, in pious self-
consciousness. Here the basis of his later system is already evident.
The ultimate assurance that there is a truth to be known and that
art participates in life is based neither on knowledge itself nor on
artistic imagination. Religion alone provides this foundation. Pious
self-consciousness first gives access to the superior reality of the
absolute totality which is simultaneously greater than the world of
finite appearances while present and effective in it.

Dilthey summed up Schleiermacher's relation to his romantic
friends: "Like every genius he was lonely in their midst and yet
needed them."[86] "He lived among them as a sober man among

---

85. *Monologen*, pp. 45 f. *Soliloquies*, pp. 35 f.
86. Dilthey, *Leben Schleiermachers*, 1st ed., p. 260.

New Insights

63

dreamers."[87] Schleiermacher's efforts to describe the religious in
religion in the new language of the romantics with its concepts of
universe, infinite, and individual were not in the least understood
by the advocates of supernaturalistic theology. Therefore, for Sack,
his ecclesiastical superior, Schleiermacher's ideas were simply the
proof of an unbecoming conceit and thirst for glory. Sack spoke
his mind to Schleiermacher on this point. Particularly offensive
for him was Schleiermacher's questioning of the Enlightenment
conceptions of a personal God and individual immortality. Schleiermacher replied to his fatherly friend in a respectful yet firm manner:

> My ultimate purpose has been to exhibit and establish, in the
> present storm of philosophical opinions, the independence of
> religion from every metaphysics. It never occurred to me that
> my religion was in conflict with Christianity in the name of a
> particular philosophical conception. . . . On the contrary I am
> convinced that I truly have the religion which I should proclaim
> — even if I have quite a different philosophy from most of my
> listeners.[88]

Schleiermacher's new language was provocative to the older generation.
In his biography of Schleiermacher, Schenkel reported: "The
Speeches went off like Congreve rockets into the paper tabernacles
of the prevailing Enlightened theology."[89] Schleiermacher was
bound to his romantic friends more by the renunciation of the Enlightenment and its supernaturalistic dogmas than by the positive
things he wanted to say.

In the encounter with his romantic friends he participated in their
cultural world and used their language. But he ultimately did not
succumb to the temptations of romantic fantasy and sentimentality,
of their originality and sentimentality, because his decisive religious
and theological conceptions were not rooted in romanticism. As
indicated above, the novelty of his piety and the systematic development of his ideas are discernible already prior to his Berlin period.
The higher life of Christian faith rests on the encounter with the
revelation of Christ. He himself understands this as being grasped
by the new communal life created through Christ.

87. Ibid., p. 439.
88. *Briefe*, III, p. 284.
89. Daniel Schenkel, *Friedrich Schleiermacher: Ein Lebens- und Charakterbild*
(Elberfeld, 1868), p. 139.

His systematic work in theology and philosophy soon led him beyond romanticism. Scholarship became for him much more than speculative play with ideas and concepts; it became the serious service on behalf of truth for the overcoming of fanaticism and empty skepticism.

The systematic period of his thought, which brought greater conceptual clarity and a clearer profile to his theology and philosophy, thus organically followed the intuitive-creative period. But we must first deal with the ethics of romanticism and Schleiermacher's argument with the romantic interpretation of human life in community.

E. CONFIDENTIAL LETTERS ON LUCINDE

The consciousness of the individual's uniqueness is precisely the prerequisite for a deepening of life in community. Romantic ethics and anthropology thus enriched and provided new insights into the understanding of friendship and love between the sexes.

The presupposition for the new ethics of love and marriage is the romantic view of woman's individuality and the conviction that, in the relation of the sexes, body and spirit are a unity. Love aids both partners in discovering their humanity. The lover seeks to find the image of God in the other through the "silver glance" of love, and then with the help of his beloved to discover and unfold this Godlikeness as the true humanity in himself. The experience of sharing love is thus joined with the discovery of one's own true self, which can only be found by overcoming eudaemonistic egoism. Consequently, the romantic view of marriage should not be confused with so-called modern free love as the "emancipation of the flesh," with ethical permissiveness. Schlegel's *Lucinde* and Schleiermacher's *Confidential Letters on Lucinde* do not deal with "free love" but with romantic marriage.[90] According to Schlegel's own intentions, *Lucinde* was a glorification of true marriage. This intention is already embodied in the Christian name used for the title. The name Lucinde has the same meaning as the feminine name Luciane and may be translated as the "illuminated" one. Schlegel apparently took this name from the Spanish poet Cervantes. Romantic marriage is not, to be sure, a sacrament; it is also not the dutiful companionship of the Lutheran marital state. Rather it is the mystery of the happy communion of two people. The sanction for this marriage consists in the belief that each individual, each self, completes itself in a genuine harmony, a true humanity, by indissolubly uniting itself with a "thou."

90. *S. W.*, III/1, p. 421.

Marriage is therefore indissoluble. A romantic marriage established on love should — by its very nature — carry in itself the guarantee of duration. Divorce contradicts the very essence of living together as man and wife. It only reveals the fact that the union of the husband and wife had not been a true marriage. A true marriage leads the lovers beyond the limits of the finite and the chronologically limited, bringing to both lovers the experience of the infinite because it signifies deliverance from the individual's isolation. Hence only love is experienced as real and as the encounter with the original divine source (*Urgrund*) of life. Perhaps one may formulate it this way: for Friedrich Schlegel love is God. But this statement is only correct when it is reversed; according to the biblical testimony, God is the subject. "God is love."

The profounder meaning of Schlegel's *Lucinde* was completely distorted through the impossible literary form in which Schlegel cast his ideas. Schlegel wanted to offend the moralizing Philistines through a succession of paradoxes and romantic irony. Hence his work is a chaotic mixture of disjointed ingenious insights, fairy tales, allegories, and tasteless autobiographical sketches and indiscretions. All in all this writing was not a real novel; it is most tedious and as a poetic work it is worthless.

Schleiermacher was deceived by the novel's poetic and spiritual content, and at the request of his friend and of Dorothea Veit (whom Schlegel later married) he even came to the defense of this inferior work. But in reality this defense was more than a vindication of Schlegel's "love story." Schleiermacher's *Confidential Letters on Lucinde* were meant to express the romantic conception of marriage. Unfortunately he did not recognize the artificiality and formlessness of Schlegel's writing and he sought to cover the failure of this work with the good wishes of a friend. In a letter to Goethe on July 19, 1799, Schiller judged Schlegel's *Lucinde* more trenchantly than Schleiermacher: "Furthermore, this work should not be read through completely since the vapid prattle makes one much too ill. He allows himself everything and he himself declares that audacity is his goddess. This writing is the pinnacle of modern un-form and un-nature."

In his apology for his friend, Schleiermacher presented romantic marriage much more positively and clearly than Schlegel could. Schleiermacher criticized above all the marriages of the Enlightenment which were contracted for the sake of external interests, containing only the form but not the spirit of marriage. In these he saw a "desecration of the holiest bonds of human existence." In the *Letters on Lucinde*,

in which five people — three women and two men — correspond
with each other, love is presented as an unbroken totality which cannot
endure analysis and dissection.   In love the spiritual and the physical
are most intimately bound together.   The unacceptable alternative
to true love is isolated sensuality.   Such isolated sensuality is understood as a necessary evil of nature, which must be tolerated, or as
torpid and unworthy philandering which only raises the natural drive
to a sophisticated level without purifying and humanizing it.   Love
is a divine spark which cannot be dissected into spirit and flesh, will
and nature, without desecration.   An anxious and narrow feeling of
shame is brought about by the consciousness of deep-seated corruption
and general perversity.   Genuine modesty, by contrast, is the moral
attitude which frees men from the bondage of these drives and discovers
in love the beautiful and refined.   Wieland's erotic writings were
for Schleiermacher immoral and deformed.   Wieland went to almost
any length in describing sensual lust, something which is not truly
representable artistically.   Real and genuine love, in which the
spiritual and physical are unified, is the true mystery of life, opening
men to the infinite.   The fine arts and poetry transfigure this synthesis
of the spiritual and physical, and they show how real love finds its
divine determination in its relation to the good and the beautiful.

Marriage is supposed to make one out of two.[91]   The loving
individual seeks the beloved thou in order to unite both together
into a whole.   The mark and symbol of this most profound community
is the union of the spirit and erotic sensuousness.   But "objective
representations" of the merely animalic life must be recognized as
shameless.[92]

Schleiermacher's marriage ethic is a significant refinement and
deepening of previous interpretations of love and marriage, leading
beyond the marriage ethics of the Reformation and much beyond
that of the Enlightenment.   The new aspect is the inclusion of romantic
anthropology into the ethics of marriage.   Love and marriage are
not a mere process of nature which one endures or by which one
is tempted.   They are not simply a burden of duties; love rather
is the understanding of the other and in this understanding of internal
unity, the elevation of life is experienced as inner happiness which
purifies sensuous enjoyment.   This interpretation of marriage by
Schleiermacher is still open and unfinished in the *Confidential Letters
on Lucinde*.   It still contains too much of Schlegel's romanticism,

---

91. *Denkmale,* p. 129.
92. *Vertraute Briefe über Fr. Schlegels Lucinde, S. W.,* III/1, p. 460.

too much of the subjectivism of indulgence. Real love, its moral magnitude and moral seriousness, first comes into being when it is elevated beyond the mere subjectivism of indulgence. Should it not also be possible to fit love into an encompassing moral order of life? The unity of the spiritual and the sensual-erotic is not a mere gift of nature that easily comes to men. It is the goal of moral effort and growth. Schleiermacher's second defect lies here. Owing to the enthusiasm of his aesthetic vision he failed to recognize the severity of the tension between spirit and sensuousness and misjudged the necessity of subordinating the life of love and marriage to the sanctity of life's moral orders. Owing to his metaphysical vision of the unity of the spiritual and sensual, Schleiermacher failed to recognize the extensive power of passion and its destructive effects in life. Finally, however, he still admits that in the individual life there is no perfect love; love finds its perfection only in death.[93]

Dilthey has asked how Schleiermacher ever came to write the *Confidential Letters on Lucinde*, for despite its occasional deeper moments it is not worthy of Schleiermacher.[94] Dilthey is expressing here what the majority of Schleiermacher's friends and students have also sensed. The basic defect of the writing, according to Dilthey, is that Schleiermacher too hastily transferred the principles of the new romantic ethics to life itself and in doing so violated solemn moral interests.[95] Despite his good intentions of helping his friend, Friedrich Schlegel, Schleiermacher should actually have condemned Schlegel's work. The chief weaknesses of *Lucinde* according to Dilthey are: (1) the unity of the spiritual and physical is not believably represented by Schlegel; (2) an egoistical, subjective desire for desire itself breaks through time and again in Schlegel; (3) *Lucinde* expresses a foolish hatred of marriage as an objective moral order of human life. Love is not first sensual enjoyment but both an act and offering to accomplish the communal moral tasks of marriage and the family. Schleiermacher was indeed sensitive to all this but did not express it. Thus he found himself in the situation of halfheartedly defending a lost cause. In later years Schleiermacher no longer enjoyed this writing and in his sermons on Christian marriage he completely changed his views on marriage as a moral order. Divorce should be experienced as a common guilt with deep shame.[96]

---

93. Ibid., p. 501.
94. Dilthey, *Leben Schleiermachers*, 1st ed., p. 506.
95. Ibid.
96. *S. W.*, II/3, p. 250.

Schleiermacher's personal relations with particular romantics are also significant for the evaluation of his relationship to romanticism and romantic ideas. Especially decisive was his friendship with Friedrich Schlegel. This friendship was a relation of two extremely dissimilar partners, and in this dissimilarity lay the explosive material for the dissolution of their friendship. Schleiermacher's selflessness and considerateness time and again tried to uphold the friendly association with Schlegel. But Schlegel's restlessness, his desultory leaping from one thing to another, his egoism and suspicious behavior endangered their association both in their personal life and in their common work and gradually led to the breach in their friendship.

After 1802 their estrangement increased rapidly. Schlegel left Germany in a hurry, as if on the run. His erratic wanderings began with a trip to Paris and finally led to his conversion [to Catholicism] and, thus, his separation from Schleiermacher. In a letter to Ernst von Willich in 1801, Schleiermacher states:

> But the total difference in our ways of feeling, his quick volatile being, his infinite irritability, his deep inexhaustible tendency to postpone things make it impossible for me to deal with him in the honesty which I would long for, and cause me to speak to him about things in a way that is foreign to me, simply in order to make sure that he does not misunderstand me. Yet for him there are always still secrets in my heart — or else he would make up some.[97]

But Schleiermacher spoke up for his estranged friend with courageous resolution. For example, when Sack, his ecclesiastical superior, reproached Schleiermacher for having close connections with persons of suspicious principles and morals, he retorted: "I will never be the close friend of a man of reprehensible character; but neither will I ever, from the fear of other men, deny the consolations of friendship to a man falsely judged."[98]

This retort did not prevent Schleiermacher from gradually seeing more clearly Friedrich Schlegel's many failings and from drawing from this realization the appropriate conclusions. In a letter to Eleonore Grunow in 1802 he emphasized "that in some of its expressions Friedrich's overpowering, stormy sensuality was disagreeable to me and to some extent contrary to my taste; I have also spoken with disapproval of the ease with which he at times brings a twisted

---

97. *Briefe*, I, p. 277. *Letters*, I, p. 267.
98. *Briefe*, III, p. 282.

approach to his own affairs."[99]   Seen as a whole, one must agree with
Dilthey's judgment:

> Schleiermacher, more secure and manly because of the battles
> he was waging at this time, became increasingly conscious of all
> the differences that separated him from all those, without exception,
> who made up the circle of romantic comrades. Those who study
> this correspondence will always marvel at meeting in the midst
> of this gifted company (Schlegel, Tieck, Fichte, Schelling,
> Bernhardi, — not one of whom — I am writing this with care!
> — is free from duplicity and temperamental, arbitrary shifts of
> judgment) a man of such thoughtful, moral-religious temperament
> in whose entire correspondence one could not find a single instance
> of even momentary unfairness or of double dealing. Here was
> a man totally free of the selfish tendency to see people only from
> his own point of view, free from any intention to use them, free
> even from that temperamental restlessness which leads to heated
> and distorted judgment.[100]

Schleiermacher left Berlin in 1802 and decided to accept a poorly
endowed position as court chaplain at Stolp in Pomerania. With
this departure and separation from the romantic friends, the first
creative period of his thought ended and a new period of his life
and intellectual work began.

F. ELEONORE GRUNOW

The period of Schleiermacher's association with the romantics
was also the time of Schleiermacher's attachment to Eleonore Grunow,
the unhappily married wife of a Berlin clergyman. Schleiermacher
became acquainted with her in 1799 through some of his relatives
who were related to the Grunow family. Both Schleiermacher's
friends and enemies were offended that for years he courted this
woman although she lived with another minister in a childless and
very unhappy marriage. Schleiermacher held the view that in marriage
every woman had an inalienable right to her own individuality. This
romantic conception of individuality was for him in agreement with
the view that a marriage in which a woman is prevented by the moral
unworthiness of the other partner from developing her own individuality
is no longer a marriage but a subversion of mankind's holiest bonds.
Therefore, he considered it his duty to dissolve such a marriage

---

99. *Briefe*, I, p. 305. *Letters*, I, p. 294.
100. Dilthey, *Leben Schleiermachers*, 1st ed., pp. 531–32.

which was really no marriage. In his later sermons on marriage
and in his Christian ethics he took another point of view. According
to his later view marriage is indissoluble. A misalliance and unsuccessful marriage must be borne by Christians penitently. But
if the state nevertheless dissolves such a dead marriage, the church
can bless a second marriage only with a profound remorse for the
imperfections of the church.

But Schleiermacher did not hold this later viewpoint at that time.
Consequently he waited years for Eleonore to dissolve her marriage
outwardly as well as inwardly. They regarded themselves as secretly
betrothed. Schleiermacher left Berlin in order to permit her full
freedom in the decision. For years she was unable to reach any
final decision. Even as she had left her husband and initiated the
divorce proceedings with the help of her brother she once again
returned to him for reasons of conscience and abandoned the divorce.
Eleonore felt it her duty to continue her unsuccessful marriage, even
at the cost of her life. Schleiermacher wrote at that time to his friend
Reimer: "It pains me that you are so silent about her. The weakness
she is guilty of is the weakness of a pure humble soul melting into
mildness and she surely deserves from all who know her fate and
deed, that they treat her with love and compassion, but above all
with love."[101]

No one can reproach Schleiermacher with having opposed the
existing order by insisting on the right to passion. It was his moral
interpretation of true marriage and of love as the understanding and
uniting of two individuals which led him to his attitude. Later
he not only respected Eleonore Grunow's decision, he even approved
of it.

Many of Schleiermacher's friends did not wholly understand
what it was about Eleonore that captivated him so that he courted
her for approximately six years. She was no romantic figure; she
lacked the broad culture and versatility of the typical romantic woman.
Sentimentality, hypersensitivity, and intellectual playfulness were
alien to her. She was also no beauty. She is described by contemporaries as tall, lanky, and acerb.

Regrettably only a few of Eleonore's letters to Schleiermacher
are preserved and almost all the numerous letters from Schleiermacher
to Eleonore have also been lost. Dilthey still had Schleiermacher's
letters to Eleonore about one hundred years ago when he together

---

101. *Briefe*, I, p. 363. (This letter is omitted from the Rowan translation
of *Letters*.)

with L. Jonas published Schleiermacher's correspondence under the title *Aus Schleiermachers Leben in Briefen*. But, out of respect for Schleiermacher's privacy, he included only a few of them in the collection. The rest, according to Meisner's information, had been lost by the end of the nineteenth century. Hence the sources are lacking by which one could more closely come to know Eleonore's life and character and her relationship to Schleiermacher. One can, however, draw the following conclusions from the sparse information: Schleiermacher did not seek the typical romantic woman in Eleonore, and she was not such a woman. He cherished in her not her education but the richness of her feeling, its flexibility and strength.[102] To both, love meant the intuition and understanding of the other in the depths of his being. Their influence on each other was powerful. "Of all the persons who have stimulated me and contributed to my development there is none that can compare with you in the influence you exerted on my feelings and on the purer manifestation of my inner life."[103]

Schleiermacher particularly loved in Eleonore her abundance of feelings and her unusual ability to communicate. From Stolp he wrote to her:

> Rightly enjoy the wealth of feelings now within you. It compares to a moment in a great piece of music wherein the uninitiated believe they hear contradictory tones but in fact all is in harmony, a harmony which long remains only with those who have perceived all the tones, and whoever cannot do this will still enjoy — if he is not lacking awareness — each single sound for itself.[104]

It is difficult for us today to appreciate fully this form of love as an understanding based on shared feelings, as the exaltation of life through ardent fantasy.

Schleiermacher's understanding of love can be drawn from this communication to Eleonore:

> I wish the devil would take half the brains in the world . . . and in their place we could receive but one quarter of the fantasy which we now lack in this fine world. But he will be on his guard for surely he must know that this would be bad for his kingdom. . . . But how much is required, dear friend, rightly to see a

102. Heinrich Meisner, ed., *Schleiermacher als Mensch: Familien- und Freundesbriefe*, vol. I (Gotha, 1922, 1923), p. 230.
103. Ibid., p. 288.
104. Ibid., p. 257. *Briefe Schleiermachers*, ed. Hermann Mulert (Berlin, 1923), p. 144.

man! To do so a man must not only know himself, but he must have found *everything* within himself. True innocence and purity of heart will never achieve such a knowledge of human nature. But a man who can discover within himself at least an element of every kind of perversity and corruption (and the essence is wholly present in each element), and if he can then also uncover in himself a trace of all that is great and noble, while being at the same time vain enough to construct out of his own imagination the whole completed pattern from these elements — lo, such a man alone can have insight into people. How happy I am to know that in this I have your own permission to include you.[105]

Schleiermacher is not only a man of feeling, imagination, and reflection, but a man of moral action, of good intentions, and of self-restraint. A strong motive in his attachment to Eleonore was his intention to assist this woman, who was frequently tormented by depressions and anxieties, to freedom and inner peace through understanding, compassion, and even by sharing her suffering. Special attention should also be given to the confession that Schleiermacher put into the mouth of Eleonore in his *Letters on Lucinde*: "In finding limits and strictly holding on to them I have at all times remained a heroine."[106] Both of them concealed nothing from her husband and strictly observed the limits their consciences set for them.

Schleiermacher's development led him into romanticism, but it also led him through it and beyond it. At the dedication of the marble bust of Schleiermacher that was placed in front of Trinity Church in 1904, Wilhelm Faber, the General-Superintendent [Bishop] of Berlin, characterized this development with this observation: "Through the fantastic flowering of romanticism, in which there was no lack of blossoms surrounding the serpent, to the "cool" heights of philosophical reflection, from the enchained world of the beautiful into the better world of moral Good: along this way he was led, past many an abyss."[107]

---

105. *Briefe*, I, pp. 342–43.   *Letters*, I, p. 330.

106. *S. W.*, III/1, p. 486.

107. T. Kappstein, *Schleiermachers Weltbild und Lebensanschauung* (Berlin, 1921), pp. 34–35.

III.

THE PERIOD OF SYSTEM BUILDING

A. BEGINNINGS IN STOLP

Following a visit with his sister in Gnadenfrei, Schleiermacher began his pastoral duties in Stolp in 1802. Stolp was a provincial city in Pomerania, near the Baltic coastline. Its Reformed congregation was very small, comprised of about fifty families. Schleiermacher's official duties also included the pastoral care of a large number of very small Reformed congregations near Stolp and as far away as West Prussia which had maintained their independence from the larger body of the Lutheran church. These experiences in the Reformed *diaspora* became motive and cause for Schleiermacher's initial proposals for union at this time.

In the fall of 1802 he wrote to Alexander Dohna: "My leisure hours are sparse enough. The busy-work which is so annoying and is not even worth mentioning ruins much of my time; and then there are the disagreeable trips from which I am not even completely free for six weeks during the good seasons."[1] He avidly gave himself to his preaching. His criticism of his own sermons contains an undertone of dissatisfaction and resignation: "Today the sermon is the only means of having a personal impact on the common outlook of a large number of people. In reality its effect is not great for it does not achieve much. But if one takes up and deals with the matter as it should be — not just as it is — and if there should be only two or three who really listen, even then the result may still be beautiful."[2] "This calling has become more and more dear to me, even in its unpretentious form and in its unhappy relation to the spirit of the times. If I had to give it up I believe I would grieve even more deeply for all that I have now lost."[3] He gave confirmation lessons with real devotion; Plato was to him the great example and teacher in catechizing.

---

1. *Schleiermachers Briefe an die Grafen zu Dohna*, ed. Justus Ludwig Jacobi (Halle, 1887), p. 22.
2. *Briefe*, I, p. 338. *Letters*, I, p. 328.
3. *Briefe*, I, p. 362. *Letters*, I, p. 346.

Two large scholarly works were of decisive importance for his
further intellectual and scholarly development.   He worked at his
Plato translation for a time and then on his first great scholarly work,
Outlines of a Critique of Previous Ethical Theories (*Grundlinien einer
Kritik der bisherigen Sittenlehre*).   He wrote the latter in eleven
months of intense work and it was published in 1803.   This relatively
dry and highly detailed inquiry, however, gives a clear view of the
transformation in his character and life.   After the intoxication of
his intuitive romantic period in Berlin came the sobering activity of
quieter and more demanding methodical work.   He was at first
profoundly sobered by the analysis of previous ethical philosophy.
"How many dead letters on the most holy, the most living of subjects!"[4]   "When I imagine how . . . the old men will wonder that
I have come to be such a sober and thorough critical thinker, and
will wait to see whether I shall be able to survive such a transformation!
But they will soon discover that I am still the same old mystic."[5]
Later Schleiermacher self-critically called this book a "forest of
oriental cactus" which is difficult to penetrate, even though in the
end everything has grown from one root.

This work contains a critical polemic and radical examination of
ethical systems in history.   Only Plato and Spinoza are in some
measure judged favorably.   Kant and Fichte were particularly
critically examined.   The book had little effect.   Fichte refused to
read it and many readers reacted as did Spalding who admitted,
"I came away from your *Outlines* as someone comes away from algebra
with Gellert's agonized groan against Kästner: And you understand
all this?   I read it without interruption — but how!   Like a bur-
rowing mole.   Nothing, I understood nothing of how the pieces fit
together."[6]   Schleiermacher himself became discouraged.   In his
letter to Brinkmann of December 14, 1803, he complained about the
many people who overestimated his learning.   Everything would
come to a bad end.   He would always remain a dilettante in philosophy,
and if nothing could be preserved in this field as systematic works
of art, then soon not even a trace would any longer be found of him.[7]
Nonetheless, the preliminary statements for the outlines of his later
system can be seen in this collection of critical shavings.   He wanted
to develop further the subjective and formalistic ethics of Kant and

---

4. *Briefe*, I, p. 354.   *Letters*, I, pp. 340–41.
5. *Briefe*, I, p. 366.   *Letters*, I, p. 348.
6. *Briefe*, III, p. 367.
7. *Briefe*, IV, p. 89.

Fichte into an objective and material ethics of values. In addition he emphasized the idea of individuality which should be the expression and organ of the whole. Finally, the threefold division of ethics into theories of goods, virtues, and duties, was conceived here for the first time.

His pastoral activities provoked his critical spirit to write his *Modest Memorandum concerning the Protestant Church in Relation to the Prussian State* (*Unvorgreiflichen Gutachten in Sachen des protestantischen Kirchenwesens in Beziehung auf den Preussischen Staat*). Schleiermacher did not recommend actual union. As one might have expected from the author of the *Speeches* he rejected the Enlightenment leveling of confessional differences. Schleiermacher proposed a cultic union in which communicants would be mutually admitted to the Lord's Supper. He did not seek a new liturgical order or a new interpretation of the Lord's Supper as a basis for this union.

His proposals for reform were simply a cry of distress; he knew there was no hope that they could change the situation. In a letter to Reimer of November 11, 1803, he called his proposals "a rocket which helps nothing except that the darkness is seen better."[8]

B. ACADEMIC ACTIVITIES IN HALLE

While at Stolp Schleiermacher received a call to a professorship in ethics and pastoral theology at the newly established University of Würzburg. This recently established institution was part of the enlightened *Kulturpolitik* of the new Bavarian state which had annexed new areas — including Protestant lands — since the secularization of the religious territories in 1803. In education this new Bavarian state strove for equality of rights for all confessions and for national management of the entire educational process. Consistently, it also established alongside the Catholic a Protestant theological faculty whose first professor was the rationalist Heinrich Eberhard Gottlob Paulus (1761–1851). Schleiermacher at first hesitated to accept this call; his friends warned him against it since the future of the Protestant theological faculty was neither clear nor certain. Paulus and Schelling had failed in their lecture series as a result of Catholic opposition.

Schleiermacher nonetheless accepted the call because he was assured of an academic position in which he could also pursue preaching.

---

8. *Briefe*, III, p. 370.

At this point the Prussian throne intervened and called him to the hitherto totally Lutheran faculty at the University of Halle as *Professor Extraordinarius* and as University Preacher. The Prussian government had a double political intention in this appointment. It wanted to make Halle into the first and most distinguished university of Prussia. The University of Berlin was not yet founded. The expectation was that new professors who were striving to overcome the Enlightenment would establish the ascendancy of the University of Halle. Thus a great many hopes were placed on young and provocative scholars such as Steffens, the philosopher of nature, and the theologian, Schleiermacher.

The government's second intention was to take a step on the road toward union by appointing the Reformed Schleiermacher to a Lutheran theological faculty. The Halle faculty did not fundamentally resist Schleiermacher's appointment, but arranged that he be called *Professor Extraordinarius*. He accepted this appointment although he received a more modest stipend than that promised him in Würzburg, and despite the fact that he had the prospect of receiving a position at the Berlin cathedral. He preferred to remain in the service of the Prussian state. Moreover, the combination of an academic teaching position and service as the university chaplain attracted him. After one year Schleiermacher was admitted to the full faculty as *Professor Ordinarius*. Thus the Lutheran faculty at Halle became the first integrated faculty in Prussia.

In October, 1804, Halle was a city of 13,000 "residents" in addition to civil servants, professors, students, scholars, and soldiers. Essentially it was a university town. There were a host of other educational cities in addition to this one founded by Francke. In the Fall of 1804, Halle University had 796 students; the enrollment rose to 1280 in 1806, the year it closed down. In 1804 the school of theology had 347 students; by 1806 the enrollment had risen to 473.

The eighteenth century was a golden age for the University of Halle, for the most famous representatives of the Enlightenment were active there at that time. The philosopher Christian Wolff won ascendancy through his philosophical system which was an enlightened reformulation of Leibnitz's philosophy. Further, the enlightened historical criticism investigated the older Protestant dogmatics and particularly the theory of verbal inspiration of the Bible. The best-known advocates of this historical-critical Enlightenment theology were Baumgarten, Semler, and Michaelis. The historical outcome of this Enlightenment theology was the critical dismembering of orthodox Protestant biblical theology and doctrine.

Since the 1780s, however, a significant intellectual change began to affect Halle; although it continued to extend Enlightenment thinking, it also introduced an entirely new form of scientific thought and inquiry. The change was manifested in Halle by four important new appointments to the faculty: in 1783, the classical philologist Friedrich August Wolf; in 1787 the professor of medicine Reil; and in 1804 Steffens the philosopher of nature, as well as Schleiermacher. These four scholars came together as advocates of a new spirit seeking to overcome the Enlightenment.

Schleiermacher at first was given a cool reception in his own department. In the eyes of his associates he was the "mystical colleague," a new kind of heretic; he was suspected of being a follower of Schelling and of that pantheism present in the new concept of life after the manner of Goethe. Niemeyer was the most distinguished member of the faculty. As the great-grandson of August Hermann Francke he went through Francke's institutes and gained special prominence through his pedagogical researches. Like Melanchthon he advocated a combination of the Christian faith with humanism rooted in antiquity. From this perspective he sought to coordinate the pedagogical ideas of the times. Using the ideas of Wolff and Lessing he developed the principle of education and defined its tasks. All human powers should be so developed and cultivated that the ultimate goal of man — morality — will be achieved. Belief in God was for him a means toward moral education.

Schleiermacher's old philosophy teacher, Eberhard, who still taught at Halle, completely rejected his former student. The following statement by Eberhard was preserved in Schleiermacher's correspondence: "It has now come to the point that an open atheist has been called to Halle as a theologian and preacher."[9] These words of this old Enlightenment thinker sum up what all the advocates of the Enlightenment felt about the new theology and philosophy of religion. They did not understand transcendental philosophy's criticism of the Enlightenment concept of God and of the supernaturalistic metaphysics still affirmed in the Enlightenment. The critique Schleiermacher and his friends made of Enlightenment religion and its supernaturalistic view of God was for them pantheism and hence also atheism.

The other members of the theological faculty — Vater, the orientalist, and Nösselt — were critical theologians. Nösselt especially was a typical enlightener. He interpreted the proclamation of Christ

9. *Briefe*, III, p. 403.

and the apostles as the accommodation Christ made in his preaching
to the then prevailing mythological conceptions. He explained
away the accounts of demons, angels, the possessed, and the New
Testament miracles by reference to natural and psychological-his-
torical processes. Even at that time there was an Enlightenment
"demythologizing." Yet in spite of all their critical reservations
the Enlightenment theologians still retained a belief in a personal
God, in his wise rule of human history, and in the destination God
set for mankind. God wants to lead men to enlightenment and
happiness and bring them to perfection in a future eternal life. Nösselt
was Schleiermacher's special colleague in that both lectured on the
same subjects: systematic theology, hermeneutics, dogmatics, and
ethics.

Schleiermacher's pietistic colleague, Georg Christian Knapp, was
even farther from him. Despite Knapp's undistinguished status as
a scholar he had the best-attended classes. He embodied the alliance
between orthodoxy and pietism, but his adherence to dogma had
been shaken by the Enlightenment. He still used the New Testament
miracles, interpreted supernaturally, to prove the divinity of Christ and
Christ's promise to be with his disciples as proof for the inspiration
of the apostles and Holy Scripture.

This faculty of rationalists, supernaturalists, and late pietists was
the background for Schleiermacher's first theological activity as a
scholar and professor. The intention of his theological work and
study at that time was defined by this opposition. Schleiermacher
himself clearly saw "that I am a thorn in the flesh of most of my
colleagues here."[10] In contrast to the reception he received here,
Schleiermacher found open acceptance and friendship in other academic
departments and nontheological circles. In the home of the composer
Reichardt, in Giebichenstein, he first learned to appreciate the contemporary music of early romanticism.

The philologist Friedrich August Wolf was not an easy man for
Schleiermacher to be friendly with. Occasionally Wolf gave vent
to his wit and sarcasm against theology and its spokesmen. On the
other hand, he had to acknowledge the seriousness and significance
of Schleiermacher's philological studies. Subsequently he even had
to admit Schleiermacher's superiority in interpreting Plato. Wolf
also introduced Schleiermacher to Goethe, who visited his disciple
Wolf at Halle in the summer of 1805. But Schleiermacher discovered

10. *Briefe*, II, p. 49. (This letter is omitted from the Rowan translation of
Letters.)

in 1805 at Halle, as well as in a later visit to Weimar in 1814, that he had no access to Goethe, who remained distant.

Schleiermacher's friendship with Steffens, the philosopher of nature, was of the greatest importance for the formation of his philosophical point of view. Until that time Schleiermacher had based his philosophy of culture on history. Although he left a place in his philosophical system for the philosophy of nature, which he called "physics," he never lectured or wrote on this subject. Dilthey justifiably used Steffens's philosophy of nature to fill out the gaps in his interpretation of Schleiermacher's system; in this manner he demonstrated that Steffens's philosophy of nature in fact exactly dovetails with Schleiermacher's system.[11]

As a young professor Schleiermacher devoted himself enthusiastically to his lectures. In his exegetical lectures he occupied himself mainly with Paul and saw in him the key for understanding primitive Christianity. From his studies in the Pauline letters came the critical, one might almost say "form-critical," work on 1 Timothy, in which he proved its non-Pauline character through stylistic criticisms.

The greatest emphasis, however, was on his lectures on ethics, dogmatics, and hermeneutics. Schleiermacher did not rely on detailed notes as the basis for his lectures. He first prepared an overall plan for the course and made only a few notes and cues for each individual lecture. He gave his thought free rein, making his lectures artistic and graceful discourses that captivated and electrified his listeners, but also made it difficult to follow him or take notes. One of his students (Börne) characterized his teaching method as follows: "He taught theology as Socrates would have taught it had he been a Christian."[12]

In these lectures the outlines of his later philosophical and theological systems emerged. Dilthey has rightly observed that once Schleiermacher had firmly grasped these outlines he remained true to most of them in his later development. This is particularly noticeable in the basic conception of his philosophical system, which he first achieved in ethics and later in dialectics. It is very regrettable that he did not leave a publishable version of his philosophical ethics, though he had lectured numerous times on the subject. These lectures were held during the winter semesters of 1804/5, 1805/6, and 1811/12, and during the summer semesters of 1816, 1824, 1827,

---

11. Cf. Twesten's examination of corresponding statements by Schleiermacher in his lecture on ethics. A. Twesten, *F. Schleiermachers Grundriss der philosophischen Ethik* (Berlin, 1841), p. xcvii.
12. L. Börne, *Sämmtliche Werke*, II (New York, 1858), p. 183.

and 1832. The basic outline of his ethics is already recognizable
in the two courses of lectures that he gave at Halle; the later versions
were only expansions of this basic outline. Hence it is advisable
to inquire into and examine the beginnings of his theological and
philosophical system in connection with the exposition of his system
as a whole, to which we will return in a later section. At the moment
we are chiefly interested in the new elements Schleiermacher introduced
into his philosophy of religion and theology. It is of utmost importance
for the interpretation of Schleiermacher to find the connection linking
the *Speeches* to *The Christian Faith*. This link also passes through
Schleiermacher's philosophical lectures because in them he developed
his new conception of the meaning of religion in the context of
philosophical discussion.[13] Further sources are the second edition
of the *Speeches* in 1806 and *Christmas Eve*.

1. CHRISTMAS EVE

What was the new element in his theological-philosophical system?
In defining the essence of religion Schleiermacher dropped the concept
of intuition and identified the essence of religion only as the feeling
of unity, of the universe, totality, the eternal. It should be recalled
that this concept of feeling is not to be interpreted psychologically.[14]
Feeling is the original act of the spirit, it is immediate self-consciousness, which is posited and affected by the actions of the universe.
The believer experiences this "self" as a whole, as autonomous, yet
above all as finite givenness. In this feeling the unity of the self
is given by revelation as the organ and symbol of God.

Schleiermacher introduced this change because he wanted to
distinguish religion from metaphysical speculation even more clearly
than he had in the first edition of the *Speeches*. The concept of
intuition could also entail the speculations of "intellectual intuition"
in Schelling's sense. Such speculations Schleiermacher intended to
avoid. In this feeling mankind has communion with God as absolute
unity and totality. We experience our being as being in God.[15]
Religion is also the feeling that grants us the awareness that God
lives and acts within us. Concepts, words, and symbols have only
secondary significance for the life of religion. They are mere forms

---

13. Cf. Dilthey's examination of the concept of religion in the various outlines of *Ethics: Leben Schleiermacher*, vol. II (Berlin, 1966), pp. 551 ff.
14. See above, p. 39.
15. *Reden*, p. 60. *Speeches*, p. 94.

of expression, representations, symbols of this life. Furthermore, religion is now receptivity, passivity, and not productivity. E. Hirsch, who in his *Geschichte der neueren evangelischen Theologie* has instructively and vividly examined Schleiermacher's life at Halle and earlier in Berlin, sees here the influence of Fichte on Schleiermacher. But this influence is only traceable to his use of the concept of feeling in a formal epistemological sense. Substantively the essence of the religious process is totally different for Schleiermacher than it is for Fichte. Schleiermacher always regarded Fichte's philosophy and interpretation of religion as forced. Religion and communion with God is for Schleiermacher above all receptivity, immediate self-consciousness made definite. The self's act of freedom then follows from the basis of its being determined. Freedom is based on man's dependence on God.

What then was the essence of Christianity for Schleiermacher? In addition to his first volume of sermons, his *Christmas Eve* provides information on this question. Following a sudden inspiration, Schleiermacher wrote *Christmas Eve* in December, 1804, so that it was ready for publication in January, 1805. In contrast to the *Speeches* and *Soliloquies* this work was not published anonymously. In the preface to the second edition, which he finished in November, 1826, and published in 1827, he admitted in retrospect:

> Times have changed since this little book first appeared almost twenty-one years ago. The movement of destiny which then menacingly marched upon us has played out its role, and the great battle has splintered into a thousand fragments. The religious differences which here confront each other, while essentially remaining the same, still have significantly changed in color and tone so that most of them no longer retain the same truth they once did.[16]

Nevertheless Schleiermacher rejected the idea of changing the work and making it more appropriate to the new situation. He sought only to express himself more carefully and clearly. The meaning and purpose of this writing remained the same as in 1804. "It may be a gratifying sight, and itself not an unworthy Christmas gift, to see that the most diverse interpretations of Christianity are not only peacefully present together in an ordinary living room . . . but also to see how they amiably permit themselves to be mutually compared."[17]

---

16. *S. W.*, I/1, pp. 463 f.
17. Ibid.

The literary form of this work is patterned after Plato's dialogues. *Christmas Eve* is a conversation among friends about the meaning of the Christmas Eve celebration and the biblical account of Christ's birth. Participants in the conversation are the host and hostess (Eduard and Ernestine), an engaged couple (Ernst and Frederike), Agnes, the youthful Caroline, the adolescent and somewhat precocious Sophie, Leonard, and finally the Herrnhuter Joseph, who arrives at the end.

The three women begin with accounts of Christmas experiences. The celebration of Christmas conveys the religious meaning of the relationship of mother and child. Every mother is a Mary and mother love is the eternal element in the life of a woman, the foundation of her being. As Mary did, she perceives in her child the pure revelation of divinity. The ensuing dialogue of the critical, reflective men delineates the theological and philosophical perplexities in the celebration of Christmas. Historical-critical rationalism is represented in Leonard; Joseph represents a naive Christianity of feeling alone in which all scholarly criticism is rejected; the speculative theology and philosophy of religion of Schelling's school is advocated by Eduard. Schleiermacher's basic conception may perhaps be found most clearly in Ernst, to whom he had for that very reason given his own Christian name which he had received from his godfather and uncle, Samuel Ernst Stubenrauch.

The dialogue begins with a historical criticism by Leonard, the Enlightenment figure. The historical Jesus stands closer to John the Baptist than he does to the apostle Paul. About the life and teachings of Jesus there is little that can be known with historical certainty. The contemporary Christmas celebration is indeed a vital and powerful reality, but it hardly has actual historical background. The story of Christ's birth is legend. The contemporary Christmas celebration only symbolizes childlike joy. As night is the historical cradle of Christianity, so this festival is also celebrated at night. The candles and lights are the Christmas star over the stable, without which the Christ child could not be found in the darkness of history. This bland, Enlightenment position, the first to be thrown into relief, is criticized by Ernst and Eduard. It is interesting to compare the brief handwritten notes for Schleiermacher's 1806 church history course with this criticism. In this 1806 lecture manuscript Schleiermacher rejects the reflective empiricism of the Enlightenment view of history. It results in efforts to discover insignificant causes for important events in history and, therefore, sees the outcome of history as something accidental just because it is misunderstood as something determined.[18]

A better treatment of history is needed, "for history derives from epic and mythology, and these clearly lead to the identity of appearance and idea."[19] "Accordingly, it is precisely the task of history to make the particular immortal. . . . Thus, the particular first gets its position and distinct existence in history by means of a higher treatment."[20] Historical understanding must be confirmed by a combination of speculation and empiricism. "However weak the historical traces may be if viewed critically (in the lower sense), the celebration does not depend on these but on the necessary idea of a Redeemer."[21] The historical foundation of Christmas may be weak. Yet despite this, Christmas is not merely a universal celebration of childlike joy. On the contrary it has a quite specific and real relation to redemption, to the Redeemer and his birth. We finite men do not live in the unity and harmony of primordial nature. We live in the separation of spirit and flesh, and we require redemption. Hence for us Christians there is no other principle of joy than redemption. "And for it [the experience of redemption] in turn there must have been a first point, the birth of a divine child."[22] In the first bud of the new life we see at the same time its finest blossom, its highest perfection.[23]

These christological ideas were further clarified in the second edition of *Christmas Eve* in 1827. The festival of Christmas depends on the necessity of a Redeemer. But this is not simply postulated; rather Christmas rests on the experience of an enhanced existence, which cannot be traced back to any other beginning than this one (the Redeemer).[24] "So it is actually to Christ and his powers of attraction that the creation of this new world is indebted. And whoever acknowledges . . . that Christianity is a powerful present reality and effective pattern for the new life, hallows this celebration."[25] The higher life, mediated by the Redeemer, is thus not attained by a deductive conclusion about the Redeemer; rather the Redeemer's

---

18. *S. W.*, I/11, p. 624.
19. Ibid., p. 625.
20. Ibid.
21. *S. W.*, I/1, p. 518.
22. Ibid., p. 517. *Schleiermachers Weihnachtsfeier*, ed. Hermann Mulert (Leipzig, 1908), (a critical edition based on the first edition), p. 117.
23. Ibid., p. 119.
24. *S. W.*, I/1, pp. 518–19.
25. Ibid., p. 519.

power is apprehended and experienced in this higher life itself. The basic christological interpretation that Schleiermacher later developed in *The Christian Faith* is already present here. Hence Dilthey judged that *Christmas Eve* is the best introduction to the study of Schleiermacher's dogmatics.[26]

The young Halle professor was just then preparing his lectures on dogmatics. The foundation and point of departure for his dogmatic investigations is the reality of the living community of Christians. The basis of this reality is found in Christ — not in the historical Jesus, but in the Christ whose image is efficacious in the community (according to Schleiermacher's later dogmatics) simultaneously as "corporate act" and as "corporate possession."[27]

Simultaneously with his dogmatics Schleiermacher worked out his basic conception of philosophical ethics as a philosophy of life and history. These speculative ideas find their expression within *Christmas Eve* in the third speech by Eduard. Schleiermacher gives a speculative interpretation to the familiar opening to the Gospel of John. He locates the spiritual and higher meaning of the Christmas celebration in the incarnation of the Word in flesh. The flesh is the earthly, finite, physical, and the divine Word is thought, knowledge. "The Incarnation is therefore the coming of original and divine reason in that form. What we therefore celebrate is nothing other than ourselves, what we are together, or human nature, or whatever else you wish to call it, seen and known through the divine."[28]

In these views Schleiermacher was doubtless referring to the eighth of Schelling's *Lectures on the Method of University Studies*, which he had published only a few years earlier.[29] Schleiermacher was by then already critical of Schelling's speculative view of Christ. In his discussion of Schelling's lectures he found "the kind of freedom of determination, which could be the key to Christianity, somewhat distorted."[30] Unlike Schelling, Schleiermacher did not want to present the idea of Christianity as a pure speculative concept. His

---

26. Dilthey, *Leben Schleiermachers*, vol. I, 2nd ed., p. 775.

27. Schleiermacher, *Der Christliche Glaube nach den Grundsatzen der evangelischen Kirche im Zusammenhange dargestellt*, 2d ed., ed. Martin Redeker (Berlin, 1960), § 88, 3. An English translation is given in *The Christian Faith*, trans. H. R. Mackintosh and J. S. Stewart (Edinburgh, 1948; New York, 1963).

28. *Schleiermachers Weihnachtsfeier*, 1st ed., pp. 125–26.

29. Cf. the discussion of *Christmas Eve* by Schelling in the *Jenaer Literatur-Zeitung* of 1807: *Sämmtliche Werke*, I/7 (Stuttgart and Augsburg, 1856–61), pp. 498 ff.

30. *Briefe*, IV, p. 586.

concept of the Incarnation sought to retain the contingency of its entrance into the historically concrete. In this he also departed from Plato's theory of the ideas. The Platonic ideas are archetypes of pure being. Consequently it is not possible for these archetypes to appear in the finite and historical. The world of contrasts and becoming, the finite world can only be the reflection of the ideas and archetypes. Schleiermacher also distinguishes between eternal being and finite becoming. But eternal being enters into the becoming of history. The Spirit, that is, the ideas reveal themselves in the historical process of mankind by bringing mankind to self-consciousness. But man cannot live in the world of the archetypes and ideas. Individual men live in the world of opposing realities, of becoming, of duplicity and distortion. This duplicity and distortion, however, is overcome when the archetype of mankind enters history and unites individual men into community. This deliverance of individual men from duplicity and distortion is redemption. The fundamental thought of Christianity is this liberation of men for the higher life of mankind. Christ is this archetype which embodies the idea of true humanity. Man-in-himself is not God but the Spirit of the earth (*Erdgeist*). This Spirit is the knowledge of the earth in its eternal being and its constantly changing process of becoming.[31]

Thus in the idea of mankind the Spirit unfolds in the mode of our earth. The community of this higher life is the church. But this church must have a point of origin and this point must be Christ, for he bears this self-knowledge in himself. "In Christ we see the Spirit, according to the mode of our earth, forming itself for the first time into self-consciousness in an individual."[32] These philosophical speculations determine Schleiermacher's philosophical ethics. The church is nothing other than the community of mankind, in which the moral process of man's becoming man and the becoming truth of his existence is brought to perfection. Hence the Christian faith is mankind's higher self-consciousness. Speculative knowledge is the mark of the members of this ecclesiastical community. Naturally, nonphilosophical Christians can also have this higher Christian self-consciousness, but only in "feeling" and not in "knowing."[33] Humanistic self-understanding of man's true higher life and the Christian life of faith are closely bound together in *Christmas Eve* — indeed they are finally identical. This is a point of view which,

31. *Schleiermachers Weihnachtsfeier*, 1st ed., p. 126.
32. *S. W.*, I/1, p. 523.
33. *Schleiermachers Weihnachtsfeier*, 1st ed., p. 128.

following the turn in his thinking after 1811, Schleiermacher later rejected.[34]

In *Christmas Eve* the Halle professor linked the genuinely human with the Christian. The Christian joy of Christmas is the perfection of humanity. On the other hand, everything genuinely human is part of the higher life of the Christian faith. Christological speculation combines with the idealist notion of humanity. At the end of the critical dialogue Schleiermacher takes back the christological speculations through the objections of Joseph the Moravian against the "evil principle," namely, against Leonard, the reflective, dialectical, hyper-intellectual man. "This speechless object requires . . . a speechless joy."[35] Joseph feels like a child born anew into a "better world where pain and grief no longer have any meaning."[36]

Political events, particularly Prussia's defeat in the war with Napoleon, determined the further course of Schleiermacher's life. The city of Halle was captured and occupied by French troops after battles in the streets. Schleiermacher gave refuge to his friends Gass and Steffens — and the latter's family as well — in his lodgings at Märkerstrasse. There they were victims of plunder and were required to take on the quartering of soldiers. The friends were hit hard by the expulsion of the students from Halle and then by the dissolution of the university itself. Despite all this Schleiermacher remained in the city. He was firmly convinced that a better future awaited Prussia and Germany. The destruction of the old Prussian state was for him only a transitional stage. What was old and feeble had to fall in order that a new Prussia and Germany might develop even more strongly. This was his hope. "What was built on sand must collapse in this time of storm."[37] "The scourge must pass over everything that is German; only under this condition can something thoroughly beautiful later arise out of this. Bless those who will live to see it; but those who die, may they die in faith."[38]

With a few other professors and representatives of the cultural life of Germany he decisively repudiated Napoleon as a foreign conqueror and dictator. When the French official who was billeted with him asked that he witness Napoleon's entry into Halle, Schleier-

---

34. *Der Christliche Glaube*, § 14, 2.
35. *S. W.*, I/1, p. 524.
36. Ibid.
37. A letter from Schleiermacher to Karl August Varnhagen, November 17, 1806, in *Reminiscenzen* by Wilhelm Dorow (Leipzig, 1842), pp. 90 f.
38. *Briefe*, II, p. 77.

macher asked to be excused. It is interesting to compare this repudiation of Napoleon with the respect that Goethe and Hegel had for the French conqueror.

An unshakable belief in Prussia's recovery gave him the inner peace and strength to devote himself to his scholarly studies in these turbulent times. He advanced in his Plato translations, wrote a review of Fichte's *The Characteristics of the Present Age* (*Grundzüge des gegenwärtigen Zeitalters*), and composed his *Commentary on the First Epistle to Timothy* (*Sendschreiben über den Timotheus-Brief*), which made an important contribution to the literary criticism of the New Testament at that time. Schleiermacher also decided to remain at Halle for the time being, hoping that Halle would remain Prussian and that his university would be reopened.

As long as he could get hold of "potatoes and salt" he would remain in Halle and await Germany's fate. He turned down a very enticing call — which would at once have removed his economic worries — as pastor to the *Stephanskirche* in Bremen.

In addition to scholarly activities he became involved very fruitfully in preaching during 1806 and 1807 in Halle. At the time of his appointment Schleiermacher had attached great importance to organizing worship services in this academic setting. The University Church was first put at his disposal on August 3, 1806. At the opening service seven hundred students were present in the congregation to hear Schleiermacher's sermon on Romans 1:16. By the middle of September the University Church was appropriated by the Prussian military and used as a storehouse for grain. Schleiermacher transferred his preaching activity to the *Ulrichskirche*. Gradually it became evident that he could not remain in Halle. New political and scholarly tasks drew him to Berlin.

C. ACTIVITIES IN BERLIN

1. PATRIOT AND POLITICIAN

There awoke in this son of a Prussian army chaplain, during his stay in Halle, a Prussian and German patriot who became closely associated with the reformers of the Prussian state and its political ideas.

Just like these reformers, Schleiermacher had demanded a political and social restructuring of the Prussian state even before its collapse. These ideas of reform originated in the new nationalism. During this time Schleiermacher became an advocate of a new political ethics

which discovered, from the perspective of the newly emerging Protestant ethics, the values of homeland, people, and the state; this
political ethic also ushered in a new period for the Protestant interpretation of the state and introduced the sermon as a political service
on behalf of public concerns of the state. Schleiermacher's ethical
thinking had originally given the most prominent place to the idea
of individuality. Schleiermacher now moved from the idea of individuality to that of the moral self which manifests its freedom in
service to the people and the state. Human life is lifeless if it has
no part in the life of the state and the people. To live under foreign
domination, without a state, without homeland, is no real life at all.

The idea of individuality was further applied to the historical
evolution of the people as a social individual. God, the Lord of
history, avails himself of distinct orders in his providential care for
the world. To these orders also belong the historical individualities
of people and states. Any residue of romantic-aesthetic piety was
now eliminated in this theology of history. The history of mankind
is no longer an object of aesthetic contemplation. The course of
human history is no longer a harmonious peaceful whole and a process
of continuous perfection. The history of mankind is a life of struggle,
of decisions, as well as of catastrophe and destruction, sacrifice and
suffering. But it is precisely through this sharp clash that the will
of God achieves its purpose. Ultimately justice and truth will be
victorious.

In his section on Schleiermacher's political attitudes Dilthey
rightly delineated a change and greater maturity in Schleiermacher's
piety and view of God during this time.[39] Christian faith is no
longer simply a passive attitude of immediate self-consciousness
which he calls feeling; rather faith is now essentially commitment,
i.e., impulse, will, action. From the more passively delineated
feeling of absolute dependence and the inwardness of immediate
self-consciousness there came now a resolute faith in providence.
This belief in providence refers not simply to the suffering and prosperity of individual Christians, but relates to the action of God in
the whole of history. Schleiermacher is confident that the divine
law which rules in the religious conscience is identical with the divine
power which rules history. God is not just the infinite, the universe,
the absolute totality as the ground and unity of the polarities of the
world; God is the Lord of history, he is the Lord of everything valuable
and good in the world.

---

39. W. Dilthey, *Gesammelte Schriften*, vol. 12 (Stuttgart, 1963), pp. 1 ff.

The collapse of the Prussian state was in Schleiermacher's view not an accidental misfortune, for he acknowledged in it the presence of God's will which leads through defeat to victory. The sermon he preached in Berlin on March 28, 1813, on the occasion of the outbreak of war, was based on the text from Jeremiah: "At any time I will declare concerning a nation or kingdom, that I will pluck up and break down and destroy it." He took this text not as a threat against France, but rather heard in it a judgment upon his own people. The collapse of the Prussian state is God's judgment for having forgotten the old virtues and, in a rising tide of vanity and dissipation, of no longer listening to the voice of God. Salvation is returning to God. What is required, therefore, is to recognize God's work in the individual ethos of the German nation, in the historically formed Prussian state, and to follow his command. God will protect the people who want to maintain their unique meaning and spirit, which the Lord God gave them, and who want to preserve their freedom and independence. For this homeland and this freedom one must risk his life. Schleiermacher is well aware of the inscrutable ways of God which set limits for men, and of the enthusiasm and arrogance by which we promptly want to advance beyond these limits. When standing up for his fatherland a Christian should not rely on others or his own planning; he should put his trust in the power of God and obediently go the way God leads.

This is not a nationalism which absolutizes the people and state. The new national fervor is not a substitute for a lost Christian commitment. The twentieth-century reader, who has experience with completely secularized and hence unrestrained nationalism and chauvinism, must keep this difference in mind. An objective historical understanding requires this differentiation between the origins of German national consciousness against the background of a Christian humanism and the secularized degenerate nationalism of the twentieth century. The patriotic preacher of the German war of liberation in his 1817 pamphlet "On the Proposed Synodical Form of Government for the Protestant Church of Prussia," had asked very critically, as a matter of conscience, whether the revival of piety during the war years was not merely a dream and self-delusion. "Recently, to be sure, we have accomplished great things under the banner of piety which the world has admired; the world indeed is astonished at our apparent transformation. It (the world) will soon want to know how much truth there is in this allegation and whether it was actually God or merely necessity and revenge that motivated and guided us."[40]

In his later Christian ethics, Schleiermacher formulated this even more clearly: "Where the unity of the people is the final point of reference, there one finds nothing but self-love and the absence of morality."[41]   Independence for the social individualities of people and state and autonomous arbitrary authority are completely distinct.

It was a rigorous, determined, manly piety that motivated the young professor.   Dilthey believed this was evidence that something of the spirit of his Reformed ancestors still lived in him.   But one should also see the other side.   One of Schleiermacher's guiding beliefs was that fear of God overcame fear of men.   The defense of people and country is based on theonomy.   Fichte in his *Addresses to the German Nation* speaks in terms of the imperative "you shall"; Schleiermacher has a different basis for his argument: it is God's will.   His state is not an autonomous state of well-being and welfare. The person who personally experiences the impulse of the divine Spirit through faith is the one who will really work for the proper self-determination of human and political freedom.   When Christianity assumes responsibility for the formative processes of talent and character, such moral development does not only come out of the natural man alone but is upheld by the divine Spirit as well.[42] Thus in the struggle against Napoleon, Schleiermacher rejected all halfheartedness and indecision.   He was prepared to take up arms in defense of the nation and he participated in militia exercises. Nevertheless, he was aware of the tension between fighting for the freedom of national self-determination and the commandments about Christian love for one's neighbor.   The war is justified only for the sake of the peace it wants to bring about.   Only the idea of eternal peace is fully Christian.   This eternal peace cannot be established here on earth through treaty and substantive guarantee.   Schleiermacher's theology of history is sufficiently realistic to estimate rightly the results of national egoism and the demonic will to conquest. Eternal peace is the eschatological demand of God's kingdom; it is a goad in Christian consciences, but it cannot be realized on earth.[43]

Schleiermacher proclaimed this political ethic mainly through his sermons, which attracted large throngs of profoundly moved wor-

---

40. *S. W.*, I/5, p. 255.
41. *S. W.*, I/2, *Christliche Sitte*, p. 476.
42. Ibid., p. 481.
43. Ibid., p. 485.

shipers. Steffens reported on Schleiermacher's effectiveness in the pulpit at Berlin: "How he elevated and settled the mind of its citizens . . . ; through him Berlin was as if transformed. . . . His commanding, refreshing, always joyful spirit was like a courageous army in that most troubled time."[44] Schleiermacher's political sermons were effective not because he played on political events or in the usual way called upon government as an authority under which we should lead a quiet life. His preaching style was not the emotional style of the fanatical sects. Its effectiveness was due to the fact that he let this political ethic arise from Christian faith in a new way and showed how a strong new impulse for political action proceeds from Christian faith, particularly from the Christian belief in providence and from the theology of history.

In 1808 began a brief episode of Schleiermacher's life in which he entered practical politics. At that time Prussian patriots came together and by secret agitation sought to prepare for a popular uprising and national war against Napoleon. Such a national committee existed in Berlin, headed by Count Chasot. The real power behind this circle, however, was Eichhorn, then an assistant judge of the superior court and later Prussian Minister of Education. The members of this patriotic coalition traveled in the various provinces of Prussia seeking to unite their friends, the majority of whom they found among the many discharged officers of the Prussian army and officials of the lost Prussian provinces. A political trip also brought Schleiermacher to Königsberg. He made Stein's acquaintance there and also consulted with Gneisenau and Scharnhorst. He was received in a private audience by both Princess Wilhelmina and Queen Luise, who stood especially close to the patriotic circle. In his study of Schleiermacher's political views, Dilthey collected the available evidence of Schleiermacher's political activity from his letters. Schleiermacher went the way of agitation, but not the way of conspiracy. He did not join the secret "League of Virtue" (*Tugendbund*), although he did participate in the work of the free committees. The goal was a popular uprising against Napoleon in the winter of 1808/9. But the politics of the Czar and the Erfurt Diet ruined this venture for the patriots. Only in 1811 under more propitious circumstances was the Prussian war-party revived by Stein.

Another political role for Schleiermacher was his brief career as an official in the Department of Public Instruction in the Ministry of the Interior. The oldest son of the house of Dohna, Alexander,

---

44. Heinrich Steffens, *Was Ich Erlebte*, vol. VI (Breslau, 1842), pp. 271 f.

became Stein's successor as Minister of the Interior from 1808 until
1810. He appointed Schleiermacher as Director of the Berlin
Academic Deputation and then to the Department of Education in
the Ministry of the Interior. By means of memoranda, which are
still preserved and have been collected by Kade,[45] Schleiermacher
cooperated in the restructuring of Prussian public education. When
Minister Schuckmann, whose friendship Schleiermacher did not
enjoy, became secretary of the Berlin Academy of Science in 1814,
he took the opportunity to relieve Schleiermacher of his position.

After 1814/15 Schleiermacher aroused the mistrust of Prussian
politicians who were filled with anxiety about revolution. He wanted
to see Stein's reforms put into effect, but he also wanted to see the
creation of a constitutional monarchy with a constitution and a
parliament, as the king had promised his people in 1813. Because
of these views the conservative group in Prussia, who wanted to
prevent the liberalization of the Prussian state, regarded Schleiermacher
with suspicion.

He particularly aroused the distrust of the ultraconservative
group in Prussia by his activities as a journalist and editor in 1813.
In that year a newspaper called *The Prussian Correspondent*, published
four times a week, was founded by Niebuhr. On January 25,
Schleiermacher had to take over its management. He soon came
into conflict with the Prussian censor. An article on July 14, in
which he criticized Prussian politics for not being decisive enough,
gave particular offense. Above all he spoke out against a premature
conclusion of peace with Napoleon. All Prussian patriots thought
as Schleiermacher did; three months later Napoleon was beaten at
Leipzig. During these three months, however, the censor had the
opportunity thoroughly to examine Schleiermacher's articles. Minister Hardenberg even goaded the king to strong disapproval and
immediately received an order of the Cabinet: "I commission you
to request his [Schleiermacher's] resignation and instruct him to
leave Berlin within forty-eight hours and to leave the country through
Swedish Pomerania. You are also responsible to see that this order
is promptly executed." However, this order was not carried out
and Schleiermacher heard nothing of it. On July 19 Schleiermacher
received a reprimand. It stated that the newspaper article had advocated the necessity of overthrowing the Prussian form of government
through violent measures. This was high treason. Schleiermacher

---

45. Franz Kade, *Schleiermachers Anteil an der Entwicklung des preussischen
Bildungswesen von 1808–18* (Leipzig, 1925).

was told to abstain from all political involvement; it was inappropriate for him as a clergyman and teacher. If he would not listen, he should expect immediate dismissal from his official duties. Schleiermacher told the publisher of the newspaper that the whole affair amused him.[46] He added, "This is all of one piece, and they call it a decisive victory over the Stein party. These are the first fruits of Scharnhorst's death. Still, let it pass, the cause of good will yet win."[47]

Schleiermacher courageously continued to edit the paper until the end of September. But again he quarreled with the authorities. On October 22, 1813, Hardenberg administered still another reprimand. Then on December 30, 1814, *The Prussian Correspondent* discontinued publication.

a) *Schleiermacher's Experiences in the Period of Reaction against the Agitators*

Schleiermacher's dispute with the senior member of the law faculty at the University of Berlin, Councillor Schmalz, occurred during this period. In 1815 Schmalz published a work on political associations in which he also discussed Scharnhorst and his relationship with him. Schmalz was himself a Freemason and had belonged to the League of Virtue; but now he attacked his former like-minded friends as revolutionaries. Niebuhr and Schleiermacher answered this work. Seldom did Schleiermacher use such sharp polemical language. Niebuhr and Schleiermacher charged that Schmalz's writing suspected everyone who wished a constitution to be guilty of high treason, since a constitution would diminish the power of the princes. Schleiermacher's relation with the conservative party in Prussia at that time was now shattered. The Prussian king prohibited the continuation of this literary war, and Schmalz received the decoration of the Prussian Order of the Red and Black Eagle. When Schleiermacher's friends and colleagues asked from behind the scenes why he had not also received the decoration of the Eagle, Schleiermacher answered with the biblical quotation, "Wherever the carcass is, there the eagles will be gathered together."[48]

Prussian universities especially, but also other German universities, were defamed because German students were associated with the murder of the poet Kotzebue on March 23, 1819, by seminarian

---

46. *Briefe*, II (July 24 , 1813), p. 305.
47. Ibid.
48. A. Hausrath, *Richard Rothe und seine Freunde*, vol. I (Berlin, 1902–6), p. 109.

Karl Sand.   De Wette, a professor of theology at Berlin and a colleague
of Schleiermacher, wrote a letter of condolence to the mother of the
executed student.   He was much maligned for this pastoral act,
and had to submit his resignation from public service to Prussia.
Schleiermacher and the Senate of Berlin University stood up for
De Wette, but he had to give up Prussian service nonetheless.   Now
Schleiermacher also found himself under suspicion.   Even friends
such as Gneisenau, from the earlier years of reform, withdrew from
him.   Hegel, his colleague at Berlin, came to oppose Schleiermacher
after the De Wette affair and even permitted himself some cynical,
disdainful comments in the introduction to his *Philosophy of Right*
and *Philosophy of Religion*.   For him nationalistic ideas were "intellectual pap."

Action against Schleiermacher came in 1823.   During a search
of Ernst Moritz Arndt's home letters were found which Schleiermacher
had written to his brother-in-law, containing some incautious comments
against the Prussian king.   In the investigation Schleiermacher
was able to demonstrate the innocence of the affair and the proceedings
were discontinued.   Nonetheless, Schleiermacher's relation with the
Prussian king was severed for years.   Finally in 1830/31, on the
occasion of the French July Revolution, a change occurred.   In a
Parisian newspaper it was reported that Schleiermacher was the
leader of a liberal revolutionary political party in Berlin.   Schleiermacher, who was a loyal Prussian, became so indignant that he published a rebuttal in the *Allgemeine Preussische Tageszeitung*.   He
wanted nothing to do with the French Revolution, and in particular
with the July Revolution of 1830.   The decided advocate of freedom
and patriotism was at the same time a determined Prussian.   For
him this included acceptance of the Prussian monarchy — although
it did not exclude the desire for a constitution.

The king relented after Schleiermacher's disavowal.   He even
consulted Schleiermacher regarding the reconciliation with confessional Lutheranism which wanted to secede from the Prussian
State Church, and he bestowed on him as a mark of reconciliation
the medal of the Red Eagle, third class, the first and only decoration
Schleiermacher received from his king.

2.   PROFESSOR AND FOUNDER OF THE
UNIVERSITY OF BERLIN

Schleiermacher's decisive role in the founding of the University
of Berlin is not always sufficiently recognized in the literature of

the university's history. This is the case because Schleiermacher
had not played a leading role at the outset of planning for the
university.

After the collapse of the Prussian state in 1806/7 and the loss
of the western provinces, all the western universities and most out-
standingly Halle were lost to Prussia. The urgent desire thus developed to build a third university in Berlin (in addition to Koenigsberg
and Frankfort/Oder) and to call a good number of the professors
from the University of Halle to Berlin. As a result a deputation
of Halle's professors traveled to Memel to deliver this wish directly
to the Prussian king. King Friedrich Wilhelm III concurred and,
according to the report of Professor Schmalz, formulated there the
famous and often quoted statement, "The Prussian state must make
up through intellectual power what it has lost in physical power."

Cabinet Minister Beyme invited a group of scholars for an evaluation
of forthcoming plans for the university. Fichte was included while
Schleiermacher was overlooked for the time being. But Schleiermacher came forward on his own with an anonymous work entitled
Timely Thoughts on German Universities from a German Viewpoint
(*Gelegentliche Gedanken über deutsche Universitäten im deutschen
Sinne*), which appeared in Berlin in the spring of 1808. Even before
its publication, however, Beyme had advised him that he was being
considered for an appointment to the University of Berlin. He
received the final notification of appointment on July 14, 1809.

Meanwhile, Beyme's plans had come to a standstill because Minister
von Stein did not fully support them. Stein had doubts about
locating a university in metropolitan Berlin. He would have preferred
to build in Potsdam. The actual founding of the University of Berlin
finally took place under Wilhelm von Humboldt. In 1809 he took
over the direction of the Department of Worship and Instruction
in the Ministry of the Interior, which was headed by Schleiermacher's
friend Count Alexander von Dohna. In a short time he was so
successful in expediting the financial arrangements that as early as
the spring of 1810 the king was able publicly to decree the founding
of the University of Berlin. Humboldt quickly went to work and
convened a commission including Süvern, Uhden, and Schleiermacher.
In this way Schleiermacher became one of Wilhelm von Humboldt's
closest collaborators. Humboldt, as a Graecophile, had first considered
the classicist Wolf, but he was alienated by his arrogance. Humboldt
took up the ideas in Schleiermacher's prospectus in his own memorandum. The following ideas from Schleiermacher's prospectus
were the ones that Humboldt emphasized: Schleiermacher, like

Fichte, opposed the establishment of a technical school of higher
learning. This plan was of immediate concern because in France
the older, predominantly church-sponsored universities had been
dissolved and technical schools of higher learning and special studies
were established in their place. It is to Schleiermacher's credit
that he carried through the views, previously stated by Fichte, in
the concrete planning and structuring of the university.

These German scholars, influenced by idealist transcendental
philosophy and its new understanding of science, rejected the technical
schools because the science they had in mind was a universal and
coherent science understood as a system of the unity and universality
of man's total knowledge. Consequently the university should not
become a technical academy but should itself represent the totality
of knowledge. "The totality of knowledge should be shown by
perceiving the principles as well as the outline of all learning in such
a way that one develops the ability to pursue each sphere of knowledge
on his own."[49] Hence genuinely creative and productive scholarly
work is not possible unless it is rooted in the scientific spirit as expressed in philosophy.

Schleiermacher formulated this view thus: "There is no productive
scientific capacity in the absence of the speculative spirit."[50] By
speculation Schleiermacher did not mean empty speculation; he
meant rather the highest consciousness, the scientific spirit that cannot
isolate itself like a spectre, but that permeates all scientific work,
including also the particular projects of empirical research.[51] For
this reason the philosophical faculty came to predominate over the
other faculties. Fichte went so far in his forceful defense of speculation that he sharply diminished the significance of the other faculties.
He did not even want to take the theological faculty into consideration
as an institution in its own right. In contrast it is to Schleiermacher's
credit that he gave expression not only to the new concept of science
but also to the distinctiveness and independence of the special branches
of science. Organizationally he allowed the distinctive work of
the specialized sciences — theology, jurisprudence, and medicine
— to make its contribution within the university as a whole. He
also received support from the particular specialists within each
discipline. Reil, the Professor of Medicine, likewise interpreted
medicine not as a separate science, but classified it among the natural

49. *S. W.*, III/1, p. 558.
50. Ibid.
51. Ibid., pp. 558–59.

sciences, which in turn have a place within the framework of the sciences as a whole. The advocates of the cultural-historical sciences similarly wanted to treat their specialized disciplines only within the whole of learning.

The second idea from Schleiermacher's prospectus that Humboldt emphasized was the connection between research and teaching. The university should occupy an intermediate position between the scientific technical schools and the academy. It should combine research and teaching so that young students would be encouraged not merely to assimilate a specialized form of learning in all its details. The student should be captivated by the idea of knowledge and understand all specialized learning in terms of the entire framework of knowledge and he should derive the impulse for his own research from that.

The third main idea in Schleiermacher's prospectus concerned the relation between the university and the state: the state should allow freedom of research and teaching. Wilhelm von Humboldt also agreed with this. But the problem came with the question of how far state financing and state control were compatible with the supervision of a university. Humboldt and Schleiermacher were both convinced that the state should not intrude into the free life and spirit of scholarship. Scholarship, from this point of view, best serves the state if the state in no way encroaches upon the freedom of research and teaching. Moreover, if scholarship fulfills its final aim in seeking the idea of truth, then it could also serve the new Prussian state of the reform period as a community of justice and culture. These views have been stated in Humboldt's own memorandum on the organization of science. There he writes:

> The state must not demand from universities those things that directly and straightforwardly refer to itself. Rather it must retain the inner conviction that if the universities achieve their final aim they will also fulfil its [the state's] purpose. Indeed, its purpose will be fulfilled in a more profound way and in a way that is much more comprehensive and brings to bear quite different powers and levers than the state itself could set into motion.[52]

As an associate of Humboldt and as a member of the organizing commission, Schleiermacher had a decisive influence on the beginnings

---

52. Wilhelm von Humboldt, "Über die innere und äussere Organisation der höheren wissenshaftlichen Anstalten in Berlin 1810," *Werke*, vol. IV (Stuttgart, 1964), p. 260.

of the University of Berlin.   Furthermore, the Minister of the Interior,
Alexander von Dohna, personally called his friend Schleiermacher
for advice on many occasions.   The theology faculty was also a
subject of Schleiermacher's report.   Upon his suggestion De Wette
and Marheineke were appointed; De Wette as a New Testament
scholar and Marheineke essentially as a historian of the church and
doctrine.   Schleiermacher's basic principles are found in a memorandum for developing a theology faculty that he presented to the
commission on May 25, 1810.   He adhered to the division of the
theological discipline into four parts: exegetical, historical, dogmatic,
and practical theology.   But he did not request a specific professorial
chair in practical theology since he essentially wanted to leave the
concern for practical-theological development to the church.   Furthermore, specialization in theological scholarship at the beginning
of the nineteenth century had not yet gone so far as to appoint a
Professor Ordinarius for a single specialization.   Schleiermacher
requested three professors but expected that each *Ordinarius* could
represent two theological disciplines so that each subject would be
covered twice.   He requested two levels of academic rank in theology.
"Highest respect should be given" to the honored Doctor of Theology.
As the lower grade he recommended the Licentiate of Theology
which should be the prerequisite for *Habilitation* and, in addition,
a qualification for higher church offices.

As a member of the commission Schleiermacher also naturally
exercised considerable influence in the appointment of professors
to other faculties.   He particularly took pains to find a counterbalance
to Fichte, for it was quite certain from the beginning that Fichte
would be the first philosopher called to Berlin.   He made efforts
to have his friend Steffens appointed, but this was accomplished
only twenty years later.   The first statute of the University of Berlin
and the School of Theology also goes back to Schleiermacher's influence.   Above all he wanted to establish a genuine self-government
for the entire academic community.   The state should concern itself
essentially with the external organization.   The real weight of academic
self-government naturally rested on the faculty.   The core of the
faculty consisted of the full professors, plus the associate professors
and instructors.   This was not meant to give special privilege to
the full professors, but rather was intended to insure that the faculty
and thereby the university as such was independent and accountable
to itself.   Furthermore, Schleiermacher also requested the suspension
of all censorship for all publications appearing under university
auspices.   But on this issue he had only partial success.

His strongest influence on the university's life was through his effectiveness as a teacher and scholar, as a reinterpreter of the new Protestant theology, and as a co-founder and formulator of the new cultural-historical sciences and their method of understanding which had its origins in German transcendental philosophy.

It is understandable that in September, 1810, Schleiermacher was named the first dean of the theological faculty. He occupied this position four times (1810/11, 1813/14, 1817/18, 1819/20). He held the Rectorship in 1815/16. After the age of fifty he resigned all purely administrative offices since he wanted to devote himself exclusively to his calling as a teacher and scholar. His lectures at the University of Berlin were extraordinary. The extent of his educational activity was astonishing when one also recalls that in addition to his teaching he filled the pastoral office at Trinity Church, that he was secretary for the Prussian Academy, that he was otherwise called upon as an author and scholar, and also that he kept up a very lively and extensive correspondence with his friends.

The catalogues that have been preserved from the University of Berlin give insight into this academic activity. In the summer semester he lectured in philosophy from six until seven o'clock; for five days a week he lectured in theology from seven until nine o'clock, for a total of ten hours a week. Apart from the Old Testament he dealt with almost all areas in theology. Besides dogmatics, which he frequently repeated, he taught encyclopedistics and Christian ethics. In addition there were also his lectures in exegesis, church history, and practical theology.

In philosophy he lectured in the areas of dialectics, ethics, psychology, pedagogy, aesthetics, and hermeneutics. It is most regrettable that Schleiermacher did not finally publish these lectures in book form. Only his fragmentary comments and notes have been retained.

After Schleiermacher's death, his students — including Jonas, Alexander Schweizer, Lücke, Lommatzsch, and George — sought to pass on the content of his lectures to future generations. They had at their disposal Schleiermacher's own lecture notes plus a range of more or less carefully recorded student transcripts. They sought to compile and coordinate these remains, some of them quite fragmentary and dissimilar. Consequently the reading of these pieced-together lectures is unusually difficult. They do not provide a clear picture of either the structure of Schleiermacher's system or the stages in the development of his philosophical thinking. This kind of transmission has done extraordinary damage to the impact of Schleiermacher's philosophical thinking and diminished the understanding and appreciation of his philosophical accomplishment. One of Schleiermacher's most important nineteenth-century disciples, Wilhelm Dilthey, attempted, several decades after Schleiermacher's death, to present in detail his philosophical thinking and system. Unfortunately these works by Dilthey also remained fragmentary and only now after many decades have they been published from Dilthey's literary remains.[53]

The transmission of Schleiermacher's theological thinking was more successful. Schleiermacher himself published *The Christian Faith* in the two editions of 1821/22 and 1830/31; he also published two editions of his theological encyclopedia [*Brief Outline of Theological Study*] in 1810 and 1830. In addition there is a host of smaller works. Both his letters to Lücke are informative about his basic theological intentions. Schleiermacher may have been even stronger in speaking than he was as a writer; he was the preacher in the pulpit and the lively teacher in the classroom. This raised his impact upon that generation but it has diminished his influence on theology and cultural history generally. Unfortunately there was no attempt in the nineteenth century to undertake a scholarly edition of his collected works which would have examined the available manuscripts from a critical perspective and would have transmitted to us a better text of his writings than that which we now have in the *Sämmtliche Werke*, first published in mid-nineteenth century. Today it would be very difficult to prepare a scholarly edition of his collected works since many manuscripts were lost in the nineteenth century. Despite the difficulty, Protestantism, as well as theological and philosophical scholarship, owes such an edition to one of its most significant scholars.

3. SYSTEMATICS

a) *The Theological System*

Schleiermacher's biographer, Dilthey, described the ultimate aim of his biography as the "resolution of the great historical question of how completely scattered elements of culture . . . are moulded in the workshop of a single mind to form an original whole, which, in its turn, creatively enters into the life of the community."[54] Dilthey tried to exposit Schleiermacher's system as theology and philosophy.

---

53. W. Dilthey, *Leben Schleiermachers*, vol. II, ed. M. Redeker (Berlin, 1966).
54. Dilthey, *Leben Schleiermachers*, vol. I, Preface.

He wanted to demonstrate how Schleiermacher "in the deepest awareness of his being, elevated the universal experience and understanding of the most various spheres of life to the level of philosophical consciousness," and how a universal understanding of the cultural world thus arose.[55] In this regard Schleiermacher's intellectual growth inevitably led him to develop a unified system of theology out of the intuitive understanding of the Christian faith of his youth. Dilthey is correct in this assessment: Schleiermacher was a systematist.

It is right, therefore, in our interpretation of Schleiermacher, to treat his theological and philosophical thinking as a system. For Schleiermacher, theology and philosophy are independent and self-contained systems, but together they complement one another in terms of a larger whole, which one might compare to an ellipse with two foci. In this section we will try to examine both systems in their particularity and simultaneously to show their complementary relationship.

The development of modern science in the course of the nineteenth and twentieth centuries has led to a distrust of systems and systematization, since the idealist conception of science at the beginning of the nineteenth century saw in the making of systems the special character and true goal of scientific investigation. Today we must free ourselves from a false critique of systematics. Schleiermacher's system of theology is not a formal-logical construct of concepts, as one would usually expect to find in older Protestant dogmatics and would usually hold up as an example of the road to theological error.

In all periods of Protestant theology the necessity of understanding proclamation and theology as a common structure of meaning held together by the center of the revelation of Christ has been recognized. Hence the question about the internal coherence of the subject matter of theology is methodologically justified. For Schleiermacher the question of where the center of his life and thought lay and what the center of his theology might be arose early. Schleiermacher himself spoke much more clearly and decisively about his theology than about his philosophical system. For the investigation of the philosophical system we are dependent upon a few of Schleiermacher's original essays on particulars and mainly on the lecture notes on dialectics and philosophical ethics. He expounded his theological system in two programmatic and epoch-making publications. These are the *Brief Outline of Theological Study* (1st ed. 1811; 2d ed. 1830)

---

55. Ibid., Introduction, p. xxiii.

and the famous *The Christian Faith* (1st ed. 1821/22; 2d ed. 1830/31).
It has justly been said of the latter that, aside from Calvin's *Institutes*,
that there has been no system in Protestant theology which, *qua*
system, has attained the status of Schleiermacher's *The Christian
Faith*.

(1) *Conception and Development of the System*

The line of development in his theological system-building leads
from the insights of the *Speeches* and *Soliloquies* to *The Christian
Faith* of 1821. It does not move in quite so straight a line as is
commonly supposed. In the period from 1806 to 1811 Schleiermacher
stood closer than ever to the idealist philosophy of identity and
Schelling's metaphysics in particular. A kind of Christian speculation
was now added to his initial insights. It is already recognizable
in Eduard's third speech in *Christmas Eve* (1806), and in addition
in the various lecture notes of this period on ethics and dialectics,
insofar as they touched on questions of the philosophy of religion.
Evidences of his theological thought as contained in his early lectures
on dogmatics are sparse, since Schleiermacher apparently destroyed
nearly all his manuscripts that antedated the publication of *The
Christian Faith* in 1821. In Twesten's literary remains a transcript
of lectures from 1811 was found, a valuable addition to our previous
knowledge.[56]

During this time Schleiermacher adopted a middle position
between Jacobi and the speculative metaphysics of Schelling and
Hegel. Schleiermacher did not follow Jacobi's alternative of being
a heathen in the head and a Christian in the heart. As far as Jacobi
was concerned, metaphysical speculation about unity and totality
leads to atheism and determinism and for him it was incompatible
with the experience of faith, in which feeling was immediate self-
consciousness. Schleiermacher wanted to tie together feeling and
the speculative understanding of the universe. They are the two
sides of our spirit, which correspond to one another. The immediate
consciousness of God in us must therefore not only express itself
in both sides of our being but also in equal measure. For if the
two were of diverse kind, the consciousness of God would have to
be split. But then it would not be the consciousness of God. The
totality of religious feeling must be like the totality of scientific
understanding, though this is not meant to deny that the manner

---

56. My colleague, J. H. Hörcher, who examined Twesten's literary remains
for me, discovered this transcript.

of moving from the universal to the particular can differ in each case. Inasmuch as the analysis of feeling is the task of dogmatics, whereas the scientific construction or elaboration of the consciousness of God falls to philosophy, it follows that dogmatics and philosophy cannot be antagonistic, that what is given in feeling must also be given in understanding. So say the written notes which the young Twesten took in Schleiermacher's lectures of 1811. Schleiermacher had expressed similar thoughts in his lectures on ethics of 1805/06.[57] For Schleiermacher, then, theology and philosophy constitute a system in which each complements, but does not contradict, the other.

Schleiermacher drastically modified these ideas between 1811 and 1814, although certain elements of this Christian speculation are retained in *The Christian Faith*.[58] Even later on, Schleiermacher considered reason and its domination over sensuousness as a manifestation of the Spirit of God. But it is indisputable that from 1811 to 1814, between the ages of forty-three and forty-six, Schleiermacher reorganized the fundamental ideas of his system. We can also observe a similar development in his christological speculations. In Eduard's speeches in *Christmas Eve*, the Platonic idea of an archetype was combined with the new humanism of idealist philosophy. Christ is the archetype of man, manifested in the life of mankind through the incarnation of the Logos. The deviation from Plato is immediately evident — the archetype enters history, whereas this is not the case with the Platonic ideas. But even this christological speculation was as completely transformed as his metaphysics of the Spirit. In his Christology a Zinzendorf-like piety centered on Christ, the principle of Christ's living communion with his followers and the soteriological motif of redemption and reconciliation became so pronounced that speculation about Christ took a secondary place, even while it was retained in connection with the Pauline speculation concerning the Adam-Christ relationship.

(2) *Basis and Method of Schleiermacher's Mature System*

Schleiermacher's programmatic *Brief Outline of Theological Studies* ushered in a new epoch for the self-understanding of Protestant theology. In accord with the new systematics of the sciences, all the theological disciplines were integrated into the vital whole of

---

57. Schleiermacher, *Werke: Auswahl in vier Bänden*, vol. II, ed. O. Braun and D. J. Bauer (Leipzig, 1913), p. 103.
58. Cf. *Der Christliche Glaube*, 2d ed., § 13.

a unified yet clearly articulated organism. Older Protestant dogmatics with its method of *loci* could no more develop this conception than could the theology of the Enlightenment. Individual theological disciplines were simply considered *seriatim*, without any delineation of their internal connections. When Schleiermacher arrived in Halle in 1804, the theological faculty had just published an entirely inadequate introduction to theological studies. Schleiermacher's *Brief Outline* tried to grasp the unity and divisions of theology from one dominant point of view. For him this principle of unity was not absolute knowledge, from which all else could be deduced, but the direction of theology toward one specific task. The goal of theology is to provide meaningful guidance for the Christian church. "Christian theology is the sum total of those matters of scientific knowledge and discipline without whose possession and application coherent guidance of the Christian church, i.e., a Christian church governance, would be impossible."[59] Schleiermacher grants that perhaps the Christian faith itself does not require such an "apparatus," but the Christian church does nonetheless. Theological scholarship is necessary for life and for the Christian church. Schleiermacher — as did orthodox Protestantism[60] — interpreted church government to be first of all the mandate of the spiritual office, and not, as in the language of the present day, the highest management of the legal institution of the church and the administration of church order.

This ecclesiastical theme in theology was somewhat incautiously formulated by Schleiermacher. It was not Schleiermacher's intention pragmatically to distort this ecclesiastical theme, as happened later in the nineteenth century, in reference to the spiritual office(s) of the proclamation of the gospel and the administration of the sacraments. "Ecclesiastical" does not simply refer here to the usefulness and applicability to church practice. From the principles of usefulness and applicability one could with equal ease derive a fundamentalist dogmatics and the insubstantial modern theology of accommodation. Neither corresponds in any way to Schleiermacher's intentions. For Schleiermacher the task was "to present more clearly the distinctive nature (of Christian life) in every future moment";[61] "to represent

---

59. Schleiermacher, *Kurze Darstellung des theologischen Studiums*, critical edition, ed. Heinrich Scholz (Leipzig, 1910), § 5. English translations are available in: *Brief Outline of the Study of Theology*, trans. W. Farrer (Edinburgh, 1850); *Brief Outline on the Study of Theology*, trans. Terrence Tice (Richmond, Va., 1966).

60. Cf. *Confessio Augustana*, article XXVIII.

61. *Kurze Darstellung*, § 84.

the idea of Christianity according to the distinctive understanding of the Evangelical Church in ever increasing clarity in this church and to win ever increasing forces for it."[62]

Thus the ecclesiastical theme in theology leads to the question of the nature and truth of the Christian faith and life. Theology is self-reflection of the church on its own substance. The proclamation and activity of the church — its teaching, its worship, and its polity — must be analyzed phenomenologically, and pneumatically tested, founded, and refined. Ecclesiastical interests, i.e., participation in church life, must be unified with the scientific spirit.[63] Faith and the critically constructive spirit of inquiry do not stand in contradiction, but enter into a vital relationship. Church-mindedness is the precondition of theology.

It is important in this connection to see how Schleiermacher applied his new understanding of science to theology. Theology is not a "speculative" but a "positive" science. In this juxtaposition, "positive" denotes the theological exposition of the contents of Christian revelation — in contrast with the natural theology of the Enlightenment, which identified revelation and reason. Positive science tries to explore that which is actually given, concrete historical life, rather than making speculative deductions. Schleiermacher's concept of "positive theology" has nothing to do with the distinction between conservative-positive theology and critical-liberal theology which was made later in the nineteenth century.

Schleiermacher's turn away from Schelling and the latter's metaphysical understanding of science was a result of this definition of theology. Schelling sought to derive all science from absolute knowledge. According to Schelling's philosophy of identity there are two manifestations of absolute being: first in nature — in which case the real takes priority over the ideal — and secondly in reason and history — in which case the ideal outweighs the real. In a modified form Schleiermacher adopted for his own philosophy the structuring of the sciences from the philosophy of identity. The two principal sciences are natural philosophy and philosophical ethics; the latter includes the philosophy of history, of culture, and of society. Thus the overarching and fundamental philosophical science is the transcendental-philosophical foundation of dialectics, which ontologically investigates the relationship of thinking and being as well as the method and logic of scientific cognition.

---

62. Ibid., § 313.
63. Ibid., § 258.

Schleiermacher, however, did not insert theology into this system of major speculative sciences. He clearly separated the secondary forms of positive science from the truly speculative sciences. He thus reiterates the view of the *Speeches* that the certainty of the truth of faith cannot be proven through metaphysical speculation. He confessed with considerable passion that his faith in Christ could not be derived from philosophy.[64] Hence the propositions of dogmatics are not established by philosophy but are expressions of the pious Christian state of mind. Scientific speculation, the intuition of Absolute Being, seeks to grasp the idea of the highest being through rational thought; dogmatic propositions, in contrast, are nothing but "analyzed reflections of the original pious state of mind."[65]

"The Evangelical Church has the single-minded consciousness that its distinctive formulation of dogmatic propositions does not depend on any philosophical form or school, and does not even proceed from any speculative interest at all, but only from the interest of the satisfaction of immediate self-consciousness through the sole means of Christ's genuine and unfalsified foundation."[66]

The organization of theology is also understandable in terms of this definition of theology as an ecclesiastical and positive science. Schleiermacher distinguished three principal disciplines: historical, philosophical, and practical theology. Included in historical theology are biblical exegesis, church history, dogmatics taken as the phenomenology of doctrines considered valid in the church, and statistics. Historical theology is the "real body of theological study." It is concerned with the material, the stuff of theological thinking. If it remained isolated it would be threatened by spiritless empiricism. "To be sure, philosophical theology presupposes the material of historical theology as something already known, but it should itself establish the foundation for the truly historical understanding of Christianity."[67] By the term "historical understanding" Schleiermacher meant a view of the essence and truth of Christianity as evidenced in historically concrete life. The somewhat unfortunate term "philosophical theology" could lead to misunderstandings, as though philosophy were in its turn to intrude upon theology. Ultimately, however, the concept of philosophical theology only involves a question of methodology and not an exchange of divine revelation

---

64. *S. W.*, I/2, *Sendschreiben an Lücke*, p. 616.
65. *Der Christliche Glaube*, 1st ed., § 2.
66. Ibid., 2d ed., Addendum to § 16.
67. *Brief Outline*, 2d ed., § 65.

for philosophical speculation. What is meant is the question concerning what is normative, essential, and distinctive in working out the given content of perception. Tertullian had long since claimed that any philosophical discussion about God from a standpoint outside the faith does not deal with God but with demons. This damning judgment was maintained in theological language through the centuries. It would be unjust to condemn the basic structure of Schleiermacher's theology on account of the accidental use of the term "philosophical theology." This basic structure of theology does away with the reliance on scriptural proof based upon the literal citation of the Bible or the creeds, so typical of older Protestantism. Dogmatics should not lay the foundations of Christian faith, but should clarify its inward nature. In such a representation itself lies the proof of its thruth. The Christian faith does not arise through obedience to any doctrinal norms, but through the living community with the Redeemer. But because we have been brought to faith by Christ, Scripture and creed take on new meaning as the witnesses to faith. Thus, by critical and constructive treatment of the biblical and traditional teachings of the church and of the whole range of historical "materials," dogmatics should help lead to an expression of the Christian faith which would correspond to its true character.

No theology can deny that its interpretation of science and its method are influenced by the contemporary philosophy of science. Schleiermacher's theological method also cannot conceal its origins in the new concept of science offered by German transcendental philosophy. He himself attributed only formal significance to this influence, a claim we still must examine. His thinking is determined by two methodological principles: (1) by the differentiation between idea and appearance in transcendental philosophy, and (2) by the idea of an organically related whole. Schleiermacher wanted to overcome the opposition between a mere empiricist, historical, psychological, and sociological analysis of life and the Christian faith, on the one hand, and speculation about God and Christ, on the other. The idea — i.e., the nature and truth of Christian faith — takes on concrete form in the Christian life; the task of theological thought can only be solved in the constant tension and mutuality of the knowledge of essences and observation of appearances.

The second methodological principle is his idea of system. Scientific knowledge which is obtained through the complementary relationship of idea and appearance can only be formed and secured within a context. It cannot be emphasized enough that this system must not be speculatively construed but must be found through

theological reflection on the nature and truth of the Christian faith
as something already given. The internal, factual coherence of
Christian doctrine is not constructed or postulated. It is instituted
by the revelation of Christ. The self-manifestation of God in the
Christian life of faith contains a system, i.e., an internal structure
which is dependent upon the truth of revelation and is therefore the
presupposition of human piety and theological reflection; it is a structure which in its own center is not dependent on theological reflection
but rather can only be discovered and made manifest.

What then is the object of dogmatics according to these presuppositions? It is the living community with Christ the Redeemer
which contains the relationship of faith between God and man.
Schleiermacher characterizes this internal experience of faith as the
pious Christian dispositions. These dispositions are the object of
theological reflection and representation. Disposition as used here
is not the sphere of the irrational and emotional; rather, in the distinctive language of Schleiermacher, it is feeling as immediate self-consciousness. Here he means a man's concentration on his innermost
self of which he becomes aware only in the self-realization of existential encounter and decision. This theological statement has been
criticized as subjectivism and psychologism. This is to misinterpret
its meaning in much the same way as the basis of modern existential
theology is falsified when the methodical reference of all theological
statements to human existence is condemned as subjectivization of
the Christian faith. Schleiermacher wanted to pursue theology, not
existential ontology. God, according to the assumptions of critical
transcendental philosophy, is not an object in this world nor an object
of a metaphysically constructed transcendent world. Hence the
reality of the living God is not comprehended through metaphysical
speculation — a claim Schleiermacher untiringly reasserted. Schleiermacher's theology does not deal with reflection on the isolated
self, and definitely not with mere introspection of immediate self-
consciousness. A transsubjective relationship is intended, a determination of immediate self-consciousness through God. It is
precisely the Christian faith in redemption which, in the new being
of the human self through Christ's salvation, experiences that the
reality of God as the author of self-consciousness manifests itself
in the making of the human self.

The same is true for statements about the world. Theological
assertions about the world do not refer to the world as an object of
knowledge, but to the lordship of God over the world and in the
world. Schleiermacher, proceeding from transcendental philosophy,

affirms — and this is the decisive aspect of his theology — the non-objectifiability of God. The result of this rejection of the older metaphysical objectification of God, however, is not the agnostic uncertainty which results in the assertion that no one can know whether there is a God or not. The criticism of the older metaphysical conception of God itself followed from the new revelatory experience of God's reality which overwhelms man and posits and determines the human self, and thus persuades it of the reality of God. Redemption by Christ posits a new self in justification and rebirth, thus showing the reality of God. In this way Schleiermacher discovered anew the authentically theological in theology; and in opposition to the enlightened faith in reason, to supernaturalistic metaphysics, and pantheistic dissolution of God's divinity, he witnessed once again to the reality of God as the Father of Jesus Christ.

(3) *The Structure of* The Christian Faith

The skillful construction of *The Christian Faith* is markedly different from the customary organization of dogmatic systems. How is this structure to be interpreted according to its fundamental theological conception? *The Christian Faith* has a monistic tendency because of its view of God; the omnipotence of God is understood not in the sense that God can do whatever he wills but in the universalistic sense that in reality he is the cause of everything. Despite this reappearing monistic tendency the main part of *The Christian Faith* is dualistic and arranged around the antithesis of sin and grace, i.e., around the human need for redemption and the actual redemption by Christ. This principal part was preceded by another preliminary section conveying a theology of "universal God-consciousness" without reference to the antithesis of sin and grace. One could say in simplified formulation that Schleiermacher builds the theology of the second and third articles of the Christian creed on that of the first article. In it the theological content of the pious Christian's feeling of creatureliness and confession is depicted: "I believe that God has made me and all creatures."

Schleiermacher interpreters disagree about the meaning of this theology of "universal God-consciousness." Time and again some thought they had caught him on the paths of natural theology or speculative philosophy. Schleiermacher himself emphatically contradicted this.[68] He was not concerned here with natural theology for in the reality of historical life there is no natural but only positive

---

68. *Der Christliche Glaube*, 1st ed., § 2, 2; 2d ed., § 63.

religion. Therefore this universal God-consciousness never exists
in isolation and independence; it exists only as one dimension within
the Christian faith in redemption. For the Christian faith in God
there are no "sacred moments apart from Christ."[69] There is "no
relation to Christ . . . which is not also a relation to God. Our
proposition is thus simply the most general expression of the vital
connection between the first and the second part of our exposition."[70]
The separate treatment of the first article [of the Apostles' Creed]
on creation is thus merely an abstraction.[71] However, Schleiermacher
held that this abstraction was necessary.

Moreover, he prefaced this first part with an introduction of
thirty-five paragraphs. In addition to a doctrine of theological
knowledge this introduction contains a religious philosophical
inquiry into the nature and truth of religion, a developmental survey
of the history of religions, and a theological classification of the types
of religion in which Christianity constitutes the highest stage.

The author of *The Christian Faith* acknowledged in his open
letters to Lücke that he would have preferred to preface *The Christian
Faith* with the presentation of "the full Christian consciousness. . . .
Then no one could have failed to recognize that the exposition of
the distinctive Christian consciousness is the true and real purpose
of this book."[72] Schleiermacher argued against this arrangement
for two reasons: (1) Because of his distaste for anticlimax; he did
not want to start from the important and then descend to the less
important. A scientific investigation is not a banquet at which one
first distributes the good wine and later the poor wine. The main
reason, however, was a different one. (2) Schleiermacher considered
it necessary to rid Christian faith in God of all unnecessary metaphysical
and mythological ballast in order to testify to the pious experience
of the reality of God when confronted with the modern scientific
world view. When based on critical transcendental philosophy the
scientific world view should not entail the tendency toward pantheism
and atheism. It must remain open to the reality of the living Lord
of nature and history as he is professed in the Christian faith. In
order to guide this discussion about natural science and theology to
the point where a bond between both could be established, he proceeded
with this abstraction of "universal God-consciousness." This God-

---

69. Ibid., 1st ed., § 39.
70. Ibid.
71. Ibid., 1st ed., § 78.
72. *S. W.*, I/2, p. 609.

consciousness is contained in the Christian faith in the Redeemer as a universal claim available to all people. But there is an additional theme. His conception of scientific system led him to include the specifically Christian within the larger framework of the definition of the nature of religion. In the first edition he even made this formulation: the student of religion must take a standpoint "above" Christianity in order to define the specifically Christian.[73] That occasioned a heated polemic against Schleiermacher. Even Twesten, his loyal student, wanted to take his standpoint only "in" and not "above" Christianity. Consequently Schleiermacher dropped this formulation in the second edition of *The Christian Faith*. He did not seek to separate himself from the Christian faith but only to formulate in theoretical terms the universal tendency contained in Christian faith. The term "above" had only a logical-theoretical meaning and did not imply transcending in the sense of overcoming.

An apologetic theme is present in the religio-philosophical arrangement of the Introduction. It is not Schelling's speculative philosophy that is conspicuous but Schleiermacher's modification of Kant's critical transcendental philosophy. On the one hand, Schleiermacher wanted to indicate that religion in its certainty of truth is independent of the general claim to truth by the human mind; on the other hand, however, he wanted to show that religion is a necessary component of life in human history. It is religion alone which provides the deeper foundation for the union of the human spirit with the ultimate Ground of Being and thus protects science, art, and morality from skepticism and degeneration.

Here in the Introduction, then, Schleiermacher borrows from the field of philosophy. He does not deny that scholarly theological work needs this assistance from philosophy. Theological scholarship is not bound to any single philosophy, but not every philosophy is suitable for this cooperation with theology either.

> A theologian can only accept one [philosophical system] which somehow preserves the distinction between the ideas of God and world, and which upholds the antithesis of good and evil. . . . On the other hand, of course, one system may suit some better while others prefer still another according to their adopted view. And in this way the appropriate balance is maintained in the total development by the interplay or co-existence of systems through their mutual or shared influence on dogmatic language and exposition.[74]

---

73. *Der Christliche Glaube*, 1st ed., § 6.
74. Ibid.

Philosophy must not be allowed to become master and judge in theological matters, but "the separation of dogmatics from philosophy can never go to the point of a renunciation of philosophical language."[75]

"Whatever dogmatics borrows from philosophy will unavoidably change once a philosophical system is antiquated, i.e., when people no longer think in that framework and a different conceptual framework has become dominant."[76]

Thus the following ingenious system emerges as the structure of *The Christian Faith:*

> Part I. The theological content of general religious self-consciousness as universally presupposed in Christian piety.
>
> Part II. The theology of Christian religious self-consciousness: the theology of redemption through Christ as seen in the opposition of the doctrines of sin and grace wherein the doctrines of sin and grace are distinguished.

By the same method the two (or three) parts are given a tripartite arrangement.[77]

There is theological inquiry into:

> 1. the religious self-consciousness
> 2. the concepts of the divine attributes in their relation to man and world
> 3. theological cosmology

The sequence of these three perspectives is different in parts I and II. Part I contains the following sequence:

> 1. theological analysis of human self-consciousness
> 2. the doctrine of God
> 3. cosmology

In the theology of redemption [Part II] the sequence is:

> 1. the analysis of religious self-consciousness
> 2. cosmology
> 3. the doctrine of God (as the culmination)

All three areas of doctrine are thus treated three times. For instance, the doctrine of God is arranged as follows:

> Part I. the doctrine of God's eternity, omnipresence, omnipotence, and omniscience
>
> Part II, 1. the doctrine of God's holiness and justice
>
> Part II, 2. the doctrine of God's love and wisdom

---

75. Ibid.
76. Ibid.
77. Ibid., 2d ed., § 35.

The doctrine of the Trinity is treated separately at the conclusion of the dogmatics.

(4) *The Principle of the Feeling of Absolute Dependence*

In the Introduction to *The Christian Faith* Schleiermacher presented a definition of the essence of religion. This definition tried to accentuate the religious in religion in order to use this concept as a principle of interpretation which characterizes that which is distinctive in the Christian faith. On the other hand, it is at once clear that the essence of religion can be grasped neither in a purely speculative nor a purely empirical manner. This religious principle of interpretation must have been drawn from a concrete — i.e., positive, historical — religion. When defining the essence of religion, the theologian, proceeding from a religio-philosophical standpoint, is bound to the specific Christian experience of revelation. Schleiermacher omits the *Speeches'* definition of religious essence which is there expressed as intuition and feeling of the universe, or characterized as the sense and taste for the infinite. He retained only the category of feeling as the original act of the Spirit as that which ontologically precedes human knowing — including speculative knowing — and human willing. This feeling Schleiermacher describes as immediate self-consciousness. In handwritten comments in his lecture notes on proposition 8 of the first edition he interpreted the word "immediate" self-consciousness as meaning "original" self-consciousness. This self-consciousness is completely independent of metaphysics and morality in its self-certainty and distinctiveness. It is a fully independent domain; even more, it is the place and domain in which the original positing — rather, the de-positing — of human self-consciousness occurs.

Two elements are present in immediate self-consciousness: "a self-positing *(Sichselbstsetzen)* and a not-having-posited-oneself-thus *(Sichselbstnichtsogesetzthaben)*."[78] The first element is the being-for-itself of the particular or "the being of the subject for itself." The other element is that of being together with others and being determined through others. Both elements of self-consciousness are described as self-acting and susceptibility, as freedom and dependence. Self-consciousness is related to that which is its other, that which affects self-consciousness, in a reciprocal way. Over against the other it is partly free, partly dependent. This other is always co-posited with self-consciousness. It is the totality of everything

78. Ibid., 2d ed., § 4, paragraph 1.

finite. This totality is what we call world. Partly we depend on
this world of the finite, partly we are free from it. In the sphere
of the finite there is no feeling of absolute freedom, but neither is
there a feeling of absolute dependence.

Apart from this relationship to the world, however, one also finds
in immediate self-consciousness the feeling of absolute dependence.
It is differentiated from world-consciousness because it entails
absolute dependence. The determinative element in this feeling of
absolute dependence, which is essential to self-consciousness, cannot
be the world; it can only involve the eternal and absolute now transcending the world. This determining now can only be God; for
God is the absolute, infinite unity which differentiates itself from
the world by encompassing and transcending all the contradictions
of the world — e.g., thought and being, reason and sensibility. As
the final unity God is transcendent in relation to the world at the
same time that he is the decisive power which unifies the world's
contradictions and thereby creates and preserves life in this world
and thus vitally permeates it. The infinite power is absolutely
superior to the finite world and yet operative in it.

The reality of this God-relation, the determination of the finite
by the infinite, is not an object for metaphysical speculation but
an experience of immediate self-consciousness. Already in the
Speeches Schleiermacher had stressed that the universe creates its
own admirers. Schleiermacher now indicates that the feeling of
absolute dependence and the God-relation, which he described as
an "immediate existential relation" in the open letter to Lücke, were
one and the same. Absolute dependence is the "fundamental relation"
between God and men, encompassing all other relationships, called
forth by an original revelation of God to men.

God-consciousness and self-consciousness are intimately linked.

> But any idea that God is somehow contained in this or that
> place is excluded, because all external givens are objects which
> can evoke a reaction of their own, no matter how slight. To
> transfer this conception to any perceptible object, unless one is
> aware that it is a purely arbitrary symbolism, is always a corruption,
> whether it be a momentary transferal as a theophany or a con-
> stitutive transferal in which God is represented as a perceptible
> and permanent particular.[79]

With this the non-objectifiability of God is clearly shown.

---

79. Ibid., 2d ed., § 4, 4.

This theological interpretation of the feeling of absolute dependence
as the co-presence of God in self-consciousness[80] has often been
challenged by interpreters of Schleiermacher. Schaeder already
raised the objection that Schleiermacher's definition of the nature
of religion does not start with God but with man, and that he does
not arrive at the object of religion until he deduces God as the cause
of the feeling of absolute dependence from self-consciousness.[81]
This objection is inaccurate. As far as Schleiermacher is concerned,
reflection only yields a theological conception of God, of human
self-consciousness, and of the world, but not piety itself; for the
feeling of absolute dependence is already a God-relation which
Schleiermacher also calls God-consciousness. Particularly inappropriate is the objection made by F. Flückiger that the feeling of absolute
dependence is simply naked consciousness of human being and existence.[82] It was precisely this misunderstanding Schleiermacher
fought against as the "nonreligious explanation of this feeling."[83]
It is rather God-consciousness which is clearly differentiated from
consciousness about God (i.e., the notion of God). It is God's
living relationship with man, of the Creator with his creation, and
not a matter of being at one with the world. The relationship of
man to the world, however, is determined partly by the feeling of
dependence and partly by the feeling of freedom.

Only when one eliminates the feeling of freedom in world-consciousness, when "everything particular is extinguished in a general
feeling of necessity and leaves no room for the spontaneity of life,"[84]
then there remains only a feeling of necessity in regard to the world
and a pantheism develops which is incapable of distinguishing between
God and world. Schleiermacher, however, put great stress on
maintaining the transcendence of God as absolute totality, in contrast
to the finite world as the totality of all opposites and differences.
Schleiermacher at all times passionately defended himself against
the charge of pantheism. "It is quite inconceivable how one could
attribute pantheism to me, for I fully separate the feeling of absolute
dependence from any relation with the world."[85] "Ruinous pantheism

80. Ibid., 2d ed., § 30, 1.
81. E. Schaeder, *Theozentrische Theologie*, I (Leipzig, 1909), p. 18.
82. F. Flückiger, *Philosophie und Theologie bei Schleiermacher* (Zollikon-
Zürich, 1947), p. 36.
83. *Der Christliche Glaube*, 1st ed., § 36.
84. Ibid.
85. Ibid., 7th ed., p. 29, footnote.

which would make man a part of God is clearly excluded by the
statement that absolute dependency is the same thing as dependency
upon God."[86]

In his utter dependence on God man simultaneously realizes that
all finite being, and thus the world, also depends absolutely on God.

Religious affection according to Schleiermacher is not something
incidental or transitory but an "essential element of life."[87] For
Schleiermacher this affirmation took the place of all proofs for God.
Critics promptly challenged this, claiming to have found here an
unacceptable apologetic, a transformation of theology into philosophy.
They contend that this is not a theological conception but one taken
from transcendental philosophy, that Schleiermacher was not trying
to erect a specific concept of religion but sought to establish a religious
a priori for the sphere of religion as the innermost presupposition
of all religious life and experience. In transcendental philosophy
the *a priori* represents the necessary and universal validity of rational
principles. Thus, for the religious sphere, the feeling of absolute
dependence would constitute approximately the same sort of *a priori*
as was the categorical imperative for the moral realm, or as the categories
of the understanding were for scientific cognition. The frequent
understanding of the *a priori* in neo-Kantian terms easily leads to
the mistaken notion that this definition of the principle of the absolute
dependence of human self-consciousness leaves man in isolation,
so that God ultimately becomes a product of the human mind and
the God-relationship is postulated and constructed by man on the
basis of this *a priori* principle. Strong objections must be raised
here, for Schleiermacher had no intention of being so understood.
The faith-relationship of God and man, for him, is an original and
immediate relation created by God; it cannot be based on speculation
and metaphysics or on transcendental-critical rationality.

It cannot be denied, on the other hand, that Schleiermacher
utilized the concepts of transcendental philosophy for interpreting
the principle of absolute dependence. G. Wehrung has shown this
with particular thoroughness in his book *Die philosophische-theologische
Methode Schleiermachers*.[88] The principle of absolute dependence is
"that which remains identical in all particular manifestations of
piety . . . , which relates to the outpourings of the religious life in

86. Ibid., 7th ed., vol. II, p. 500.
87. Ibid., 1st ed., § 37; 2d ed., § 33.
88. G. Wehrung, *Die philosophische-theologische Methode Schleiermachers*
(Göttingen, 1911).

the same way that the self-positing of each person relates to all the expressions of one's personal existence as such."[89]

Schleiermacher's explanations in the Introduction and in Part I of *The Christian Faith* reflect something of a discrepancy resulting from the invasion of categories from transcendental philosophy. They mix theological with philosophical thinking. Perhaps we can find the key to this division in § 20 of the first edition (second edition, § 13, postscript).

The authentically Christian in Christianity and authentically religious in religion can neither be caused nor forced by reason. But it nevertheless may be presented in a reasonable manner. The transrational in Christianity, therefore, cannot be contrary to reason, which relates to the fact that this reasonable presentation is identical with the "observed self-consciousness."[90] The most inward self-consciousness and objective consciousness, i.e., the totality of everything rational, cannot, according to Schleiermacher, contradict each other even though the content of religious self-consciousness is in no way produced by reason. And when Schleiermacher passionately attacks speculation and metaphysics he is indeed justified in respect to Schelling's speculations, at least as found, for example, in the ninth lecture on the "Method of Academic Studies." With a clear conscience Schleiermacher uses the categories of critical transcendental philosophy to interpret the piety of Christian faith, not to establish it; for him reason too is a creation of God and ultimately it is piety which gives it its basis and certainty of truth.

Schleiermacher himself was conscious of the incomplete and tentative character of the first part of *The Christian Faith* which dealt with God as Creator and the world and humanity as the creation of God. Owing to his theological method Schleiermacher proceeds from the feeling of absolute dependence. Dogmatic propositions should "represent," as he explicitly formulated it in the second open letter to Lücke,[91] the living God-relation of the feeling of absolute dependence and the experience of faith which it entails. However, the theology of this consciousness of absolute dependence, isolated from the second part of *The Christian Faith*, is an abstraction, requiring further explanation, completion, and greater depth. The same holds true for the dogmatic propositions on universal God-consciousness in *The Christian Faith*.

---

89. *Der Christliche Glaube*, 1st ed., § 36.
90. Ibid., 1st ed., § 20, p. 112.
91. *S. W.*, I/2, p. 618.

An omnipotence whose goal or means of movement I do not know, an omniscience whose concern or valuing of the objects of its knowing I do not know, an omnipresence whose form of emanation and attraction I do not know — these are surely indefinite and barely living conceptions. But it is quite a different matter if omnipotence makes itself known in the consciousness of the new spiritual creation, omnipresence in the activity of the divine Spirit, and omniscience in the awareness of God's grace and good will.[92]

Schleiermacher admits that were Parts I and II to be reversed "the propositions of the first part — which as there presented probably only deserved to be regarded as mere externals — would have a warmer hue and would likewise appear in a proper Christian light, if instead they had first been brought up after Christology and ecclesiology and after the development of divine love and wisdom. . . . In such case the worst and crudest understanding, namely, that my theology in *The Christian Faith* has a speculative tendency and rests on a speculative base, would be prevented as far as possible."[93]

Nevertheless Schleiermacher retained the original arrangement. He explained his basic motive for doing so in the second open letter to Lücke: he was certain that theological work would have to do justice to a pressing need of the times. This need consisted in a discussion with the free and independent work of scholarly research — a discussion which is clear, genuinely honest, and bears future developments in mind. He was certain that the goal of the Reformation was to make an eternal pact between Christian faith and free inquiry. The foundation of this pact is already available. It is necessary, however, to become much more conscious of the task in order to solve it. This pact does not mean capitulation to modern science, nor a mere defense of a feeble apologetic.[94] But it must be possible that the Christian faith and philosophy can exist in the same person, "that one can be and remain a true philosopher as well as a genuine believer, and in the same way that one can be devout and yet have and maintain the courage to enter into the farthest depths of speculation."[95]

At this point one should examine the question whether, for an interpretation of the first part of *The Christian Faith*, one must

---

92. Ibid., *Sendschreiben an Lücke*, p. 608.
93. Ibid., p. 609.
94. Ibid., pp. 617 f.
95. Ibid., p. 649.

necessarily draw on the philosophical trains of thought from the *Dialectics*,[96] a matter of long-standing controversy in Schleiermacher interpretation. Schleiermacher himself wanted to pursue theology throughout the whole of *The Christian Faith*. He denied that his systematic ingenuity in dogmatics was substantively determined by philosophy. This intention is most clearly stated in the conclusion of his second open letter to Lücke. He did not want to produce a philosophy of nature and a metaphysical world view, but a theological doctrine of creation. Creation is supernatural; it relates, however, to the natural connection of things. The supernatural is primary and the natural secondary; the natural is dependent upon and derived from the supernatural. It will be our task to inquire whether Schleiermacher truly carried through this theological intention.

(5) *Theological Analysis of General Religious Self-Consciousness*

The main problem in the first part of *The Christian Faith* is the relation of the creative power of God to the natural order as it is viewed in scientific research, namely, as an object for knowledge and for the technological subjugation of nature. Schleiermacher was the first person systematically to take hold of this problem that had arisen with the advance of the natural-scientific world view in the modern period and to resolve it in an entirely new way. He rejected both solutions proposed by Enlightenment theology: first, the supernaturalistic theory which cannot directly relate God's creative power to the causal nexus of scientific knowledge but can only assign him and his omnipotence to a sphere that lies outside the scientifically knowable order or that annuls this natural order; second, Schleiermacher also rejected the opposite solution which in pantheistic naturalism identifies God's creative work and the causal nexus of nature.

Schleiermacher's train of thought for the solution of the problem is as follows: "As indicated in the feeling of absolute dependence God can only be described in such a way that, on the one hand, his causality is differentiated from that found in the natural order, and thus is opposed to it, but, on the other hand, is equated with it in terms of its extent."[97] The formulation of § 51 in the second edition is similar. The absolute divine causality also encompasses the causality of the natural order. God's omnipotence should not be thought of as potential omnipotence; God not only can create what he wills, rather he effects and determines *everything*, including the

---

96. *Friedrich Schleiermachers Dialektik*, ed. Rudolf Odebrecht (Leipzig, 1942).
97. *Der Christliche Glaube*, 1st ed., § 65.

natural order, including the evil in the world, and even death and finitude. The omnipotence of God is thus experienced as "omni-activity" in the feeling of absolute dependence. Therefore the supernaturalistic solution to the dilemma which finds God's omnipotence mainly in the gaps of the natural order or misinterprets his omnipotence as the arbitrary intervention of the natural order is impossible. Schleiermacher sees the supernaturalistic solution as a limitation of God's creative power.

On the other hand, the divine causality stands in contrast to the causal nexus of nature; they are the same in compass but different in manner. "The distinction, however, is most easily understood by the fact that the natural order . . . appears as something completely temporal while the condition expressed in religious self-consciousness can only be apprehended as something perfectly timeless. This opposition, when interpreted as a divine attribute, leads into the concept of eternity."[98] This means that the omnipotence of God is an eternal omnipotence and, as such eternity, is opposed to the finite natural order. Here one sees how completely Schleiermacher had adjusted himself to a way of thinking that had been created in the realm of natural science by Kant's critical transcendental philosophy. According to Kant's critical analysis of scientific thinking the natural order and its causality are bound to space and time; that is to say, this causality is temporal and finite. Now this epistemological consequence of Kant's critical transcendental philosophy stands face to face with the theological statement: God is eternal, i.e., he is not bound by time, he is timeless and yet determines all temporality; he is not bound by space but determines all spatiality, because in his "omni-activity" he is omnipresent. This conception of God is not a limiting concept of metaphysical speculation, but is a specific theological assertion about God's eternal and omnipotent creativity as revealed in the feeling of absolute dependence.

Here is something genuinely new in Schleiermacher's idea of God, a theological solution vis-à-vis the new picture of nature and world that resulted from modern natural science and its interpretation in critical transcendental philosophy. It has often been rightly emphasized that the Christian view of God was forced by Kant's and Fichte's transcendental philosophy to relinquish the older super-naturalistic metaphysics and objectivity and to think about God and his activity nonobjectively. This is difficult for many Christians because they cannot quite comprehend something like the non-

---

98. Ibid., 1st ed., § 65, 1.

objectifiability of God; they think that God and his action have been relocated in the inwardness of the human spirit and that one no longer dares to relate the religious belief in God's "omni-activity" to the world which opens itself to the so-called modern natural science.

Schleiermacher's theology of creation, however, is no retreat; it is a look forward to a changed picture of the world and the relationship between God and world. God's primordial actuality and omnipotence must not be thought of as an object and a power of this world. God's activity must also not be thought of as an extension and interplay of natural powers. For then the sovereignty and absolute superiority of God, i.e., the difference in kind between the causality of God and the temporal-finite causality, would not be taken seriously.

Schleiermacher intends to interpret the divine causality not supernaturally and not pantheistically-naturalistically but existentially with the help of the immediate experience of creatureliness in the feeling of absolute dependence. The seriousness of this for him is seen in his treatment of a series of specific questions. Schleiermacher first of all sharply rejected attempts to understand natural causes, i.e., the causal nexus of natural occurrences, as a form of intermediate or proximate causation between God and world.[99] Mosheim's theory of a *gubernatio immediata* or *inordinata* Schleiermacher regards as totally false. This formulation contradicts basic religious feeling "because it represents God as bound within the ordinary course of nature."[100] According to that view the primordial causality of God and the causality of natural law would be equated; but they cannot be equated. God's eternal activity is the pre-condition, the source of the entire finite order of causality. God's eternal omnipotence is — speaking metaphorically — light, eternal light. The finite causality of the natural is only the shadow of this eternal light. No one could claim that the light is determined by the shadow; rather the reverse is true.[101]

"The divine omniscience is not related to divine omnipotence in the way that human reason and will relate to each other; it is rather only divine omnipotence seen in its spiritual aspect."[102] To this Schleiermacher added the following important explanation, in which the omnipotent spirituality of God is differentiated from a perceiving and sensitive world soul and also from human spirituality.

---

99. Ibid., 2d ed., § 47, 2.

100. Ibid.

101. See H. Scholz, *Christentum und Wissenschaft in Schleiermachers Glaubenslehre* (Leipzig, 1911), p. 163.

102. *Der Christliche Glaube*, 1st ed., § 69.

Spirituality means nothing more than what we previously called
inner vitality, and it is much more important to establish the
difference between the feeling of dependence on the Supreme
Being and that feeling which might derive from a blind and dead
necessity, than it is to determine precisely what the similarity is
between God and that which we term Spirit. About that we
will have more to say below. However, we know no better way
to designate that difference than to contrast the dead and blind
with the living and conscious because for us conscious life is the
highest thing. Even while we say this, however, we are aware
that *we cannot think of God's consciousness as anything like our
own* — just as the biblical *pneuma* would not lead to that — and
we are aware that to keep the relation of dependence pure we must
guard against thinking of God as some sort of perceiving and
sensitive world soul.[103]

It is appropriate at this point for the interpretation of Schleiermacher's theological thinking to introduce his views of natural order
and order in life generally, as found, for instance, in his *Dialectics*
and philosophical *Ethics*. Along with the scientific thinking of his
time Schleiermacher rejected the interpretation of nature as a chain
of mechanical causation, as it was seen in the French Enlightenment
of the eighteenth century as well as in the materialistic natural
philosophy of the later nineteenth century. This mechanistic causal
nexus is something dead. But nature, man, and the world are alive.
Nature is the whole of living powers.[104] But it is also not understood simply in terms of biological vitalism. The natural order is
neither a causal mechanism nor purely a biological process, but an
order of individual unities of force and life which are, on the one
hand, self-determining and hence partially free, but, on the other
hand, limit each other and hence are partially dependent. The
feeling of absolute dependence goes beyond this opposition of partial
freedom and partial dependence. The power of God which is attested
to in the feeling of absolute dependence is not the same kind of
spiritual-psychical power manifested in the world. God is the unity
and totality bringing together the antithesis of material existence
and spirit, hence the source of all finite life.

Thus the whole traditional doctrine of creation requires complete
restructuring. Creation is not a mythical process of remote times nor
an event at the beginning of the history of the earth. As Christians
we can only speak of God's creative action as we become immediately

103. Ibid., 1st ed., § 69, note.
104. Ibid., 1st ed., § 40, 2.

aware of it in the feeling of absolute dependence. Two truths are conveyed to us: (1) God, as Creator, creates and preserves our human existence and instills in us the religious feeling of creatureliness. (2) In this feeling of creatureliness we became certain that God vitally permeates the entire world. God's creation and preservation are the same in content. God creates the new beginning of life in continual succession and thereby preserves life. We must not impose upon God the temporal sequentiality of our thoughts. Thus creation has no beginning in time.

Schleiermacher vigorously disputed the idea that this theology of creation presents an isolated natural theology. The revelation of the omnipotence and omniscience of God in creation is not an isolated process. The content and final goal of God's eternal omnipotence is the redeeming love in Christ. "God is loving omnipotence or omnipotent love."[105] The creative activity of God is also at work in unredeemed man. The unredeemed God-consciousness in its powerlessness, however, is incapable of comprehending the content and direction of the divine creative activity. *Therefore the disrupted God-consciousness must be redeemed through Christ in order to comprehend in religious self-consciousness God's omnipotence and its final purpose.*

As a result of this clarification and purification of the theology of creation the *concept of miracle* must also be renewed and freed from the mistaken impressions of supernaturalistic metaphysics. All occurrences are miracles insofar as faith experiences them as acts of God. Thus the miracle of piety cannot be a magical-mythological spell or a supernatural miracle which is used to fill in the gaps within the causal nexus of nature.[106]

What is the role of miracles in the New Testament? Schleiermacher accepts as credible the New Testament reports about Jesus' miracles and the resurrection. However, our conceptions and knowledge of the natural order do not suffice to integrate miracles into the natural order. The miraculous in the miracle, however, is not that which is scientifically knowable, but the creative will of God active in it. We Christians of today no longer depend upon the miraculous in the New Testament for our life of faith. Our assurance of faith rests upon the living communion with Christ. Today we are no longer influenced by the physical presence of Christ, but rather by the spiritual activity of the Redeemer.[107]

---

105. Ibid., 2d ed., § 167.
106. Ibid., 2d ed., § 34, 2.
107. Ibid., 2d ed., § 103.

The New Testament miracles are therefore not part of the basis of our living faith in Christ but part of our confidence in Holy Scripture.   Hence we should not confine ourselves to the individual miracles of Jesus today but should turn to the total spiritual miracle of his life of redemption which is the decisive redemptive reality today, yesterday, and for the future.   Christ is the culmination of God's miraculous acts, "the absolute miracle."[108]   "We acknowledge that this [the miracle of redemption] — apart from Him — could not have been accomplished by all the powers of nature known to us."[109]   Christ is the miracle of all miracles, superior to all miraculous occurrences in our finite world; and thereby he is also the end of miracles in the sense of supernaturalistic phenomena.

(6) *Theological Interpretation of the Christian's Religious Self-Consciousness*

Schleiermacher's doctrine of sin has come under constant and intense criticism in recent theology.   Even his contemporaries, especially pietists like Tholuck, believed that they had discovered here the Achilles' heel of his theology.   For Tholuck and his friends the doctrine of sin was one-sidedly made into a critical criterion for evaluating a theology, whereas in the period of the Reformation this standard was the doctrine of justification.   As the result of this particular pietistic norm they found that Schleiermacher had erred precisely in his theological interpretation of sin.   Characteristic of this view is a journal entry by the young Wichern who attended Schleiermacher's lectures on dogmatics.   Looking back on this lecture he judged, "that according to this teaching evil has exchanged its black color for grey."[110]

In contrast, Karl Barth more recently, in connection with his exposition of nothingness, has called Schleiermacher's doctrine of sin a positive and promising effort even though he rejected Schleiermacher's total theology as a "theology of consciousness."[111]

Rather than making hasty judgments our inquiry should focus first of all on the contribution Schleiermacher's doctrine of sin has made to the history of theology.   Schleiermacher refuted the superficial and moralistic misinterpretation of sin in the Enlightenment,

---

108. Ibid., 7th ed., § 103, p. 117.

109. Ibid.

110. *Briefe und Tagebuchblätter D. Johann Hinrich Wicherns*, vol. I, ed. D. J. Wichern (Hamburg, 1901), p. 125.

111. Karl Barth, *Church Dogmatics*, III/3 (New York, 1961), pp. 319 ff.

placing himself in considerable opposition to the spirit of his times and his friends during a period dominated by the optimistic belief in progress and a correspondingly high self-estimate of man as the exemplar of humanity. His teachings of the need for redemption and the sinfulness of men contradicted the optimistic, moralistic self-regard of the Enlightenment as well as the prevailing philosophy of humanity. He convincingly presented, from the perspective of the Christian belief in redemption, the religious meaning of sin as the disruption of and radical opposition to God-consciousness.

The concept of sin is for him not a psychological, sociological, or even moral category. To the contrary, this concept has a distinctive Christian and theological meaning; the proper knowledge of sin comes from the inner experience of communion with Christ and the God-consciousness present in it. In dependence on the Pauline statement in the seventh chapter of Romans, he defined sin as "the positive antagonism of the flesh against the spirit."[112] In the first edition he explained the opposition of flesh and spirit as the antagonism between "that in us which produces pleasure and aversion," and "that in us which produces God-consciousness."[113] One should beware of reading the antagonism of sensibility and reason into this opposition of flesh and spirit. Even though he uses the concept of sensibility for his interpretation, its opposite — "spirit" — is not abstract rationality and not that reason that is productive of ideas. The opposition of flesh and spirit is for him the antagonism between God-consciousness and the irreligious world-consciousness of historical existence, the latter understood as activity of the flesh for its own sake and as self-enclosed finitude.

Only when one sees this teaching in its full implications does it become clear that "sin" has a specific religious and Christian meaning; *the consciousness of sin is the experience of the need for redemption* within the context of the Christian's faith in redemption. Sin is, then, "complete incapacity for the good."[114] It is original sin [*Erbsünde*], inherent in man, an internal and timeless predisposition toward sinning; but as original sin it is at the same time the act and guilt of every individual and the corporate guilt of mankind.[115]

Original sin is the internal and timeless predisposition toward sin. The primordial sin [*Ursünde*] is manifested in time and thus

---

112. *Der Christliche Glaube*, 2d ed., § 66.
113. Ibid., 1st ed., § 86.
114. Ibid., 1st ed., § 90; 2d ed., § 70.
115. Ibid., 1st ed., § 92.

actual sin, which is to be differentiated from primordial sin, comes into being as concrete act and guilt.[116]   Due to primordial sin mankind exists in a solidarity of sinfulness; sin is a contagious power moving from generation to generation.   It is in this sense that the idea of original sin is accepted, inasmuch as the continuity of generations of sinners is experienced in self-consciousness.   Only in the reborn, who must still struggle against sin, is this contagious power no longer effective, the power of sin having been fundamentally broken by the redemption in Christ.   But where God-consciousness has not been restored through redemption the destructive consequences of sin continue.   This applies to everything beautiful in pagan antiquity but especially to the moral achievements of civil law.[117]   Without God-consciousness even love of country, which Schleiermacher prized so highly, is only intensified sensuousness and at best a righteousness of the flesh.   "Hence even the best in this realm, to the extent that it exists independently of the power of God-consciousness, can only be counted as a disposition, wisdom, and morality of the flesh."[118]

Schleiermacher treats the basic issue in the third section of his doctrine of sin, under the title "On the Divine Attributes Which Relate to the Consciousness of Sin."[119]   The dilemma arises from the fact that Schleiermacher must understand the omnipotence of God as "omni-activity," which leads to the question whether God can also have brought about sin and evil.   If God causes everything, he must also be the author of sin.   But if one rightly claims that God could not cause the sin which he radically negates, then either man or the devil would have to be the author of evil.   Then there would actually be two gods in the world, as with the Manicheans where God and the devil are two competing powers.   But this view is just as untenable for Christian faith in God as the idea that God causes evil.

How does Schleiermacher resolve this question?   First of all, two things must be maintained: God causes everything that happens, and, secondly, God's relation to sin is marked by his negation of it through his law and his holiness and his victory over it through his redemptive act.   However, this alone does not resolve the dilemma for Christian faith in God.   Schleiermacher rejects the customary

---

116. Ibid., 1st ed., § 95.
117. Ibid., 1st ed., § 96, 4.
118. Ibid., 2d ed., § 70, 3.
119. Ibid., 1st ed., §§ 101–6; 2d ed., §§ 79–85.

theological maneuverings around the problem which so often have come up in the history of theology. The first way out of this embarrassment clings to the doctrine of God's permissive will. God, to be sure, does not cause evil but permits it in that he withdraws his supporting hand from men. Schleiermacher points out that this idea also is present in the Augsburg Confession which speaks of a human will from which God has withdrawn his hand.[120] This idea is unacceptable because it means limiting God's "omni-activity." This limitation is an anthropomorphic way of looking at things. Such a way of speaking is only permissable for *human* government and its *finite* conditions. In the case of human government there is a divided causality; God's causality, however, is always absolute.[121]

The other proposed solution consists in regarding sin solely as negation, as mere deficiency. Schleiermacher admits "the most natural thing would be to say that consciousness, which we describe as consciousness of sin, in its fullest extent is . . . nothing but that . . . vivid consciousness of the Good which we still lack."[122] Schleiermacher emphatically rejected this viewpoint because it does away with the reality of sin as well as the necessity for redemption. It "leaves so little room for the distinctive activity of a Redeemer that it can barely be regarded as Christian."[123]

Schleiermacher's own solution makes two distinctions. (1) He affirms that God cannot be the author of sin in the same sense that he is the author of redemption.[124] However, since we never have a consciousness of grace without a consciousness of sin, God has ordained the reality of sin *with* and *alongside* grace. Redemption in Christ occurs without human merit. No act of men, however good, can bring about redemption. The exclusive character of Christ's work of grace precludes any cooperation by man. God has so willed it and has therefore also ordained man's need for redemption. Thus Schleiermacher comes to the statement that God has ordained sin not in and for itself but only in relation to redemption.

Sin is the disorder and impotence of God-consciousness, and the commanding divine will causes this disorder of God-consciousness to become sin for us so that we become conscious of this sin. Occa-

---

120. Cf. *Confessio Augustana*, article XIX.
121. *Der Christliche Glaube*, 1st ed., § 103, postscript 1;   2d ed., § 81, 4.
122. Ibid., 2d ed., § 68, 3.
123. Ibid.
124. Ibid., 2d ed., § 80.

sionally Schleiermacher's formulations sound as if the accent in the concept of the consciousness of sin rests on the second part of the word and that the most important thing for him is that we are conscious of our sin; that is, God does not cause the disorder and impotence which sin introduces into the God-relationship, but rather God through his holiness merely causes a bad conscience as our sin-consciousness. But this would be a misunderstanding of Schleiermacher. What he means is that sin arises from freedom and hence from the responsible act of men. Schleiermacher expressly says that the freedom of the will precludes all external compulsion. The essence of conscious life consists in this: "every stimulation really receives its determination from the innermost center of life."[125] Therefore the sin is the sinner's own act and the deed of no one else. *By consciousness of sin Schleiermacher meant responsibility for the act that freely arises from our innermost being.* Sin is therefore a reality and not simply a way of regarding oneself. It is in positive opposition to God-consciousness and against the Spirit that evokes God-consciousness in us.

In addition to this answer — that God did not ordain sin in and for itself but only in relation to redemption — Schleiermacher also has still a second distinction. (2) God absolutely nullifies sin, so that it is nothing before him. Man, however, cannot oppose God in any such absolute way. The conflict against God's Spirit does not have the same radical and absolute opposition as does the op-position of God against sin. Thus Schleiermacher suggests the following formulation: Sin "is eternally wrought by God in and with the total development of God-consciousness."[126] Thus in the context of the whole history of redemption sin is an act of our own which is independent of this context of redemption. But this is only possible because human sin cannot be "an absolute contradiction against the commanding will of God."[127] An absolute contradiction against the will of God would be the condition of absolute hardness of heart "which we have already excluded from the human sphere."[128] In the context of Schleiermacher's thinking: *God is stronger than human sin which wants to struggle against God. Human sin cannot annul God's act of creation and redemption.* To that extent sin is ordained for the sake of redemption and therefore Schleiermacher

---

125. Ibid., 2d ed., § 81, 2.
126. Ibid., 2d ed., § 81, 3.
127. Ibid.
128. Ibid.

can also affirm that sin belongs to the conditions of the existential stage of the human race. We are not yet in the kingdom of God and for this reason the existence of sin is ordained together and along with the grace of God, for only in this way can the absolute sovereignty and majesty of God's gracious action be affirmed. We are still in the existential stage of human history where the antagonism between flesh and spirit exists. The temporality of history — the process of becoming — is ordained by God, i.e., he posits sin along with grace, and sin exists "as something which disappears before grace."[129] But that applies only to the finite, temporal becoming of human history in which the contrast between the kingdom of God and the world still holds, but which God has ordained that he might manifest the omnipotence and "omni-activity" of his grace in this human history.

Schleiermacher was not content simply to describe the relation of God to sin as a logically and factually indissoluble paradox. In the context of God's history with man he wanted to assess the proper balance between God's holy, gracious omnipotence and human resistance to it, and to give each its appropriate theological stress. The decisive perspective is the universalism of God's omnipotent love. The true Christian fulfillment of the principle of absolute dependence is the work of the redeeming love of God. Before God and from an absolute standpoint sin is as nothing. But from the standpoint of God's activity in the temporal, finite becoming of human history, sin is a juncture, a stage of humanity to be overcome. No doubt it is simpler and more convenient to refer to evil as the eschaton and as the ultimate paradox than it is to attempt to assess the correct theological weight that should be given to it within a skillful systematic description.

Even while acknowledging the theological achievement of this system, which Karl Barth himself respects, we should not conceal the fact that Schleiermacher's doctrine of sin still differs from Luther's doctrines of sin and justification and Luther's interpretation of Paul. One should first of all guard against describing any theology of human weakness as specifically Lutheran. Modern skepticism, supported by naturalistic thinking as well as by the nihilistic arguments in modern existential philosophy, does not touch the decisive point. Schleiermacher's doctrine of sin cannot be refuted simply as a theology of human weakness. Sin is a human act, it is antagonism toward God arising from the innermost center of life. Therefore

---

129. Ibid., 2d ed., § 80, 2.

it is not human weakness. It is a disorder of the God-relation
which is overcome through God's grace. The idea of God's judgment
and the threat of annihilation of human existence plays a much
larger role for Luther and his view of God. The difference between
Schleiermacher and Luther is perhaps most clearly drawn in an 1830
sermon by Schleiermacher, the theme of which he formulated as:
"Nothing need be taught concerning the wrath of God." For
Schleiermacher the biblical images of the wrath and judgment of
God were anthropomorphisms. Wrath is a psychological emotion
that has no place in the Christian understanding of God. God's
"No" to sin is identical with his redemptive love.

Schleiermacher made it clear that his doctrine of sin and grace
is antithetical to pietistic practice which first directs men consciously
to repentance and the agony of penitence in order to magnify the
blessedness of grace. Inwardly Schleiermacher stands closer to
Zinzendorf's viewpoint, according to which the fundamental disposition of Christianity is the joy and blessedness of experienced
grace. In his view the penitential agony of Halle pietism engages
in a game which is hazardous to the soul and which is, furthermore,
untrue. Nevertheless, Schleiermacher appears to have a theological
short circuit that diminishes the dialectic of judgment and grace
found in Luther. The history of God with man is construed by
Schleiermacher as extreme supralapsarianism thereby weakening the
tension between judgment and grace. To this degree the oft repeated
charge by the pietists that sin for Schleiermacher is not black but
grey has a definite element of truth. A similar criticism has been
made of Schleiermacher's principle of absolute dependence, namely,
that it is chiefly attuned to the feeling of creatureliness and the experience of redeeming grace and only puts secondary emphasis on
God's unconditioned demand of conscience (in § 11 of *The Christian
Faith* and in his interpretation of God's holiness)[130] as the teleological
purpose of piety.

Schleiermacher's doctrine of sin contains two realms, involves
two dimensions: (1) the dimension of the eternal, holy omnipotence
of God. From this perspective sin is denied and negated by God.
God is all and in all. (2) In addition, however, there is the perspective
from which one experiences in faith God's activity in the process
of finite, human existence. In this realm sin is "ordained" as something temporary, as a point of transition. It has not been sufficiently
recognized by Schleiermacher that we can in the first instance only

---

130. Ibid., 2d ed., § 83.

pursue a *theologia viatorum* and that the existential level of the *theologia gloriae* is an object of Christian hope.

(7) *Christology*

The section on the divine status of the Redeemer in *The Christian Faith* is no doubt the heart of Schleiermacher's dogmatics. His Christology has rightly evoked particular attention from both his followers and opponents. Those of his students and followers who, in the course of the nineteenth century, sought to connect the older confessional Lutheran dogmatics with his theology of the experience of faith have, because of his Christology, forgiven him for his many other departures from the older dogmatics and his transformation of biblical-mythological language into modern doctrinal formulations. For the same reasons, however, his rationalistic and left-wing Hegelian opponents attacked precisely this center of his theology. They said that he had gone only half way, had practiced a spurious mediating theology, and that his theology had resulted only in theological illusions and disguises (*Verschleierungen*); their accusations went so far as to defame the etymology of his name — Schleiermacher is the man who disguises (*verschleiere*) the naked truth.

Two methodological premises determine his Christology.

First: he redefined the relation of the doctrine of the person and the work of Christ. As to their content both doctrines stand in a relation of interdependence, i.e., they are dependent on each other. Dogmatic statements about the person of Christ are simultaneously assertions about his work and vice versa.

Second: he redefined the relation of theological conceptualization to Christian existence in community with Christ. Section 15 states that dogmatic formulations are descriptions of the pious Christian disposition set forth in speech.

Consequently some have understood his method simply as a reflection on Christian self-consciousness; they have alleged especially that his Christology seeks to draw conclusions from the religious experience of contemporary Christians and apply them to the historical Jesus because this historical Jesus is the redeeming source of the experiences of the soul. Even Wilhelm Dilthey, Schleiermacher's sympathetic biographer, rejected Schleiermacher's Christology for the reason that the image of Jesus resulting from these reflections on Christian self-consciousness is merely a subsequent construction and an unhistorical postulate.

Schleiermacher's christological statements, however, do not allow this interpretation. Schleiermacher proceeds from the belief that

Christ and his followers enjoy an immediate living community. The
relationship to Jesus is of a very special sort. It is not a relationship
of intimate and appreciative give and take of man's spiritual life;
it is rather the participation in and partaking of the life of God, an
ontological relationship to the God who is present in Christ. There
is an immediate association, a living community of the redeemed
with the Redeemer.

One could say for Schleiermacher what Adolf Schlatter formulated
with admirable simplicity — Paul Tillich makes reference to this
statement[131] — that we know no one so well as Jesus. What is
meant is the immediate life-relation which opens up for us the being
of God in him, that which is Christ-like in him; here the model of
cause and effect and the model of deductive conclusions are inappropriate. Christology deals with the self-reflection of believing Christians, the immediacy and awareness of the life revealed in Christ.
Immediate self-consciousness, already for Augustine the locus of the
authentic experience of truth and actuality, is also for Schleiermacher
the place where the truth of revelation — the truth which manifested
itself in Jesus' unique and archetypal God-consciousness — also
becomes spirit and reality in the life of the believer. The same
process is involved here as in the feeling of absolute dependence:
it is the process wherein the reality of God opens itself to us
immediately, wherein God neither is first postulated through a
deductive conclusion about the source of this feeling of dependence,
nor is the conception of God first established elsewhere in order to
show itself as reality in immediate self-consciousness.

Schleiermacher's Christology, therefore, is not based on a his-
toricized causal relationship moving from the historical effect back
to its cause, but upon the immediate existential experience of the
revelation in Christ. The questions of historical criticism about the
reports of the Gospels are no longer fundamental. What is central
is the actual present life-relation to the present and living Christ.
It is for the sake of Christ that Schleiermacher believes in the biblical
reports.

The mythological, metaphorical language of the Bible and the
revision of the biblical witness in the two natures doctrine of the
ancient church's dogma must be newly interpreted. Schleiermacher
did not want to do away with the biblical metaphorical language
and the ancient church's dogma; rather, he wanted to "formulate

---

131. Paul Tillich, *Systematic Theology*, vol. II (Chicago: The University
of Chicago Press, 1957), p. 116.

a new scholarly language" for contemporary theology.[132]   He already
provisionally and more formalistically described this existential
understanding of revelation in the analysis of the feeling of absolute
dependence and the God-consciousness active in it.   But now the
feeling of absolute dependence is also defined in terms of its content
by the revelation in Christ.   The divine dignity of the Redeemer
should not be understood mythologically or supernaturalistically.
The divine dignity of the Redeemer cannot be experienced physically
and objectively as an empirical omnipotence or empirical omniscience
as ostensibly occurs in the mythological or supernaturalistic miracles.[133]
According to Schleiermacher, this way of thinking about miracles
obscures more than it clarifies the experience of God's revelation
in Christ, it seals off more than it opens up.   The same applies
especially to the metaphysics of the doctrine of the two natures.

Schleiermacher emphatically and very clearly based this criticism
on formal-logical grounds.   The concept of nature has a totally
different content when one speaks of the divine nature than it has
when one speaks of human nature.   Human nature can only signify
the finite being of men; hence the same concept of nature cannot
be applied to God.   The divine nature of Christ can only be known
as the eternal Word of God, in the sense of the prologue of the Gospel
of John.   Thus here one cannot feign some unified metaphysical
conception of nature.   In the same way it is formally and logically
confusing to say in the doctrine of the Trinity that Christ is one of
the three divine persons, of one substance with God, yet at the same
time having both a human and divine nature according to the doctrine
of the two natures.

But this more formal and logical objection to the older dogmatic
formulation still does not get at Schleiermacher's basic interest.
The fundamental mistake lies in supernaturalistic metaphysics.   It
is still an objectifying metaphysics.   God's eternal omnipotence is
spaceless, but not in the sense in which supernaturalism conceives
of it as transcendent space in analogy to finite space.   God's being
is timeless and therefore he is also not bound by the supernaturalistic
temporality of miracles in which God's activity seemingly has a
beginning and an end.   For if God's eternity had a beginning and
an end, then it would not be clearly distinguishable from temporality.
But above all, supernaturalistic thinking falsifies the divine omnipotence
by bringing the causality of God into competition with the finite

---

132. *Der Christliche Glaube*, 2d ed., § 96, 3.
133. Ibid., 2d ed., § 93, 3.

causality of the natural order. It is precisely for the sake of divinity
and the act of redemption that the divine status of Jesus should not
be understood as a supernatural miracle.

The christological approach of the Enlightenment is equally
untenable. Jesus is not the teacher of an idea about God, or about
virtue and immortality; he is not the exemplar and bearer of a religious
principle. For then Jesus would only teach a conceptualized God;
but he cannot redeem mankind from its sins through the teachings
of religious and moral ideas.

In rejecting these wrong approaches Schleiermacher's basic intention
comes to clear and radical expression. The Redeemer distinguishes
himself exclusively from all other men by the uninterrupted power
of his God-consciousness, because "God's actual being was in him."[134]
The first edition formulated this in proposition 116; he is "distinguished
from all other men in that the indwelling God-consciousness was
the true being of God in him."

Because the God-consciousness dwelling in Jesus is the true being
of God it needs to be clearly distinguished not only in degree but
in kind from all other human God-consciousness. Even the God-
consciousness given to men together with their natural and immediate
self-consciousness cannot in the strict sense be called God's being
insofar as time and again it is "overcome" by sensuous self-consciousness, i.e., world-consciousness.

Jesus is the one original locus wherein is found the being of God,
for in Jesus we must posit the God-consciousness in his self-consciousness "as consistently and exclusively determining every moment,
and accordingly this perfect indwelling of the Supreme Being as
his own unique being and innermost self."[135] "Indeed, retrospectively
we can now say, if it is only through him that the human God-
consciousness becomes a reality of God in human nature, if it is
only through rational nature that the totality of finite powers can
become a reality of God in the world, then in truth he alone mediates
all divine reality in the world and all divine revelation throughout
the world, inasmuch as he contains in himself the entire new creation
which contains and develops the power of God-consciousness."[136]
The "rational nature" is mankind, i.e., through Christ all humanity
is placed under the Lordship of God and in this way all finite powers
of the world are shown to be in absolute dependence on God. This

134. Ibid., 2d ed., § 94.
135. Ibid., 2d ed., § 94, 2.
136. Ibid.

also means that the divine governance of the world in nature and history and the divine redemptive activity for the entire world are mediated through Christ and experienced in faith.

One of the basic assertions of Schleiermacher's Christology is that Christ, the sinless one, distinguishes himself through an archetypally powerful God-consciousness. This archetype became historical reality in the man Jesus. In opposition to Hegelian Christology, Schleiermacher insists that the final perfection of the God-consciousness, which he refers to as the archetype (*Urbild*), manifests itself in the individual concrete appearance of the historical Jesus. Normal idealist philosophy holds that it is impossible for the idea to enter fully into an individual appearance. Thus both David Friedrich Strauss and Ferdinand Christian Baur criticized Schleiermacher's Christology precisely on this point. Schleiermacher's biographer, Wilhelm Dilthey, also joined this criticism. According to the Hegelians the ray of divine light can only penetrate the world of appearances through refractions. Therefore the historical person, Jesus, cannot be assigned the prerogative of being the perfect revelation of the archetypal God-consciousness.

The concept of an archetype was a philosophical concept of that time. In Kant's philosophy of religion it was applied to Jesus in the sense of an ideal principle. It is also found in Schelling. When Schleiermacher took up this concept, he probably took it over from Plato, but he subjected it to creative transformation and opened it to misunderstanding. The particular elements in this Christ archetype are: (1) absolute perfection; (2) productiveness as the creative power of redemption; (3) originality and uniqueness in history. But what Schleiermacher really wanted to bring to expression was the revelatory power in the person of Jesus which classical Christian theology had expressed in terms of the myths of the Son of God, the Son of man, and the Logos. Underneath there is the certainty that the myth which is unhistoric in ancient mythology became historic in Jesus and on that basis Jesus should be revered as the Christ. It is this original concern of Christology that Schleiermacher wanted to express when he affirmed that *the Redeemer is archetype and reality. In Christ myth becomes history.*

It is entirely clear that this Christology of Schleiermacher stands in contrast to the dogma of the ancient church, especially the doctrine of the two natures. In this Christology there is no balancing of the complicated relationship of the two natures which does not get beyond the negations of the Chalcedonian formulation. Christ is man but also a wholly new creation. He is the second Adam —

a theme that ties Schleiermacher to Paul. But on the other hand, he is the pure being of God, and that in the manner wherein alone God can reveal himself in the givenness of immediate self-consciousness as it is understood in the existential theological thinking of Schleiermacher. It cannot be said of Schleiermacher that he advocates a purely spiritual Christology. In Christ the unity of spirit and flesh is fulfilled. For God is indeed the single origin of spirit and flesh. As a result of the God-consciousness implanted in Jesus there also arises, on the basis of this dominion of God-consciousness, a new image of the corporeality of the earthly Jesus.

But Christ is one unified person; the doctrine of the two natures is superfluous, the doctrine of humiliation and self-emptying has fallen by the wayside, and the doctrine of the *communicatio idiomatum* has disappeared with traditional metaphysics, having been replaced by the new existential concept of revelation. God's eternal omnipotence and spirituality were present in their absolute, eternal magnitude and have formed the entire life of Jesus into an instrument and image. This is what is newer and simpler in Schleiermacher's teaching in contrast to the doctrine of the two natures. Schleiermacher did not fundamentally call the ancient church's doctrine of the two natures into question; he did, however, try to transform it.

Furthermore, he reinterpreted the doctrine of the supernatural conception of Jesus as well as the doctrine of *anhypostasis* or *enhypostasis*. The supernatural conception of Jesus was certainly not to be taken in a physiological-magical sense, although he thought that the idea of the supernatural conception should be retained; the implanting of the archetypal God-consciousness in the man Jesus is for him supernatural conception. He approached in the same way the old question about whether there could be a personal core for the human nature if, in the *communio naturarum*, the divine nature of Christ is the person-forming element. Here, too, Schleiermacher stressed the agreement between the dogma of the ancient church and his own Christology. The implanted archetypal God-consciousness is the truly productive element and the humanity of Jesus is the organ, instrument, and image of the absolute, powerful God-consciousness. One can understand why his opponents viewed these deductions as logistical stunts and Kähler's claim that Schleiermacher might prove anything in this fashion. One must not impute to Schleiermacher a desire to acquire the appearance of orthodoxy by conceptual stunts. Elsewhere he had the courage to differ with church doctrine. Apparently he believed that the transformation of theological thinking would complete itself only gradually through his new concept of revelation and God, and that from the perspective of his Christology a relation to the dogmatic formulations of other historical epochs could be established.

(8) *Wherein Does the Specific Redemptive Activity of the Savior Lie?*

Schleiermacher defines this activity as the founding of a new corporate life through Christ in that he mediates sinless perfection to the faithful, i.e., the archetypal potency of his God-consciousness.[137] He also formulates it more briefly: "The redeemer draws the faithful into the potency of his God-consciousness."[138] This corporate life implanted through Christ in our life is the state of grace; "the new corporate life is the place of Christ's work in which the perpetual effectiveness of his sinless perfection is revealed."[139] In the corporate life the redeemed have the same relationship to Christ as the human nature in Christ has to the divine.[140] Christ is the person-forming, archetypal, divine power, supplying the decisive spiritual-personal impulse; and the faithful are the organ and image of his redeeming activity.

The two essential components of this activity are vocation and inspiration. In the unification of Christ with the faithful in the new corporate life the divine otherness, i.e., the qualitative rather than only quantitative superiority of Christ, is maintained as opposed to human self-consciousness. One should not psychologically obliterate the difference between the redemptive activity of Christ and the pious self-consciousness of Christians. The original God-consciousness of Jesus imbues human self-consciousness with new life; it is an analogue and image of the process of the incarnation. The influence of Jesus on the faithful is not merely that of a humanly inward, psychologically comprehensible causal relationship. The incarnation of Jesus' God-consciousness in the faithful calls an entirely new life into existence in human self-consciousness, a new life that falls outside the causal relationship of the purely psychological influences that occur in the human realm.

This incarnation of Jesus' God-consciousness in the faithful is never a magical process, requiring supernatural and metaphysical interpretation. Schleiermacher rejects this interpretation because it would mean giving up the connection with the historical appearance

---

137. Ibid., 2d ed., § 88.
138. Ibid., 2d ed., § 100.
139. Ibid., 2d ed., § 100, 1.
140. Ibid., 1st ed., § 121, 3; 2d ed., § 100, 2.

of the human, i.e., with Jesus the man, and would succumb to docetism. The impact of Christ upon the faithful is his personal spiritual activity through the word. On the other hand, this revelation of his archetypal God-consciousness is not instruction and teaching by means of doctrine and example; it is rather a spiritual-personal self-revelation and a new creation through redemption, rebirth, and sanctification.

Schleiermacher stresses his differences from the supernaturalistic and rationalistic misunderstanding of the Christ event. The rationalistic conception (which he labeled "barren" in the first edition) he called the empirical theory of redemption, and the supernaturalistic the magical. He calls his own Christology mystical. However, it is difficult to understand why so many Schleiermacher interpreters have failed to see that the concept "mystical" as used by Schleiermacher does not correspond to the present concept in religious studies. This point was already emphasized in the above discussion of the *Speeches*. The new life and the relation between Christ and the faithful is called mystical because "it cannot be demonstrated [to those] who are not touched by it; rather its truth resides wholly in the experience itself."[141] In accordance with his existential understanding of revelation, Schleiermacher states that the life-relation between the Redeemer and the redeemed is experienced as an actuality in the immediate existence and mystery of faith. Schleiermacher is clear that mysticism does not mean anything fanatical because the life-relation involves the historical Jesus in whom God-consciousness was implanted in its highest perfection. The activity of this Redeemer, in complete distinction from mysticism (as a historical religious phenomenon), takes place through the word and by Christ's spiritual-personal self-manifestation in his historical appearance.

The reconciling activity of Christ consists in incorporating the faithful into the community of his blessedness.[142] Reconciliation with God does not abolish suffering and death, but through Christ's reconciliation these evils are, for the faithful, no longer God's punishments. Thus suffering and death cannot destroy the blessedness of community with the redeemed. Due to his sinlessness Christ himself did not experience the evil of suffering and death as punishment. On the contrary, he endured his suffering and death in fellowship with God, thereby showing that this community with God overcomes suffering and death through its sinless perfection.

---

141. Ibid., 1st ed., § 121, 4.
142. Ibid., 1st ed., § 122; cf. 2d ed., § 104.

However, Christ did participate in the evils that men experience as punishment to the extent that he, without being guilty himself, also felt men's consciousness of punishment and guilt. Christ did not eliminate judgment and punishment through an expiatory sacrifice in some magical, supernatural way. But, through his spiritual deed, through the spiritual founding of a corporate life, and through his self-manifestation in word and deed, he — by acting and suffering and permeating our human life in its entirety — has drawn and bound to himself men who are sinful and aware of their guilt.[143] The redemptive activity of Christ is in the first place forgiveness and in its further consequences it is sanctification through the mediation of blessedness. "Since it is only by virtue of this compassion (of Christ) that there could be any movement toward the removal of evil, it is obviously right to relate his suffering with reconciliation in this sense."[144]

Schleiermacher, to the disbelief of both friends and enemies alike, still related this theological exposition of the "work" of Christ — which conforms with neither the ancient church's Christology nor with the Enlightenment's "divesting" of the cross of Christ of meaning — to the ancient church's dogma of Christ's vicarious sacrifice and his substitutionary suffering. In the second edition of *The Christian Faith* he gave as his reason for this his wish to preserve the continuity with the original christological doctrine, even to demonstrate his agreement with it. He saw the New Testament's and the ancient church's conceptions of Christ as prophet, high priest, and king as "revivified forms" of those images and teachings "through which divine government revealed itself in the old covenant."[145]

These theological-historical considerations of Schleiermacher are not as significant for our investigations as is the reason why he was actually convinced that his Christology was in accordance with traditional dogma as far as its basic intentions were concerned, even if it did not conform to the exact doctrinal formulations.

Finally one should not deny the inner necessity of such a death for Christ himself for in that moment he had to announce the complete dominion of the spirit over the flesh; and such a dominion can never appear to this extent either in a death from old age or fortuitous illness. Also the danger of defining the freedom in Jesus' death in a dubious manner is best avoided by subsuming

---

143. Ibid., 1st ed., § 123, postscript b.
144. Ibid., 1st ed., § 122, 4.
145. Ibid., 2d ed., § 102, 1.

his suffering obedience under Christ's high priestly office. The
reconciling sacrifice was also a free act of the vocation of the high
priest . . . conforming to an established divine order without a
trace of his own willfulness.[146]

In this way Schleiermacher is assured that he has found the deeper
meaning of the statements, often impugned, that Christ has satisfied
the divine righteousness by his free surrender in suffering and death
and thereby has freed us from the guilt and punishment of sin. The
manner in which God was in Christ reconciling the world to himself
— Schleiermacher deliberately uses the Pauline formulation — can
only "take on a perfectly vivid immediacy" for us in the sinless suffering
of Christ.[147]   Christ is he who "presents [us] pure by virtue of his
own perfect fulfillment of the divine will . . . so that we in association
with him also are objects of divine good pleasure."[148]   This is the
meaning, unobjectionable from a Christian standpoint, of that often
misunderstood expression that Christ's obedience is our righteousness
or that his righteousness is imputed to us.[149]   The righteousness
of Christ and his sacrificial death are not only the central content
of Christ's self-revelation and manifestation which should be included
under the doctrine of Christ's prophetic office; but also the high
priestly value is in the communion with Christ in a double sense:
(1) "that God recognizes us in Christ as partners in his obedience,"
and (2) "that we recognize God in Christ and regard Christ as the
most immediate partaker in the eternal love which sent and prepared
him."[150]

Schleiermacher sought in this way to revive the ancient teaching
of Christ's active and passive obedience. Understanding of this
rather large section of *The Christian Faith* is complicated by Schleiermacher's enormous efforts — for the sake of the continuity of Christian
doctrine — to reaffirm major formulations of older Protestant dogmatics
concerning Christ's satisfaction and vicarious atonement. He wanted
to give these older Protestant formulations a new meaning so that
they might be more easily vindicated — as he said — against Enlightenment criticism. This decision all too easily creates confusion
for today's reader. He unequivocally rejected the so-called blood
and wounds theology which he himself had still experienced among

---

146. Ibid., 1st ed., § 125, 3.
147. Ibid., 1st ed., § 125, p. 294.
148. Ibid., 2d ed., § 104, 3.
149. Ibid., 2d ed., § 104, 4.
150. Ibid.

the Moravians. This Christology falsely finds the deeper meaning of Christ's suffering in the sensuous details, splitting up the totality of Christ's suffering and its full meaning for the sake of an allegorical game with these sense particulars. But most emphatically he rejected the theory of Christ's vicarious suffering to pay the penalty for sin, a theory which stemmed originally from Anselm and then also entered into orthodox Protestant dogmatics. In the first place he condemned the keystone of this theory which held that Christ's suffering as payment of the penalty for sin was a quantitative equivalent for the sins of mankind. Christ's infinite suffering and redemption should correspond to the infinity of human sin. This rationalistic and calculating way of thinking does not touch the full meaning of Christ's suffering. His protest against the idea of the necessity of paying the price for human sin was far more passionate. He believed this idea to be repugnant to the Christian understanding of God. The assumption of an absolute necessity for divine punishment and divine repayment for the sake of satisfying the wrath of God is "hard to separate from a view of divine righteousness transferred to God from the most barbaric human condition."[151]

Beyond both these objections he had two further basic reservations. The first concerns the concept of a substitute in the suffering for punishment. Already in the crisis of faith that he experienced in Barby the idea awakened which he retained in a slightly different form for the rest of his life: that which the Redeemer does for the redeemed he cannot and must not want to do for the redeemed in a substitutionary capacity. For in that case, one could say of the redeemed that they really could have redeemed themselves.[152] It therefore contradicts the meaning of redemption to depict Christ's atonement as vicarious. Sinners cannot redeem themselves nor can they reconcile themselves with God. Schleiermacher wanted to give another meaning to satisfaction and substitution, so that substitution is not the same as satisfaction and satisfaction is not substitution.

He identifies satisfaction with redemption. In this manner he gives it a totally different meaning than this concept had in the doctrine of reconciliation in the ancient church. This can be confusing. Substitution is not satisfaction, but real substitution. There is compassion on the part of the suffering Christ for men's sins and the punishment they suffer. Today we would say that Christ shares

---

151. Ibid.
152. Ibid.

a solidarity with sinners and with the punishment of sinners. Every time an innocent person shares the suffering of a guilty person that suffering has a vicarious character. Schleiermacher, however, on the basis of the idea of the high priesthood, comes to yet another interpretation of substitution. In Christ's high priestly prayer as well as in the explanation of our prayer we have the memorable fact of this substitution. Prayer in the name of Jesus involves the certainty "of Christ's cooperation in sanctifying the same as a purification and perfection of our God-consciousness. This co-operation is his representation in the sense that only through him does our prayer come acceptably and effectively before God."[153] Even here the idea of substitution is completely changed from the older dogmatics.

For the sake of clarity we should now inquire into the positive statements about Christ's work of salvation. For Schleiermacher the suffering and dying Christ is not a human hero and example in the Enlightenment sense. On the other hand, the sacrificial death of Christ as a saving deed must not be understood as in supernaturalism in the sense of a magical act by which a sacrifice appeases the wrath of God. The salvation of Christ has its redemptive meaning in the spiritual-personal effect of redemption and reconciliation upon the faithful. The superiority of Christ in contrast to the redeemed is not only quantitatively determined as a more perfect form of God-consciousness, but he is qualitatively superior because in him, the sinless one, God is truly present and active.

Thus the suffering and the sacrificial death of Christ have a twofold meaning. On the one hand, the sacrificial death of Christ brings the proof of that which happened but once in the history of mankind: the divine Spirit rules over the flesh, i.e., over sin and man's pre-occupation with the world. On the other hand, by conquering sin and receiving the redeemed into the new community of God and man, Christ both conquered sin and abolished its consequences, so that the evils of this world are no longer punishment of sin for the faithful. Thus Christ has reconciled the faithful with God, for we now see God in Christ and we see Christ as the most immediate partaker of eternal love which has sent and equipped him.

The work of Christ is more than an illustration of his proclamation. It is act. It becomes clear in the work of Christ that the divine Word which took human form in the person of Christ is the creative redemptive act of God. From the standpoint of today's reader it

---

153. Ibid., 2d ed., § 104, 5.

would have been better had Schleiermacher not tried to connect this christological interpretation to the old concepts of satisfaction and substitution. In this context we must observe that the outcome of Schleiermacher's theology and Christology was not simply the gospel of Christmas peace arising from the teaching of the incarnation of the Logos in the flesh. Neither his preaching nor his dogmatics can do without the message of the cross.

What differentiates him from the Reformation theology of the cross is the rejection of the idea of propitiation, which he eliminated along with the idea of the absolute necessity of repayment. Christian theology from its beginnings until the Reformation was certain in its belief that the sin of men demanded expiation. Not all theologians have understood this expiation to mean that some change of mind of an angry God must be effected by an expiatory sacrifice. The core of Christian theology emphasizes reconciliation, in the Pauline sense that God himself brought about this reconciliation by the sacrifice of his Son, that God reconciled the world to himself; God is the sole actor in the event of reconciliation. The grace and love of God are reduced to sentimentality if the tension between judgment and grace, righteousness and love is not properly maintained. In Schleiermacher's theology this tension is present only in weakened form. Sinful man experiences the evil of this world as the punishment of God, and Christ redeems men from their sins through the forgiveness of sins, simultaneously accomplishing reconciliation in that he overcomes the consciousness of punishment. This relates to the fundamentals of his understanding of God. The omnipotence and authority of God's sanctifying and transforming love are so strongly sounded that sin seen from God's side dissolves into nothing. In view of the omnipotence and love of God sin is as nothing, for the omnipotence of the loving God overcomes evil and sin. In Schleiermacher's Christology everything is concentrated on the present living relationship with Christ. The biblical reports of the virgin birth, the resurrection, the ascension of Christ are not directly relevant for this living relationship to Christ. They are for dogmatics simply historical reports which Schleiermacher accepted as authentic. His idealist philosophy of nature made it possible for him to accept these reports of miraculous events in Christ's life as possible. They are inconsequential, however, for the foundation of faith's certainty.

The articles on Christian *regeneration* and *sanctification* are an extension of his Christology not only logically but also in content. This is in keeping with the organization of his dogmatics. Even his Christology is viewed in a threefold manner: its implication for the doctrine of God, its meaning for Christian self-consciousness, and its significance for the condition of the world in relation to redemption. This final lengthy section contains his ecclesiology and his eschatology as the doctrine of the perfection of the church. Schleiermacher's analysis of Christian self-consciousness corresponds to the traditional theology of salvation; it deals, therefore, with regeneration which includes conversion and justification as well as sanctification. Regeneration is the foundation and beginning of the new life, and sanctification is the continuation of the new life, the growth in grace. Regeneration then is not only the human response to the impulse coming from Christ; it is the process of grace by means of which the Redeemer establishes the new community between God and the redeemed. Schleiermacher prefers to interpret the process of regeneration and sanctification in terms of the relation of the Redeemer to the redeemed; and this living fellowship, this union of Christ and the redeemed, he explains through the analogy of the union of the divine Logos with the man Jesus in the event of the incarnation.[154]

Regeneration is understood as conversion and justification. In the first edition justification was placed first. Conversion includes repentance as remorse, change of heart, and faith. Faith is the appropriation of Christ's perfection and blessedness.[155] Repentance and faith are intimately linked and originate from the same source, the influence of the Redeemer. The faithful is forgiven his sins and adopted as a child of God. Schleiermacher vigorously disputed the view that under certain circumstances faith must be supplemented, that something extraneous, such as the fruits of faith or sanctification, must be added. Faith concerns the beginning (regeneration) as well as santification. Faith is the creation of the Redeemer. Man cannot develop it out of himself. It is never a good work of man; it can never be the instrumental cause of justification within the doctrine of regeneration.

Conversion corresponds to redemption and justification to reconciliation. The two aspects of regeneration are related in the same way that the communication of Christ's perfection and the communication of Christ's blessedness are related. Justification means forgiveness of sins and with it the adoption of the sinner as a child of God. The justification of an individual does not rest on any isolated or single divine decree. There is only one eternal

154. Ibid., 1st ed., § 131, p. 359.
155. Ibid., 2d ed., § 108.

and universal decree of the justification of men for Christ's sake.[156] This divine decree is identical with the mission of Christ. Thus there is no special decree of justification for the individual; rather the consciousness of justification and divine sonship must be awakened in every individual. Above all justification is not to be understood as only declaratory. It is the creative life-awakening act of salvation radiating from Christ. In God, thought and deed, word and act are one; thus the declaration of justification is the fact of justification.

Despite the far-reaching agreement with the Lutheran doctrine of justification, Schleiermacher's divergence from Luther on this point is unmistakable. Justification in Luther's theology is a paradoxical event, i.e., an act of God which contradicts our human conceptions and expectations. God forgives the sinner who has not earned forgiveness and then adopts him as son who had forfeited his sonship. This paradoxical focus cannot be found in Schleiermacher's formulations. The tension between righteousness and the grace of God in the justification of the sinner is missing just as it was missing from the earlier doctrine of reconciliation. It cannot be denied that the number of Christians and theologians adhering to Luther has diminished in recent Protestant history. An understanding of the paradox of God's unfounded forgiveness and the idea of expiation has disappeared for a majority of Christians in modern times. Thus Schleiermacher is not an isolated case. He is the spokesman for a major theological movement and development. In his theology, justification is taught on the basis of grace and faith; but it is no longer Luther's doctrine of justification.

Also in other particular items he departs sharply from the dogmatic tradition. We need only mention as examples his rejection of the concept of the sacraments, his criticism of infant baptism, and his opposition to the so-called third use of the law for the reborn. On the basis of his Christology he lessened the tension between law and gospel which had until then been normative for Lutheran theology. In the first edition he undid this tension outright when he stated: "The consciousness of the law to which the moral feeling relates is a stage in the divine communication; it is nothing other than the divine love viewed at a certain point of development."[157]

His position on *eschatology* has most often been criticized. It has often been claimed that he totally dispensed with eschatology. Schleiermacher himself is not without blame for this criticism. The

---

156. Ibid., 2d ed., § 109, 3.
157. Ibid., 1st ed., p. 684.

critics of Schleiermacher's eschatology generally start out from his philosophical ethics. The central theme of his philosophical ethics is the sovereignty of the spirit over the flesh, the influence of reason on nature, on which rests the progress of human history and culture. Schleiermacher's philosophical ethics is for this reason a persuasive exposition of the nineteenth century belief in progress. Is not the belief in progress, even though it be only taken in the realm of cultural-historical philosophy, the virtual end of all Christian eschatology?

Schleiermacher also includes in his dogmatics explanations of the divine governance and formation of the world which appear to exclude an eschatology of the Christian belief in redemption and perfection. The divine wisdom is a divine self-revelation which structures and orders the world through redemption. The world is now the "absolutely harmonious work of divine art."[158] For us the revelation of divine wisdom in its temporal progress becomes more and more the perfect expression of the omnipotent love of God. Therefore divine wisdom is "the ground whereby the world, the stage of redemption, is also the absolute revelation of the Supreme Being, and therefore good."[159] In the first edition Schleiermacher even asserted that the world is the stage of redemption and therefore the perfect revelation of the divine wisdom, that is to say the best world.[160] Thus Christ's revelation itself is the perfect redemption for men and for this world. Schleiermacher concludes from this "that we should not look for a greater divine revelation than the one which has been brought about in the human race by means of the redemption through Christ."[161] Thus the perfection of Christ's revelation appears to preclude any revelation of perfection in eternity. This contradicts what Schleiermacher teaches in the second edition of *The Christian Faith*, §§ 157 ff., concerning the consummation of the church. The church cannot attain its perfection in the course of human life on earth. Schleiermacher hopes that the influence of the Redeemer upon the church will increasingly grow stronger in order that the glory of the Redeemer will be ever more clearly reflected. But even if an ever increasing number of men were to be taken up into the community of the church and partake of the corporate life of Christ, there would still be no reason to expect a

---

158. Ibid., 2d ed., § 168, 1.
159. Ibid., 2d ed., § 169.
160. Ibid., 1st ed., § 185.
161. Ibid., 2d ed., § 169, 1.

perfection of the church in the era of man's life on earth. At all times the church struggles with the effects of sin and the resistance of the world. The church is never the consummated church triumphant but must always remain the church militant.

Two motives of faith and hope are present as the promise of the Christian faith: first, the consummation of the church beyond man's life on earth in the kingdom of God, and, second, faith in the continued existence of the human person. This hope is already contained in the faith in Christ. The faith in the Redeemer entails the belief in the unchanging union of divine essence with human nature in the person of Christ. Included is the belief in the survival of the human person beyond death. Through the corporate life with the faithful the person of the Redeemer mediates the reality of personal being, the survival of which is assured to the redeemed. Schleiermacher differentiates this Christian belief in a personal eternity very clearly from the belief in immortality found in general God-consciousness. Here he has clearly disassociated himself from the *Speeches* where he left open the question of personal survival because true immortality would already be given in the revelation of God now present in this life. Now in *The Christian Faith* Schleiermacher departs from this position. He admits that in both of these motives of the Christian hope the tendency is present to imagine objectively the consummation of the church as well as the person of the redeemed. On the other hand he rejects any knowledge through faith of this eschatological condition of perfection because the experience of redemption allows no statements about the condition of perfection.[162] Since Christ is the end of all prophecy the church can acknowledge no gift of the spirit which constructs the shape of the future "whereon our action can assert no influence whatsoever, since it lies beyond all human experience . . . ; indeed, in the absence of any analogy it is hard to understand the image rightly or grasp it securely."[163]

Even if the belief in the reality of a consummated church and personal survival is in the contemporary life of faith an "effective power in us," we still have no right to speculate about the mode and manner of this continuance. For our whole imaginative faculty relates to spatio-temporal existence only. The eternity of God is, however, outside space and time. For this reason we can no more imagine life after death as "some continuing progression into infinity than [we can imagine it as] a static perfection, for our powers of

---

162. Ibid., 2d ed., § 157, 2.
163. Ibid.

perceptive imagination are insufficient."[164] Hence the biblical representations of the "last things," as well as the sayings of Jesus and the Apostles belong to the sphere of prophecies and visions.

Schleiermacher gives a comprehensive and simplified interpretation of these prophetic teachings of the New Testament. But what he actually means he explains at the conclusion of the addenda to the prophetic doctrines. Shortly after he had rejected eternal damnation as incompatible with the notion of eternal bliss, which must be thought of as a state of unchanging and serene blessedness in the "vision of God," he stated soberly and critically in conclusion that eschatological thinking will, on the one hand, move toward the mystical and, on the other hand, this prophetic sort of teaching from the New Testament will always approach the visionary, i.e., the earthly-symbolic representation of something beyond. But this means that these prophetic teachings cannot furnish any knowledge in the strict sense for faith but "can only vividly depict," by means of imaginative images, the expression of principles already known.

In the acute and penetrating exposition of Schleiermacher's *The Christian Faith* in his *Geschichte der evangelischen Theologie*,[165] Emanuel Hirsch concludes with a negative judgment on Schleiermacher's eschatology. Nothing [he says] is more painful than seeing a relentless and sincere thinker arrive at the point where, because he lacks the firmness to say a clear "No," he seeks to make ideas and images, that he himself considers to be mythical and visionary, somehow acceptable by means of dialectics and tortuous exposition hemmed in with reservations. Without trying to defend at any cost what is at times doubtlessly a far-reaching reinterpretation of biblical ideas and images, we must still recognize that, on the basis of his Christology, Schleiermacher consistently thought through beliefs concerning the eternity of God. His careful attitude toward biblical statements sometimes hampers the actual consistency of his ideas; he maintains this attitude with real constancy also in his discussion of other doctrines as, for example, the resurrection of Jesus.

Consequently, according to Schleiermacher, faith in God's eternity can only be asserted in existential statements, not in objective perceptions. The eternity of God is beyond time and yet present. It transcends the world and men, and yet is experienced through the perfect revelation of Christ in the immediate self-consciousness of

164. Ibid., 2d ed., § 159, 2.
165. E. Hirsch, *Geschichte der evangelischen Theologie in Zusammenhang mit den allgemeinen Bewegungen des europaeischen Denkens*, vol. V (Gütersloh, 1952), p. 329.

the redeemed as presence and reality. After the destruction of supernaturalistic metaphysics and the overcoming of the uncritical conceptions of space and time, no other conception of faith in the eternity of God was possible for Schleiermacher than that of supratemporality — a supratemporality which through the revelation of Christ still manifests itself as present and real in the existence of the faithful. In this way Schleiermacher's eschatological thinking comes close to the theological concepts of contemporary existential theology, which seeks to express for the faithful both the supratemporality *and* the presence of God's eternity with the help of the more highly developed concepts of space and time of transcendental philosophy in contemporary existential philosophy.

The inner content and not simply the carefully constructed logical framework of his ideas is now before us. It is essential that one should not only admire the logical skill of his systematic thinking but also remember that behind this logical construction a single theological conception is at work, which arises from the center of his understanding of faith. It is misleading to view his theology primarily as a work of art as though it were a painted flower which always remains an artificial product despite its similarity to real life. The center of his theology is Christology. Schleiermacher thinks *christocentrically*, but not *christomonistically*. In his theology Christology is correlated with the faith relationship established by God between Creator and creature, which according to Schleiermacher is posited in the absolute dependence of immediate self-consciousness. One does not grasp the uniqueness of Schleiermacher's theology by putting on it certain hats of heresy from the past history of dogmatics. Schleiermacher is neither a Monophysite nor a Diophysite, a Docetist or an Ebionite, a Manichaean or a Pelagian.

The originality of his theology, which only few of his followers and students have fully understood, is its existential understanding of revelation and the relationship of God and world. On the one hand he is no enlightener and pantheist; but on the other hand he has no use for the supernaturalistic metaphysics of Scholasticism, the older Protestant orthodoxy, and the supernaturalistic side of Enlightenment theology. He draws the consequences about beliefs in God and his revelation and about the relation of God and world that proceed from critical transcendental philosophy. He made this decision during the major transformation of European thought brought about by Kant's critique of traditional metaphysics. Wilhelm Dilthey has called Schleiermacher "the Kant of Protestant theology." In this he adopted a formulation from D. F. Strauss. This characterization is misleading if one understands it to mean that Schleiermacher's basic theological conception was occasioned by critical transcendental philosophy. We will still examine this more thoroughly by comparing Schleiermacher's theology with his philosophy. The presentation of his theological system makes clear that Schleiermacher formed his fundamental conception as a theologian. Dilthey's formulation is only correct if one understands it to mean that Schleiermacher brought about a similar upheaval in the destruction of outdated metaphysics in theological thinking as Kant did in the realm of philosophy.

The significance of Schleiermacher's theology is immediately evident once it becomes clear just how much he actually demolished. He made it impossible for scholastic thinking, which is always associated with a supernatural metaphysics and which falsifies thinking about revelation by its demand for an objective knowledge of the supernatural, to find a place in evangelical theology. To that extent he established a new theological mode of thought which had its origin in Luther's Reformation, specifically in Luther's rejection of Scholasticism. God is never an object in this finite world, especially not a particular supernaturalistic and miraculous segment or gap in this finite world. God is absolutely exalted over the world in his eternal and omnipotent sovereignty and yet he is the One who as its ground and presupposition determines and vitally permeates this world. This understanding of God's revelation is ultimately not established through man's experience of his own creatureliness in the feeling of absolute dependence, but decisively through the grace of God. Here divine omnipotence is most intimately linked with the eternal love and Spirit of God. This love is shown in the archetypal perfection of the Redeemer in his life and suffering and death, and it manifests its superiority over man and the world as the sovereignty of the divine Spirit over sin and the God-forsaken world. On the other hand it is the creative love which through Christ the Redeemer as the new Adam frees all of humanity for the higher life of faith through regeneration and sanctification.

God's act of revelation is first of all related to the religious man's immediate self-consciousness which is posited by God the Creator and liberated to personal reality by God the Redeemer. This existential concept of revelation, which is part of Schleiermacher's fundamental theological understanding, is supported by the belief in the incarnation of the divine Logos in the man Jesus and by the redemptive activity of the Redeemer. Thus Schleiermacher's theology is a revised and renewed version of Johannine theology, Christology, and eschatology. He drew the conceptual tools of his theology from the movement of transcendental and critical idealism. Thus all interpreters of Schleiermacher are faced with the question of how theology and philosophy, faith and reason, relate in his piety and theology. Here Schleiermacher's own statements stand in marked opposition to the judgments of his opponents and critics who claim that the basic conception of his theology came from transcendental philosophy, and that his Christology could only be a disruption of this basic philosophical concept. This concept, however, could not assert itself in his total system and thus his theological system is a vague mixture of philosophical and theological elements. We will have to examine this question as we compare Schleiermacher's theological and philosophical systems.

b) The Philosophical System

The usual conceptions of Schleiermacher's philosophy are mostly inexact because of the inadequate literary transmission of his philosophical ideas. Most of Schleiermacher's philosophical investigations were not handed down in publishable form prepared by the author himself. In addition to a few essays and academic addresses, Schleiermacher's philosophical writings consist of the outlines of his lectures and the lecture notes of his students, which are pronouncedly fragmentary and have widely differing value. This large number of fragments shows that Schleiermacher had not yet found a final structure for his philosophical system even when he had published his dogmatics in two editions. The fact that he completed his dogmatic system first shows where the major emphasis of his scholarly interest lay — dogmatics and theology. We should at least ask whether the emphasis within Schleiermacher's total intellectual structure should not be placed differently than has hitherto been the case. And we must ask whether his dogmatics can be interpreted one-sidedly from the standpoint of philosophy, or whether one should not also consider what influence his dogmatics exerted on his philosophical thinking within the framework of his total system.

Did he not, in a thoroughgoing modification of the objective idealist conception, so construct his philosophical system as to leave room for the distinctiveness of the Christian faith and his theology? A comprehensive view of the basic outlines of his philosophical system is made the more difficult by the fact that Schleiermacher constantly revised this philosophical edifice up to the end of his life.

The most important "conversion," not only for his dogmatics but also for his philosophy, occurred in the years between 1811 and 1814. We will try to emphasize the main points of his lectures on dialectics and philosophical ethics so that their profile, which gradually appears during these changes, becomes recognizable.

(1) *Dialectics*

It is difficult to present the basic principles of Schleiermacher's dialectics because of the varied lecture notes he left behind. The oldest outline is from the year 1811, followed by the versions of 1814, 1818, 1822, 1828, and the final form found in the lecture notes of 1831. In addition to these Schleiermacher left an introduction of about thirty-five pages which he wrote down at the end of his life for the proposed publication of the *Dialectics*. The first edition of the *Dialectics*, edited by Jonas in 1839, was based on the 1814 lecture notes. This edition has inserted into the organization of the 1814 version the deviating and complementary section from other years; it also includes extracts from the notebooks of his listeners. In 1878, Bruno Weiss reexamined the Jonas edition on the basis of a rereading of Schleiermacher's papers and made possible a better chronological identification of many of Schleiermacher's marginal notes.

Jonas's first edition, still indispensable today for the interpretation of Schleiermacher, has been criticized for two reasons. First, it did not allow the full conception of the *Dialectics* to stand out clearly enough, and, second, it is very difficult to recognize in this edition the different versions of 1811, 1814, 1818, 1822, 1828, and 1831, because these fragments are not arranged systematically enough. Wilhelm Dilthey based his interpretation of Schleiermacher's *Dialectics* primarily on the final 1831 version. He persuaded Halpern, his student, to produce a new edition (published in 1903) with the aim of "obtaining a complete and finished structure of the *Dialectics* in its most mature form."[166] Following Dilthey's suggestion Halpern made the latest form of 1831, which Jonas only published as Supplement E, the "center" and filled it out with supplements of earlier versions and lecture notes. In preparing this edition Halpern allowed himself to be guided by the evaluation of the various drafts which he took from Dilthey. The 1814 lectures, which Jonas preferred, he considered an inferior version because in it dualistic and critical tendencies arise which would contradict the prevailing principles of identity

---

166. *Dialektik*, ed. Isidor Halpern (Berlin, 1903), p. xxxiii.

philosophy. Only the lecture outline of 1818 returns to the 1811 schema of identity philosophy, and then arrives at its most mature form in the version of 1831.

George Wehrung has disputed this interpretation by Dilthey and Halpern. In his investigation of Schleiermacher's *Dialectics* he has shown the tensions within the work and the variations of its development under the influence of prevailing philosophical currents. Thus the 1814 outline appears in a new light. The ideas of critical idealism are now positively evaluated. George Wehrung admires the young Schleiermacher and the manner in which he expressed himself in the *Speeches* and *Soliloquies;* but he believed that Schleiermacher mingled the creative intuitions of his youth with alien speculative ideas, especially those of identity philosophy. The loss of substance was therefore considerable. The primacy of Spirit and Ethos came to falter because of identity philosophy, and also the significance of freedom in its opposition to the realm of necessity was no longer affirmed. Schleiermacher's philosophical thinking changed between 1811 and 1814. Now the philosophy of identity faded into the background. Proceeding from the altered outline of 1814, Wehrung emphasizes the uniqueness of the cultural-historical function of Schleiermacher's *Dialectics* within the total movement of idealism. Schleiermacher clearly differs from Schelling's identity philosophy. The source and origin of truth is not *in* us but *above* us. Science as well as the moral life exist from ultimate presuppositions which are only disclosed to faith. This ultimate presupposition is God, who cannot be conceived speculatively and is thus unknown to speculation.

Odebrecht based his own edition of 1942 on Wehrung's judgment.[167] Odebrecht takes the version of 1822 as his basis and adds new material from the lecture notes of the students. He especially emphasizes the relationship between Schleiermacher's dialectics and hermeneutics and wants to demonstrate — particularly with the 1822 version — that for Schleiermacher the way to knowledge is the dialogue, just as it was for his master, Plato. Interesting as Odebrecht's attempt may be, the mixing of Schleiermacher's original formulations from reliable sources with the lecture notes of his students, which contain variations on these formulations, is nonetheless quite precarious. This compilation of primary and secondary sources cannot replace the Jonas edition. Thus Wehrung's proposal for a new edition of the *Dialectics* seems right: begin with the orginal outline

---

167. *Friedrich Schleiermachers Dialektik*, ed. Rudolf Odebrecht (Leipzig, 1942).

of 1811; then, using the outline of 1814 as a basis, include the versions of 1818, 1822, and 1828 in synoptic parallels; and in conclusion present independently the final formulation of 1831. On the basis of such an edition one could carefully study the development of Schleiermacher's philosophical thinking, and yet, on the basis of his various lecture outlines, one could also identify the total conception which they contain.

Our investigation of Schleiermacher's *Dialectics* is in basic agreement with Dilthey's interpretation which had previously remained unpublished but which has now been made available by the author of this work.[168]   I am of the view that the basic and consistent motif of Schleiermacher's systematics is the *critical transcendental philosophy of Kant* which took on its special shape under the influence of Plato and in separation from Spinoza, Fichte, and Schelling.   His philosophy is a transcendental-critical variation of so-called objective idealism. Quite beside and beyond Schleiermacher's undeniably strong drive toward system, there is, however, another impulse at work, namely, a desire to leave the philosophical system open for the source and origin of truth as found in the Christian faith in God.

An overly detailed examination of the different variables of his development could easily be too confusing in our investigation, as Wehrung's incisive and thorough developmental-historical investigations show.   Troeltsch held that here all threads of the fabric have "unwound." We are not first of all concerned with an analysis of the different threads and connections of Schleiermacher's thinking; rather our hope is to reveal the system itself, the moving internal systematic structure of his thinking.

Dialectics is the teaching of the principles of the art of philosophical thinking.   That is to say, it is the combination of logic and metaphysics. Kant's critical transcendental philosophy and epistemology are further developed into a metaphysics of knowledge.   Knowledge is posited in relation to the rational order of the world.   The evidence and truth of knowledge are not founded solely on the *a priori* character of the principles of cognition nor on the priority of practical reason; rather they are based on the overall coherence of the system which reveals itself in knowledge and is reflected in the products of knowledge. The first argument for this system of knowledge is the agreement of all thinking men in the process of knowing.   More significant, however, is the objective side of knowledge.   Being encompasses the rational system.   This coherence of being is reflected in the

168. W. Dilthey, *Leben Schleiermachers*, vol. II, ed. M. Redeker (Berlin, 1966).

system of knowledge. Thus the agreement of being and knowing is established.

This metaphysics of knowledge is the preliminary basis for Schleiermacher's epistemology. The basic concept of Greek philosophy is still at work in this elaboration of Kant's critical transcendental philosophy; accordingly either the ideas must be reflected in knowledge, as in Plato, or knowledge must conform to being, as in Aristotle. It is the task of the first transcendental part of the *Dialectics* to establish this metaphysics of knowledge.

The methodology of the second "formal" part follows. In this methodology the purely formal logic of the traditional syllogistics was criticized and rejected, in Dilthey's phrase, with "incisive logic." Formal logic is replaced by an objective concept of the agreement of system and feeling of conviction. The feeling of conviction rests on the connection between complete knowledge and world order which, after 1818, is referred to as the transcendental ground of knowledge and moral willing.

We will concern ourselves primarily with the first part of the *Dialectics*. What is the foundation of this metaphysics of knowledge? It is best to proceed from the idea of knowledge which, according to Schleiermacher, is at work in all special sciences. The original desire for knowledge, which is active as the original motive of the Spirit in all cognition, contains two transcendental presuppositions which cannot themselves become the object of knowledge but which as *transcendentalia* determine all knowing. These two presuppositions are the agreement among all thinking beings and the interrelation between thought and being. Proceeding from the interrelation of thought and being Schleiermacher postulates the independence of the real which has an impact on man by way of the organic function of sense perception. Thought likewise has its independence, since it is bound to the idea of knowledge. Both these elements, the real and the ideal, the physical and the intellectual, are correlated as the transcendental presuppositions of all cognition and knowledge. The knowledge of the thinking subject experiences itself not simply as a nexus of accidental perceptions of unconnected thoughts; rather that which is given in sense perception is formed and transformed by thought. He postulates this interrelation of thought and being because otherwise knowledge would fall victim to skepticism. Knowledge, however, has the moral duty to rely on itself to ward off skepticism.

The unity of the ideal and the real is the infinite absolute. The unity is not an aggregate of manifolds and multiplicities but infinite absolute unity. The infinite and the one stands in opposition to the unsubdued chaos of the multiplicity of sense perceptions. This absolute unity can never be the object of cognition. It is, however, the transcendental presupposition of knowledge out of which the ultimate difference of the real and the ideal arise. It is not the object of knowledge because everything which is perceived by the senses and ordered by the categories of reason can only be finite, never infinite. Schleiermacher shows this to be true both in the formation of concepts and in the formation of judgments. Conceptualization is only possible on the basis of a distinction between thought and object. If, however, the contrast between thought and object is fundamentally negated there can be no concept of this unity as such. The presupposition of objective knowledge in transcendental philosophy cannot itself be comprehended conceptually, otherwise it would not be the presupposition of conceptualization.

We arrive at the same result when we begin from the standpoint of judgment. The judgment of the knowing subject posits a predicate which potentially is already contained in the subject. All being is already posited in the total subject of absolute unity. But if all being is posited, then particulars can no longer be predicated. Then subject and object are identical. Therefore the distinction between subject and predicate is dissolved in the absolute unity and there is nothing to be predicated anymore.[169] Thus in the absolute the opposition between concept and object and the difference between subject and predicate is overcome. Therefore the absolute is simply a limiting concept, a transcendental presupposition of knowledge but not the object of knowledge.

This critical examination of the possibilities of metaphysical knowledge of God results in the following: knowledge cannot renounce the idea of God as the transcendent presupposition of all knowing without falling into skepticism. On the other hand, an adequate knowledge of God as the absolute is quite as impossible as is an adequate formation of concepts or judgments about the absolute. Schleiermacher further clarified this result by discussing in the *Dialectics* the fruitless attempts of metaphysical speculation about God.

The first path of error often taken is pantheism. In pantheistic speculation the absolute and infinite unity of being is thought of either as power or substance. The supreme force then constitutes the prime cause for the particular forces in finite being. Perhaps this pantheistic construction can be clarified with the concept of the *natura naturans*. It involves, according to Schleiermacher, serious

---

169. *Dialektik, S. W.*, III/4, 2, pp. 506 f.

false reasoning. One cannot comprehend the relationship of the absolute to the finite by means of the categories of causality and substance. The absolute can never be a power which, as such a prime cause, determines particular finite powers. No more can the absolute unity be thought of as the original substance of which the particular substances of the finite are but modalities. The categories of cause and substance only apply to the realm of finitude. Any attempt to know the infinite, absolute being with the aid of these categories and proceeding from finite being is a serious philosophical error. Such an absolute is no longer the absolute. The Godness of God goes unrecognized in pantheism. It is hard to understand how people time and again maintained that pantheism is the metaphysical basis of Schleiermacher's *The Christian Faith*; for in that work he shows with theological arguments that pantheism is an impossibility; in the *Dialectics* he does the same thing with philosophical arguments.

A second erroneous path of metaphysical speculation is taken when the relation of God and world is so construed that God, as the highest Being of spiritual creativity, and the world over against him as formless matter are juxtaposed. The relationship of God and the world is thus conceived in terms of man's "intellectual function" as related to the object of sense perception. Once again there is a very false conclusion here. The highest idea of reason and formless matter are but limiting concepts of human thought which can only be applied to the finite world. Infinite and absolute unity is not identical with the highest idea of reason and cannot be inferred analogically from man's intellectual function. The eternal and absolute unity no longer includes the opposition of spirit and matter.

A further road to error is the attempt to proceed from the opposition of freedom and necessity, which only pertains to the finite world. If one absolutizes necessity he arrives at the notion of fate. Schleiermacher describes as especially inadequate such attempts to establish some idea of fate by absolutizing the necessary causal relationship of the finite world. It is just as false to start with the concept of freedom and to postulate God, as the Enlightenment did, as the providence which governs in the gaps of the natural order.

Both speculative concepts of the Enlightenment, the ideas of fate and providence, are impossible for they seek to apply the conceptual forms of the finite world to the absolute. The absolute infinite unity is also above the contrast of freedom and necessity. Thus the critical examination of the erroneous paths of speculation confirms Schleiermacher's conclusion.

After 1818 he also included in his considerations the area of the morally responsible will. A transcendental ground also had to be found for the certainty of will as well as for the evidence of knowledge. Here, too, two arguments require such a return to the transcendental ground. First of all, there is the agreement of all moral willing as to the ultimate direction of their will; second, the will is sustained by the certainty that objective being can be determined and formed through the moral will. However, one should not postulate this transcendental ground in the same way that Kant did. Here, too, the transcendental ground is a presupposition of moral will, but it is not its postulate.

Knowing and willing are alike insofar as they are ultimately not creative functions of the human spirit, but created functions. Quite aside from all metaphysical speculation, what one has here is an existential experience of this transcendental ground of knowing and willing in men's immediate self-consciousness, a self-consciousness which Schleiermacher calls feeling in the *Dialectics* as well as in *The Christian Faith*. In the *Dialectics* he forgoes analyzing and presenting this process of mediation of God-consciousness to human self-consciousness. For him that is a task for theology and not philosophy. The *Dialectics*, however, achieves still a further liberation of God-consciousness from the dominance of dogmatic or philosophical-metaphysical concepts. All concepts of God are inadequate and are simply conceptual *images*. And this applies especially to metaphysical concepts, e.g., the conception of the absolute as the first cause, as absolute being, or the absolute law giver, and absolute artist. It is of particular interest that Schleiermacher calls the concept of absolute being — often used in theology, yet perceived by the religious man as an abstract and empty word — a conceptual schema and a conceptual image. As a critical theologian Schleiermacher saw through the one-sidedness and inadequacy of this concept.

The difference between God and world can also be clarified by a critical examination of the metaphysical conceptual images. The idea of the world is also a transcendental idea. This idea is a motivation for knowledge to actualize itself as real knowledge and to approximate the totality as much as possible. It is the goal, the *terminus ad quem*, toward which our knowledge strives. But this idea of the world is just as incomplete and limited as the metaphysical idea of God; like Kant, Schleiermacher based this conclusion on the antinomies which appear as soon as one tries to think it through. Above all, one cannot combine in a single concept a timeless and spaceless absolute with the temporal-spatial world. But at the same time the deep radical difference between God and world must be affirmed. God is not a goal of the infinite process of cognition as is the idea of the world. This transcendental limiting concept of "world" still contains in itself the oppositions of the finite world. The idea of God is altogether different. Knowledge cannot approximate the idea of God because the idea of God underlies all knowledge. Thus those who find peace in meditation on God may forgo all science and world-wisdom insofar as it concerns the divine communion of faith. Thus God is the *terminus a quo* of all knowledge. He is above all oppositions of the finite world. In contrast the idea of world is only *terminus ad quem*, the never attained goal of a development of knowledge, but within which all the oppositions of the finite world are contained.

(2) *The Philosophy of Culture*

Schleiermacher's system of philosophical ethics and his fundamental philosophical conception reinforce and support each other. The "world-wisdom" presented in his philosophy is determined by the opposition of reason and nature. Accordingly ethics and physics are differentiated as the principal divisions of science. Ethics concerns finite being to the extent that the influence of reason predominates in it. Physics has nature as its object and represents finite being under the power of nature. Both are fundamental sciences. Hence ethics is not moral theory in the traditional sense, but the philosophy of culture, history, and society. Physics is the philosophy of nature. Specialized empirical sciences correspond to these fundamental sciences. Thus empirical subdisciplines such as historiography and psychology belong to ethics.

What is the essence of the moral? In the first place it is a life process. This process consists in the progressive influence of reason on nature. It begins with the individual man and with humanity at its most primitive levels when there is a minimum impact of reason on nature. This process is completed when all of nature, under the influence of reason, has become an organ of reason. At first this sounds very artificial, abstract, and quite removed from life. But actually it is a completely new view of the phenomenon of morality. Morality is not obedience to specific authoritative commands; it is not only the awareness of the ought in the categorical imperative, nor is it simply the intellectual recognition of ideas, but it is rather a principle that permeates all of life.

Morality therefore is also not a separate sphere of life but is active in all spheres of life, in the life of individuals, in society, in one's vocation, and in the state. Through the moral process the world order, which we call nature, receives meaning and significance. This world order is so structured that the objective rational content of life stands out. As such the world process is already determined by this rational content and that which is potentially designed as a determinant there becomes an actual event. In recent times these ideas have again become prominent in modified form in the life and value philosophy, definitively influenced by Wilhelm Dilthey, Schleiermacher's interpreter. Recently, just as in Schleiermacher's time, the content of ethics, the "teleological moment," has been rediscovered. This understanding of ethics stands in contrast to the one-sided definition of ethics as a formal norm of life and as the private-personal sphere.

What then is morality? According to Schleiermacher it is the formation of life through reason. This raises the further question: What is reason? One could formulate the results of this ethics in a simple modern manner: moral good is the purely rational deposit found in all areas of life; one acts morally when he subordinates himself to the rational law contained in every area of life and through his contribution strengthens and further develops the spiritual power of this concrete law. But that is not yet enough. Schleiermacher's ethics is concerned not only with the concrete law of the particular spheres of life but also with the whole of mankind and the whole of reason.

At this point a contrast appears which Schleiermacher identifies as the opposition of the universal and the particular, the opposition of the identical and the individual. Reason is not simply a universal principle but something concretely alive in the single individual, forming that which is individual. Furthermore, reason is precisely not an intellectuality that is abstract and remote from life, but the process of acting upon nature. Morality involves the formation of structures, not simply their prohibition and limitation. The tension between the universal rational content and the living concrete individual is the decisive consideration. The universal is not an abstract idea of a conceptual construct. On the contrary, it is the whole of reason as a life power made effective in the particular. In history one never finds mankind in and for itself, but only as the principle in the distinct individual forms of particular being as well as in such social individualities of moral communities such as the family and the people of a nation. On the other hand, that which is individual is alive only insofar as it assists in universal moral progress, i.e., in concretizing the universal and identical through its moral activity and in manifesting the universal within its concrete form. The human form of the unique individual, for instance, is a reflection of mankind and thus an organ of mankind.

What then is the good? The concept of the highest good is central. The negation in this concept can soon be recognized. Schleiermacher tries to draw the line against the formalism and legalism of Kantian ethics. He does not say, "You ought, and you can because you should"; rather he says, "Become what you already are!" Bring the universal being of reason to consciousness and thus form nature! With the concept of "the highest good" Schleiermacher relates his ethics to the classical usage, but at the same time goes beyond it. In Greek ethics this concept is an indication that the life of virtue already contains in itself the highest contentment and happiness. The good deed itself provides the greatest inner satisfaction to the one who acts morally. Schleiermacher moves beyond this view; since the highest good does not only refer to the particular it is objective, it is the rational content of life as a whole. Today we might say that it is the value and meaning of life which should be made actual.   In this way Schleiermacher leaves behind the eudaemonism of the classical search for happiness. His concern is not with the inner contentment of the individual but rather with structure and work, with overcoming the oppositions of life through concrete rational action, with community and harmony wherein not only happiness but also true peace is found.

The highest good is the decisive center that orients all appearances and life-forms of human history toward action and deed. It is the "whole activity of reason, in the form of separation and community, within this natural totality of our globe."[170] The tendency to the universal and objective is undeniable as is furthermore the limitation of moral-cultural activity to this earth. "The highest good is a perfectly self-contained whole just as our globe is spacially confined; accordingly, all human activity cannot reach beyond its domain."[171] The process can therefore never be completed since there is no perfection for this world.

There are various conceptual images, definite ideal forms, for this concept of the highest good, depending on one's point of view. The highest good appears "sometimes as the *Golden Age* in the untroubled and all-satisfying communication of personal life, sometimes as *eternal peace* in the evenly distributed dominion of the people over the earth, or as the *perfection* and *immutability* of knowledge in the community of languages, and as the *Kingdom of Heaven* in

---

170. Schleiermacher, *Über den Begriff des höchsten Gutes, S. W.*, III/2, p. 481.
171. Ibid., p. 471.

the free community of religious faith. Each of these in its own uniqueness also includes the others in itself and expresses the whole."[172] To be sure, these are only the conceptual images for a process is on this earth and bound to this earth and will never attain perfection.

Schleiermacher's ethics illuminates the consummation and growth of this moral process in the specific areas of life. Schleiermacher thinks dialectically here too and inquires into the contrasts within this process. The first contrast of the moral process is the tension between the organizing and symbolizing functions. Strictly understood, organizing means making something into an organ, i.e., through the activity of reason nature becomes an organ of reason. The fundamental exemplar is the human organism in its conjunction of body and soul and its centered unity of the self.

The moral process has the task of making the world into the "finest work of Spirit"; as the young Schleiermacher expressed it with pathos in the Soliloquies, the entire finite, earthly being should become the organ of reason.[173] But this presupposes that finite being is open to this effort of human intelligence. Thus Schleiermacher's ethics also rests on the basic metaphysical conception of objective idealism, according to which thought and being are coordinated.

The organizing function, however, requires that the reason active in it is able both to communicate and receive messages. This communication takes place through the symbolizing function. Symbolizing means making nature into a symbol for reason. Symbol signifies for Schleiermacher the re-presenting of the idea of reason in the physical and the concrete. The abstract language of identity philosophy formulates it in the following way: "Inasmuch as reason has no other being than that of knowledge its action upon nature and its union with nature is entirely a penetration of nature by knowledge."[174] Symbolizing signifies rational comprehension, understanding, and inclusion within the intelligible structure of the rational. Schleiermacher's expressions are not quite uniform and unambiguous in the different drafts of his ethics. In the earlier drafts the emphasis is on the object that is to be made into the symbol. In the later drafts the emphasis lies partially on the subject of symbolizing, and thus on the reason that presents itself in nature. This is due to

---

172. Ibid., p. 466.
173. *Monologen*, p. 15. *Soliloquies*, p. 19.
174. *Ethik, S. W.*, III/5, § 126 c.

the fact that the contrast between organizing and symbolizing was weakened and all moral action was described as both organizing and symbolizing in the later drafts.

These two mutually conditioning functions were crossed with the contrast between the identical and the individual. The total moral process thus received a fourfold organization. The organizing function in the character of identity concerns the moral cultural realm of exchange. Under exchange he understands the cooperative efforts of men in earning, working, and commerce. Organizing "in the character of individuality" constitutes property. Property is necessary for the moral process because the individual can fulfill himself only through property.

Symbolizing activity "in the character of identity" constitutes knowledge. In this it is evident that symbolizing activity is a particular form of knowing. Knowing is concerned with the universal validity of the search for truth. Symbolizing activity "in the character of individuality" constitutes feeling. Here, too, we should note that feeling is not the third psychic function in addition to knowing and willing, but that it is the primordial act of the Spirit which actively realizes and symbolizes itself in immediate self-consciousness.

Art and religion are the two cultural spheres of feeling. At first glance this fourfold division is an intellectual construct and an abstract schema. However, it offers very fruitful categories for interpreting historical-moral life. This is especially evident in Schleiermacher's interpretation of the meaning of the forms of moral community which he relates to this fourfold schema.

The basic form of all moral community is the family. All four forms of the moral process are active in it. Reason and nature are unified in the bond of marriage. Sexuality is not negated but humanized and made ethical through the moral process. In his lectures on ethics this view is formulated very abstractly: "What is unique in sexual union is the momentary unification of consciousness and the permanent unity of life which proceeds from the fact of reproduction."[175] This community can include only two persons and for Schleiermacher it is indissoluble. In marriage each partner becomes "an organ for the reason of the other."[176] Thus marriage is not described simply as an institution or a station, but as a community of understanding, of respect for the individuality of the other, and of mutual education. It is a community of being and life which

---

175. Ibid., p. 260.
176. Ibid., p. 258.

arises through internalizing and humanizing of the sexual union and is therefore the organ and symbol of moral reason.

All other moral spheres of culture are prefigured in marriage and the family. The family is a community of cooperative living which serves as an example of how personal possession can at the same time become common property. Domestic hospitality is furthermore the original form of all genuine sociability. The paternal responsibility and care for the children already contains the germ of the meaning of the state. The father's instruction of the children is the beginning of the community of learning, and the religious life of the family is the original cell of the church.

In accordance with the fourfold division of the moral process the remaining forms of moral community develop alongside the basic form of the family: the state, free association, academic and cultural life which Schleiermacher identifies as the moral community of learning, and the church. Government rests on the organizing activity in the character of identity, i.e., the moral process of reason produces regulations and laws for the external life in commerce, labor, and politics. The moral process of reason leads to the formation of justice, and the state is the form of moral community which protects, preserves, and furthers justice. It is accordingly a form of community that is determined by the contrast between ruler and ruled [*Obrigkeit und Untertan*].

It becomes quite clear that Schleiermacher thoroughly transformed the theory of the state as it had been formulated in the Reformation period. But he also deepened the modern Enlightenment theories of the state and brought to bear, in modern form, the ethical tradition of Protestant political thinking *against* the Enlightenment state. The sovereign state arises in history with the advancing sovereignty of reason over nature. The meaning of the state is not simply the warding off and taming of evil by way of an authoritarian, magisterial, and supernaturally based exercise of might and punishment. The natural basis of the state is that social individuality which is the people [*Volk*]. Through the moral process of reason this social individuality becomes the state of national culture, binding government and people into a cultural community. Thus the divine aspect of the state does not consist merely in its power, which is tied to law; rather it is the rule of reason in the life of the people. It should unify government and people, all classes and interest groups into one moral community of law.

Even more, the state is not an association or contract built by individuals to pursue the selfish or — as Schleiermacher liked to say — the eudaemonistic interests of individuals or groups who only want to obtain material welfare in the state. The state is a community of diverse individuals. Each individual should receive a place in the state which fits his individuality. The worth of the individual for the state does not lie in what he asks of the state but in the free service he renders the state as a whole. The meaning of the state lies in this moral community of justice and culture formed by free individuals.

Schleiermacher's theory of the state is not a philosophical construction as with Plato and Rousseau. It also does not seek to justify past forms of the state as was done by Romanticism or during the Restoration. Schleiermacher's theory of the state reflects his own political experiences: the impact of the Prussian state under Friedrich the Great whom his father served, the experiences of living through Stein's reform of the state and the battle against Napoleon, as well as his negative experiences with the police-state measures of the Restoration. For Schleiermacher the ideal state is a constitutional monarchy in which the prince and people work together to enact legislation; above all it is a state which is aware of the limits of its power. Science, religion, and art cannot be brought to life through governmental measures; they must be free to develop by themselves. In the area of education, governmental measures and interventions are possible in a subsidiary way only as preliminary and temporary measures. The freedom of scientific research, art, and the freedom of faith lie outside the power of the state. The process by which moral reason develops exists precisely in the state's becoming ever more conscious of the growth of freedom.

(3) *The Antitheses of Good and Evil, Freedom and Necessity*

Many interpreters of Schleiermacher find it hard to understand, even find it totally confusing, that Schleiermacher basically leaves no place for the antitheses of good and evil in his system of philosophical ethics. Finally, in the late form of his *Ethics* of 1832, he explained his decision unmistakably. In his earlier outlines, the 1805 lectures, for instance, he distinguished between a lower and a higher level within subjective knowledge. The lower level of subjective knowledge is evil because it refers only to the sensuous side of subjective knowledge. In the abstract language of his ethical philosophy evil is withdrawal from the identity of reason and order. Sensuousness leads man to egoism and eudaemonism which he attacks as evil. The higher level is the moral one; here subjective knowledge is rationally directed so that it integrates itself into the whole of the knowing process. Evil, by contrast, is the resistance of egoism and eudaemonism evoked by sensuousness. Sensuousness means more for Schleiermacher than the instinctive drives of men's animal needs. Sensuousness is finitude. The moral condition corresponding to sheer finitude is egoism and the eudaemonistic, materially conditioned search for pleasure.

In the later interpretation of his ethics evil is merely the insufficiency of reason which was hindered and remained behind in the perfection of its dominion over nature. Evil is merely something purely negative, it is "that-which-has-not-become" *(Nichtgewordene)*. In the final draft of 1832 evil can no longer be included within the moral process, but has its place only "in the universally necessary relation of the empirical-historical to the ethical which is generally included within ethical theory."[177] This decision by Schleiermacher is necessary in light of his construction of the moral process. The moral process of the progressive dominance of reason over nature is deduced from a metaphysical presupposition which can no longer be substantiated by philosophy alone but is presupposed as operative within the elaboration of his ethical system.

This presupposition is the unity of thought and being, reason and nature in the absolute ground *(Urgrund)* of life, in absolute unity and totality, which is the meaning of the philosophical concept for God. The antithesis of reason and nature contains within itself the drive to annul itself in an ever greater measure in the history of mankind through the unification of reason and nature. If indeed there were in this historical process a positive resistance by evil, then one would have to assume as the presupposition of this evil an anti-reason which opposes the moral reason. But then an opposition between God and anti-God would have to appear in the absolute unity and totality which philosophers call God. But this idea is not possible; in the moral process of reason there can be no self-division of the Spirit and no self-estrangement of human intelligence. In light of the construction of his philosophical ethics this logic is completely consistent. In this way the strange duality of his philosophical ethics becomes clear. It is not meant to be a normative moral doctrine but a phenomenology of the activity of moral reason in history. In this process there is no place for evil. Schleiermacher saw this clearly and therefore sought the locus and origin of evil in the empirical and the historical.

---

177. Ibid., § 91, p. 53.

For the same reasons the antithesis of freedom and necessity also does not belong within the organization of his ethics. Reason is in itself free; nature is determined by necessity. However, in the moral process of history there is no reason in itself or nature in itself. Despite their opposition reason and nature are always related to one another. Hence the isolated freedom of reason and the isolated necessity of nature are for Schleiermacher empty ideas. The moral process is characterized by the advance of freedom in the dominion of reason and the decrease of necessity. But this process will never be consummated on this earth, and therefore the process of reason in history is an interrelation of freedom and necessity.

What is the place of *religion* within the system of philosophical ethics and what significance does it have for the moral process? According to the division of the total cultural realm of moral reason, religion belongs together with art in the area of symbolization, indeed even individual symbolization. Individual symbolization is clearly differentiated from identical symbolization; it is the subjective knowledge of feeling as distinguished from the objective knowledge of reason. But this more formal arrangement does not accurately render Schleiermacher's real concern. The statements presented by Schleiermacher in the various drafts of his *Ethics* concerning the principle of religion as individual symbolization are uneven and fragmentary. Two ideas stand out in his analysis of religion. First, understood as feeling, religion is the immediate experience of the absolute, eternal, and divine. In the feeling of this immediate awareness the contrast between object and subject, which characterizes objective knowledge, is overcome. In feeling as immediate self-consciousness the absolute is experienced in the immediate existential givenness of self-consciousness. To that extent the drafts of the ethical system agree with the religious-philosophical sections in *The Christian Faith*.

The second idea conforms with the explanations of the philosophy of religion in the *Dialectics*. Religion is the presupposition of the moral rational process. God is the absolute unity of thought and being, reason and nature. In God there can and may not be any opposition. For nature as well as reason, he is the source and ground of being that determines the progressive unification of reason and nature. On this presupposition rests the certainty of the moral process of reason concerning the actual power of rationality in its effect on nature. The moral process of reason lives on the basis of this presupposition but is itself unable to prove it. The self-certainty of moral reason in its permeation of nature and the world, the certainty of its culture and world-forming power thus rests upon religion. This is a train of thought already expressed in the *Dialectics.*

(4) *Philosophy of Culture and Christian Ethics*

The expositions of philosophical ethics concern religion but they do not yet touch on the Christian faith. Were one to consider only the philosophical ethics he might well believe that no specific Christian ethics is possible for Schleiermacher. For there is only the moral process of reason which, by virtue of the identity of reason, permeates all spheres of life; therefore it is also active in the church and in the perfection of the church as a worldly form of religious community. Religion is the power, impulse, and final presupposition of the inward self-certainty of moral reason. It does not, however, relate to the actual content and intrinsic value of reason. The specifically Christian in the life of the Christian church would be only a presupposition for a formation of the highest good; as a moral value the specifically Christian would be valid in its universality and identity for all spheres of life; it would then unfold in individual variation within the particular spheres of life while still joining all spheres into one realm of moral reason.

This conception appears to contradict Schleiermacher's theological ethics which was posthumously published from the literary remains under the title *Christian Ethics Systematically Presented according to the Fundamental Principles of the Evangelical Church.*[178] Schleiermacher himself lectured twelve times on Christian ethics: in 1806 in Halle, in the winter semester of 1809/10 in Berlin, and, after the founding of the University of Berlin, ten times from 1811 until 1831. Although he invested a great deal of his academic activity in these lectures, the material that has been transmitted from the literary remains is not equal to Schleiermacher's *The Christian Faith.* What Schleiermacher's friend and student, L. Jonas, provided for us in 1843 are fragments from Schleiermacher's lecture notes and mainly excerpts from notebooks of Schleiermacher's closest students which he attempted to work into a whole. Hence the present available edition is not tightly organized. The transmitted material provides no sufficiently clear answer to precisely those questions which we now must pose, especially the one about the relationship between philosophical and theological ethics.

---

178. *Die Christliche Sitte nach den Grundsätzen der evangelischen Kirche im Zusammenhange dargestellt. S. W.,* I/12.

If Schleiermacher's philosophical ethics is better described in the contemporary scholarly language of today as a philosophy of history, of culture, and as a social philosophy, then Christian ethics, by way of analogy, is not a scholastic theological ethics but more a theology of contemporary Christian life within the church. In addition, Christian ethics is a theological interpretation of the relation of the individual Christian and of Christianity to the state, to society, and to culture—in short, a theology of culture and society. In the ethics of 1809 Schleiermacher introduced the aphoristic assertion: "The object of both [philosophical and Christian ethics] is exactly the same."[179] Further explanations, however, show that this identification is intended to be more formal than substantial. The extent of the realm of philosophical ethics is coextensive with that of Christian ethics. Schleiermacher defines this relation of philosophical to theological ethics in a way that is similar to the description in his dogmatics of the relation of reason and revelation in creation. *The Christian Faith* (second edition), § 46, contains the affirmation that religious self-consciousness, by virtue of which we place all that which stimulates and influences us in absolute dependence on God, fully coincides with the insight that all such things are conditioned and determined by the natural order. The world as the creation of God and nature as the object of natural science are for Schleiermacher the same in their scope. But as to their *kind*, the revelation of creation and natural knowledge are totally different.

In this way Schleiermacher wanted to prevent the separation of revelation and reason into competitive spheres as in the case of supernaturalism. The causal nexus of reason serves as the basis for God's governance of the world and the scientific knowledge of nature does not contradict faith in God; for God's revelation does not interrupt the orderliness of nature but comprehends it. One belittles the omnipotence of God if he refers the direct action of God to the gaps within the causal nexus of nature and if one only recognizes the omnipotence of God as omnipotence if it arbitrarily interrupts the laws of nature which are ultimately determined by God's order of creation.

The same relationship is true of the object of revelation and reason in the sphere of ethics. The object, i.e., the scope of philosophical and theological ethics is the same. But — to speak in Schleiermacher's terms — the mode of knowing is different. Hence Christian ethics is fundamentally different from philosophical ethics. Philosophical

---

179. Ibid., Supplement A, p. 4.

ethics bases itself on reason, Christian ethics on the Christian principle of life.[180]

However, the Christian principle of life is the redemption which occurs through Jesus Christ. This relation to redemption is not only the center of *The Christian Faith* but also of *Christian Ethics*. At the end of *The Christian Faith* Schleiermacher expressed this clearly: "The believer's experience of divine wisdom as the unfolding, redeeming love in Christ leads us into the realm of Christian ethics."[181] The action of the Christian and of Christianity in the world must be related to redemption. God's Holy Spirit asserts itself as the ultimate world-forming power, and the Christian is, in his action, the organ and symbol of this world-forming power of God's Spirit which is mediated to us through Christ.

Christian moral theory thus has a different basis than philosophical ethics. But Christian ethics also enters into the philosophical interpretation of humanity and the realization of humanity in the moral process of reason. The redemption by Christ is the one perfect unification of reason with nature. For this reason Schleiermacher does not want any particular or specific Christian social ethics alongside human ethics. Redemption through Christ is eternal salvation and the guarantee of the fulfillment of God's will in the kingdom of God; hence it is the principle of hope and certainty for the moral life. The sinless Christ, whose perfection of human reason is not possible in this finite existence, is alone the actuality and expression of perfect humanity as willed by God. This view was stated by Schleiermacher in 1809 in § 24 of *Christian Ethics*: "The idea of redemption rests on the consciousness that the growing unity of reason with organization is mediated through the absolute identity of the divine being with human nature."[182] In these passages Schleiermacher explicitly refers to the Logos Christology of Justin. But this redemption involves not only mankind, for which Christ is the new Adam, but also the world. The divine idea of redemption underlies the world order of God the Creator, and the actualization of the kingdom of God is accomplished by forming the world in conformity to this idea into an organ for the divine Spirit. Thus the world as the stage of redemption is the revelation of the Supreme Being; the world is not in opposition to God but through redemption it is the servant and organ of God and thus good.

---

180. Ibid., Supplement C, p. 164.
181. *Der Christliche Glaube*, 2d ed., § 169, 3.
182. *Christliche Sitte*, *S.W.*, I/12, Supplement A, p. 8.

The structure and exposition of *Christian Ethics* were not thoroughly carried out by Schleiermacher as was the case in *The Christian Faith*. But some further examples will serve to illustrate how Schleiermacher, with astonishing foresight into future problems, concretely pictured the process by which human culture and society become moral. His *Christian Ethics* distinguishes between effective *(wirksame)* and representative *(darstellende)* action.   This distinction corresponds to the division of philosophical ethics into the organizing and symbolizing functions.   Within this division of *Christian Ethics* Schleiermacher still retained the contrast of the identical and the individual.   The action of the Christian is illuminated through this dual perspective. But if one asks whether this distinction plays a crucial role in the concrete development of the ethics, it becomes clear that this differentiation is not decisive.   In the particular expositions the distinction between the inward and outward spheres of action is far more important.

Special attention should be called to several typical examples of his critique of culture which result from the "purifying" action of the Christian.   In this connection it is interesting to note his proposals for a reform of criminal law and his point of view on the "reform of the state."   In line with this view Schleiermacher advocated abolishing the death penalty.   His argument is interesting.   He thought that with the increasing moral development within the community of the state the effort to abolish the death penalty would grow and moreover the increasing moral conditioning of the state would so deepen the conscience that the death penalty would not only be regarded as superfluous and unnecessary but also as immoral.[183]   The death penalty is immoral for the reason that only those punishments may be imposed on a citizen which he is justified in imposing upon himself as self-punishment according to the principles of Christian ethics. But for Schleiermacher suicide is wrong because only God can decide over life and death.   Therefore no man can pass judgment either upon his own or another's life.   The death penalty is in no way expiation or retaliation.   On the contrary, every punishment is a means of intimidation and threat, hence a pedagogical measure.

On the problem of tyrannicide and violent revolution Schleiermacher likewise took a decided position.   A violent revolution is not justified because a violent change of government only replaces one tyranny with another.   But in no way is Schleiermacher a man of the restoration and reaction.   This is clearly seen in his demand that in legislation

---

183. Ibid., p. 249.

the prince and the citizens must cooperate. The contrast between
commanding and obeying must become less and less personal and
more and more functional.[184]

In the area of international law he requires that the nations create
a condition of law among themselves and not remain in the lawless
state of nature. The justification of defensive war follows from
the moral idea of the rights of the people. However, it may only
be for the purpose of reestablishing a condition of law. Schleiermacher
rejects on moral grounds the right of the individual to refuse military
service. The biblical command not to kill does not justify refusing
due obedience to authority in time of war. Schleiermacher remembered
that the Quakers and Mennonites used this command when rejecting
service in the military and in war during his time; in his opinion
such an attitude was unacceptable.

Schleiermacher believed that it was possible to humanize war.
War should not be a total war which has as its goal the annihilation
of the subjects of the opposing state. The enemy should not be
defeated by killing its subjects but by taking possession of land and
people. Above all, he hoped for the humanizing of war through
advances in armaments so that the combat of man against man would
cease. The introduction of artillery and bombardment makes this
hand-to-hand combat unnecessary. Modern war completely transformed by advances in armaments will become more human — a
deceptive hope.

He rejected forced colonization of uncivilized people in developing
countries. Instead of colonization he recommended something
modern, developmental assistance, because through colonization by
force the Christian name would be defamed among non-Christian
peoples. Also Schleiermacher's social and political views show the
extent to which he was already aware of the transformation of traditional
social forms through the industrialization resulting from machine
technology. He recognized the division and the mechanization of
labor through industrialization and mechanization as a threat to the
moral condition of human society. The transformation of society
by the machine and the concomitant dependency of the employee
should not again lead to a new slavery to work. In the new industrial
society the employee should be able to be a free man.[185]

All these proposals for the moral improvement of external life
in the world can only be understood against the background of his

---

184. Ibid., Supplement D, p. 190.
185. Ibid., p. 489.

ethical system. Moral reason which should have dominion over nature is the process presupposed by Christian ethics. The establishment of the kingdom of God out of the power of Christ's rule also manifests itself as a historical power in the human realm. It is the decisive impulse for the full development and preservation of humanity. God's command and work cannot consist in mutilating human nature but in developing and raising it to a higher level. Ultimately the hope for human culture rests not in the power of moral reason but in the higher impulses which sustain reason by the divine Spirit allowing human nature to become in Christ an organ and symbol of God. Thus hope for the world rests on the Christ-event and not on the incidental successes or failures of the formative power of human reason. Accordingly, one cannot find in Schleiermacher a particular Christian ethics of business and the state either as a parallel or counter to human ethics.

The foundation of his total system in *The Christian Faith* and in his *Ethics* is the incarnation of God in Christ. This incarnation of God brings redemption for men and establishes in men the Christian life principle which permeates and transforms human life in culture and society. The future directedness of this christological foundation of social ethics takes it beyond the merely earthly realm. Schleiermacher is convinced that the process of making culture moral *cannot* be completed on earth but leads beyond this finite world. One must not interpret this idea from the standpoint of an evolutionary principle which is seen in secular terms and has a purely immanent basis. For him evolution does not mean the autonomous progress of the human powers of the spirit and of nature. On the contrary, this development is a process that is sustained by the world-forming power of the divine Spirit as manifested in the unique revelation and incarnation of the divine Logos in the man Jesus and which therefore transcends the finite world.

This correlation of the theology of redemption with the philosophy of culture stands as a new task before us today. The correspondence of the event of redemption and culture, consisting in the dominion of reason over nature, is denied by contemporary theology and philosophy. Indeed the goal — dominion of reason over nature — has also been taken up by modern technical civilization, but in the modern technical world this projected goal is understood in a wholly different manner than in Schleiermacher's time. In the modern technical world of civilization a mindless rationality is at work. It is important to recognize this difference in order to understand correctly Schleiermacher's concept of reason. Reason as understood in Schleiermacher's philosophy of culture is the reason of humanity guided by conscience which includes the ethos of freedom, responsibility, and integration.   Since Nietzsche and the modern criticism of culture this reason of humanity has been lost for a segment of the makers of culture — although not for all — and its place has been taken by precisely that skepticism and ethical nihilism that Schleiermacher always sought to avoid.   For contemporary theology it is intolerable that one should accept a culture-destroying nihilism and the mindless rationality of technological civilization as the counterpart of Christian redemptive faith.   Catholic theology is better off because it rests on natural law.   Evangelical theology, however, needs a renewal of the conception of the human and on the basis of Christian redemptive faith must find a new ethos for culture and humanity in order to counter nihilism.

(5)   *Schleiermacher's Hermeneutics*

Schleiermacher's hermeneutics has recently received a great deal of attention in theological and philosophical discussions.   This is related to the development of contemporary hermeneutics. Hermeneutics is no longer solely a theory about the exposition and interpretation of transmitted texts.   The process of understanding is more universally viewed as "the ontological mode of existence."[186] The object of understanding is the "whole of life's experience and action in the world."   Following up Heidegger's philosophy one recognizes in the existential analysis of *Dasein* how the living relationship to the given conditions the possibility of understanding and leads to the greatest possible openness for the encounter with history.

The interpretation of writings and of personal dialogue on the basis of men's self-understanding as expressed in these works has led to a deeper and broader process of understanding in philosophy and especially in theology.   In theology this understanding has become extremely important for the discussion of "demythologizing." The traditional biblical and dogmatic concepts and images should be interpreted existentially and not objectively in order to uncover their dogmatic content.   As a consequence of this controversial situation, Schleiermacher's hermeneutics has taken on a new contemporaneity.

Schleiermacher is the founder of modern scholarly hermeneutics. He abandoned the older Protestant hermeneutics which rested on the

---

186. H. Gadamer, *Wahrheit und Methode* (Tübingen, 1965), p. xvi.

assumption of verbal inspiration, as well as the Enlightenment historical-critical disputation of biblical authority and the Enlightenment philosophy of language and history. He inaugurated a new beginning of understanding and its possibilities. Enlightenment hermeneutics had simply been an aggregate of historical-critical "observations"; this was now to be replaced by a real discipline of the art of understanding. The principles for such an understanding are, first, elucidation of the meaningful connections within language and, second, the search for the formation of language and its thought content within the creative individuality of the speaker or author. These two tasks are undertaken by way of grammatical and psychological interpretation. Grammatical interpretation not only has the details of linguistic forms as its object but the entire context of language and its spiritual content. What Schleiermacher called "psychological" exegesis was meant to clarify the origin of language in the creative spiritual process within the author's individuality.

Understanding of this intellectual creative process depends on the reversal of the original course of its formation. The original process begins in the life of the author's individuality, his uniqueness, concrete circumstances, and historical relations and leads to his language and conceptions. The reproductive understanding goes in reverse, moving from concept and text to the author's original intention and encounter with reality. Accordingly, the interpreter endeavors with the help of divination to sense the author's "seminal decision" (*Keimentschluss*). In romanticism "divination" is prophetic insight into the future; at the same time it is also a sense for the mystery of life. The presupposition for this understanding of divination is the like-mindedness of all speaking and thinking men, as well as the harmony of thought and being, upon which the philosophy of language and mind in objective idealism is founded. In its turn, this philosophy of language is rooted in the religious metaphysics of objective idealism. Another presupposition is the macrocosm-microcosm speculation according to which the universe, the infinite, the totality reflects itself in individuality, thus making the latter an organ and symbol of totality. Hence in the perspective of religious faith understanding is not only the divination of empirical man through an idea, but the understanding of the individual as the organ and symbol of God who is the totality of being, present and revealed in particular individuals. This individuality as the organ and symbol of God is something different than the creative ego of Fichte's subjective idealist philosophy.

It is not entirely appropriate to use psychology to describe this divination which needs to be supplemented through careful [textual] comparison. Divination is not simply psychological or aesthetic pleasure in reflection, because the individuals who encounter one another in understanding are in this encounter at the same time opened to their own uniqueness through the totality and the whole setting of life.

The concluding observations of Friedrich Lücke's edition of the *Hermeneutics* contain some themes from Schleiermacher's lectures on hermeneutics in 1826/27: "It is of the highest scholarly interest to know how man proceeds in the formation and use of language. Likewise, it is of the highest interest to understand man as appearance in terms of man as idea. The two are absolutely inseparable because language guides and accompanies man in his development."[187] However, this understanding of man in his more profound existence is tied to the wakening of religious consciousness: "The more it [religious consciousness] awakens and becomes present everywhere the more is man himself awakened."[188]

Schleiermacher's audacious and extremely self-confident claim to be able to understand an author better than he had understood himself has become famous. Schleiermacher himself related this "more" of understanding to the fact that even the unconscious elements in the author's original spiritual creation can be clarified by the reproductive understanding. "Since we have no immediate knowledge of what is in him, we must seek to bring into consciousness much that could remain unconscious for him, except where he himself would become his own reflective reader."[189] Schleiermacher's thesis that something unconscious is contained in the author's original productive process which must first be brought into consciousness no doubt goes back to Fichte's philosophy of the ego. Fichte bestows meaning upon the unreflective feeling as the primal act of Spirit within which the subject and object of intellectual cognition are not yet separated, because it is out of this unconscious substratum of feeling that man first awakens to himself by rising to conscious self-reflection.

The maxim of understanding an author better [than he understands himself] had a sequel in the nineteenth century. It was repeated by Boeckh, Steinthal, Dilthey, and others. Its prior history is also

---

187. *Hermeneutik, S. W.*, I/7, p. 261.
188. Ibid., p. 262.
189. *Fr. D. E. Schleiermacher, Hermeneutik: Nach den Handschriften*, ed. H. Kimmerle (Heidelberg, 1959), pp. 87 and 91. *S. W.*, I/7, pp. 32 and 45.

of interest. Bollnow and Gadamer point out that it is also found
in Kant's *Critique of Pure Reason* (second edition, B, p. 370) and
in Fichte's *Vocation of the Scholar* (fifth lecture). In addition this
author has shown that, in approximately the same period, it is also
found in Herder.[190]

Bollnow regards Schleiermacher's formula as a philological guideline
which Schleiermacher had found already available; Gadamer views
it as a principle of basic philosophical criticism in the philosophical
discussion of that time — an interpretation that is probably more
acceptable. The fact that Herder also used this maxim and that
one can also document a similar formulation in the young Luther
leads us to include this formula in a still larger context. The
fundamental idea of Schleiermacher's statement is a critical ground
rule for all theological exegesis that seeks to gain an even profounder
theological meaning beyond the literal meaning of the biblical
texts.[191]

Schleiermacher rejected an independent theological hermeneutics
for the New Testament as early as his explications in the *Brief
Outline of Theological Study*. The New Testament should first of
all be understood in the same way as every other book of literature
— as is also called for by Bultmann's contemporary existential
interpretation. But Schleiermacher cannot simply stop there. He
is forced by the content of the New Testament's proclamation to
alter the universal ground rules of hermeneutics as they apply to
the New Testament and to recognize definite religious presuppositions
of Christian existence in faith for its interpretation. This is part
of Schleiermacher's interest in separating himself from the Enlightenment's historical explanations of the New Testament because they
lose sight of the unity and wholeness of the New Testament through
isolated critical investigations and by their search for causal connections.
Schleiermacher wanted to make the unity and completeness of the
New Testament the foundation for his hermeneutics. He no longer
substantiates it with the traditional dogma of inspiration; rather, he
substantiates it christologically. Christ is the "productive point of
origin for Christianity"; he is the creative Spirit for the genesis of
Christianity and the New Testament.

As Schleiermacher directed his attention to the creative power
of Christ present in the writings that require interpretation, he also
discovered the capacity of Christianity to shape language anew on

---

190. Dilthey, *Leben Schleiermachers*, vol. II, p. liv.
191. Ibid.

the basis of Greek and Hebrew. Once again he employed his schema of the contrast between the identical and the individual. The identical is the Spirit of Christ; the individual is found in the particular New Testament writers. The individuality of the New Testament writers is a distinctive manifestation of the faith-relationship of each writer to Christ. However, that which they have in common in their dependence on Christ outweighs the separation and differentiation resulting from their individuality. Therefore Lücke's edition of *Hermeneutics* concludes with the sentence: "Even if we never achieve a complete understanding of the personal uniqueness of each New Testament writer, it is still possible to achieve the most significant part of the task, namely, grasping ever more completely the common life in them, the Being and Spirit of Christ."[192]

Schleiermacher enjoyed lecturing on hermeneutics and in his lectures he stated that he considered this to be a most fruitful area of theological scholarship. As early as 1805 he began to treat the subject of hermeneutics in lectures at Halle. He repeated these lectures at Berlin in 1814, 1819, 1822, 1826/27, 1828/29, and 1832/33. He treated this subject extensively in all periods of his intellectual activity. It is comparable to the stress he placed on dogmatics in his lectures. He delivered these central lectures on dogmatics at Berlin nine times whereas he devoted six lecture series to hermeneutics. It is extremely regrettable that so little of Schleiermacher's extensive efforts in hermeneutics has come down to us from his own hand. From Schleiermacher himself only the two academic addresses of 1829 have been published: "On the Concept of Hermeneutics with Reference to F. A. Wolf's Remarks and Ast's Textbook." Fragmentary lecture notes from 1805 to 1833 have been preserved and have been separately published by H. Kimmerle. Friedrich Lücke supplemented Schleiermacher's manuscripts on hermeneutics from the literary remains with lecture notes and he published Schleiermacher's views on hermeneutics in this form in 1838.[193] The disadvantage of Lücke's edition is that it is not clearly evident what is from Schleiermacher's own hand and what is from student lecture notes. Kimmerle's edition has the advantage of including only Schleiermacher's notes and these in their historical sequence so that it is possible to follow the development of Schleiermacher's ideas. It has the disadvantage of working with fragmentary notes that are so piecemeal and partially

---

192. *S. W.*, I/7, p. 262.
193. *S. W.*, I/7, Berlin, 1838.

so enigmatic that a supplement from the lecture notebooks would be desirable.

Schleiermacher's hermeneutics is of historical importance not only because it is the first modern treatment of hermeneutics but also because it essentially influenced Dilthey's theory of understanding. Beyond this it is a prophecy for the future. Contemporary hermeneutical discussion is once again dealing extensively with Schleiermacher's basic ideas. There are primarily two such ideas which in changed form are fructifying hermeneutical work: the idea of wholeness and the idea of individuality (understood as the opening of the self to the process of life and the matrix of historical action). Schleiermacher's metaphysics of individuality, however, does not mean a psychological or aesthetic restriction of hermeneutics, as has been charged against contemporary theological hermeneutics to some extent. In the foreground of Schleiermacher's theological hermeneutics stands the hermeneutical circle enclosing the gospel message of the New Testament and the faithful individual existence of the Christian. In the New Testament too "the whole should be understood from the particulars and the particulars from the whole."[194]

The "whole" that is referred to here is described as the "total condition of that which is Christian in the Apostolic period,"[195] or as the life of Christ in the church, or as the common life of the New Testament authors, and as the Being and Spirit of Christ which should be better and better understood.[196]

Schleiermacher anticipates a contemporary hermeneutical idea when he indicates that the exegesis of Holy Scripture, as well as the dogmatic reflection on the content of its proclamation, requires the living word and an interpretation of the language of faith. The conclusion of his *Hermeneutics* states:

> We can only reach agreement in this matter on the basis of language. We see that a person is clear and certain about his highest interest only to the extent that he knows how to communicate through language. Everything therefore which is a normal expression of the religious, which is Scripture in any sense, must contribute to making this task a universal one. . . . Even if the hermeneutical task relative to the New Testament seems quite subordinate when compared to the totality of the object of the full task of the

---

194. *S. W.*, I/7, p. 247.
195. Ibid., p. 255.
196. Ibid., p. 262.

Christian church and even if many details can probably never be completely solved . . . nonetheless, it is the most general interest which relates to the hermeneutical task . . . the guarantee of this is our view of the relation of Christianity to the whole human race and the spiritual clarity with which this has been developed in the Evangelical church.[197]

---

197. Ibid.

IV.

HIS CONTRIBUTION WITHIN THE
REPUBLIC OF LETTERS

A. THE PLATO TRANSLATIONS

Schleiermacher's extensive and determined work on the translation of Plato's writings was a scholarly activity that occupied him for many years. As a result of this work Schleiermacher became one of the most important classical philologists of his time. The plan for this exemplary undertaking originated with Friedrich Schlegel.

The movement of German idealism, which included artistic and philosophical forces, also demonstrated its importance in the encounter with the literary heritage of European intellectual history. In both a productive and reproductive way it transmitted this cultural heritage through significant translations of classical, philosophical, and poetic works of European cultural history. In 1793, for instance, there appeared the translation of Homer by Johann Heinrich Voss; shortly after, in 1799, A. W. Schlegel began to publish his translation of the works of Shakespeare. Thus the plan for the intellectual conquest of Plato's world of thought for the German idealist movement was, to some measure, already in the air. Friedrich Schlegel sensed this. He immediately won over his friend Schleiermacher to this project and hurriedly concluded a contract with the publisher, Fromm, intended to help him get out of his perpetual financial embarrassment. The initial common efforts of Schlegel and Schleiermacher did not bear fruit, however, as a result of Friedrich Schlegel's lack of discipline and restless life. These differences were one, even if not the only, cause for the gradual cooling and breakup of the friendship between Friedrich Schlegel and Schleiermacher. Schlegel emigrated to Paris, and busied himself with everything except the work on Plato, so that Fromm, his publisher, lost patience and even wanted to make Schleiermacher liable for financial losses. Fortunately Reimer, a friend of Schleiermacher, took over the further publication and the accompanying financial risk.

Schleiermacher's translation opened up a new understanding of

Plato, which had been distorted earlier during the Middle Ages and again in humanism through the Neoplatonic reinterpretation of Plato. The transcendental philosophy of objective idealism created the intellectual conditions for this rediscovery. In his biography of Schleiermacher, Dilthey has convincingly demonstrated this connection. Plato was the first European creator of a system of objective idealism.

German transcendental philosophy opened up new possibilities for understanding the metaphysics and theory of science of the Greek philosophers. Schleiermacher's work on interpretation presupposed idealistic hermeneutics which is based on the philosophy of language contained in identity philosophy and its corresponding method of translation and understanding. Schelling defined this basic hermeneutical conception as early as 1803 in his *Lectures on the Method of Academic Study*. "A man educated only in languages is called a philologist only through a misuse of the term; rather he occupies a position of the highest level with the artist and the philosopher; in fact both are united in him. His concern is the historical construction of works of art and science, the history of which he must comprehend and re-present in vivid interpretation."[1]

Later in his lectures on hermeneutics and in his academic addresses on the various methods of translation Schleiermacher himself acknowledged these principles of understanding and presented them theoretically. Two ideas shape his hermeneutics: (1) the inner context, the systematics of the work to be interpreted, and (2) the individuality of the author, expressed in the inner "seminal decision" (*Keimentschluss*) of the author. Schleiermacher applied these principles, theoretically formulated only later, already in the interpretation of Plato. His main concern was to grasp the inner systematics, the organic whole of Plato's thought and then on that basis to test the authenticity of the particular dialogues and their place in the life of the philosopher. Schleiermacher presumed that Plato had created a finished conceptual structure and then unfolded it in its various stages, proceeding from didactic points of view but also in terms of the order of his system. Schleiermacher therefore distinguished three major groups of Plato's writings on the basis of his investigations of the dialogues:

1. The dialogues from the final period of his life. These involve the systematic presentation of his philosophical teaching (*The Republic*, *Timaeus*, *Crito*, and *The Laws*).

1. Schelling, *Sämmtliche Werke*, I. *Abteilung*, vol. 5 (Stuttgart and Augsburg, 1859), p. 246.

2. In contrast to these works of his old age one finds the "elementary group" of writings from his youth (*Phaedrus, Protagoras, Parmenides*). They contain the first outlines of the principles of Plato's thought, "of dialectics as the technique of philosophy, of the ideas as its true object, i.e., of the possibility and conditions of knowledge."[2]

3. The middle group stands between these two (*Theaetetus, The Sophists, The Statesman, Phaedo,* and *Philebus*). These treat the applicability of the principles of knowledge to the objective sciences, especially ethics and physics, i.e., they deal with the relation of the ideas to actual things and thus provide an explanation of knowledge and thoughtful action.[3]

Schleiermacher's work on Plato was published in various stages: in 1804 he published the first volume which contained the early writings; from 1805 to 1809 he issued the dialogues of the second level in three volumes (II. 1, 2, 3), and after an extended delay the systematic dialogues finally appeared in 1828. It is unfortunate that because Schleiermacher no longer had the necessary energy or time at his disposal, some of these dialogues, notably *Timaeus* and *The Laws*, were not translated. The work concluded with his translation of Plato's *Republic*.

What is the significance of Schleiermacher's Plato translations? He made possible a reinterpretation of Plato on the basis of the new philosophical situation produced by the metaphysics of objective idealism. He made Plato's world of thought significant for the German transcendental philosophy of that time. This contribution was immediately recognized by his contemporaries as well as by later Plato interpreters. The classical philologist Boeckh, a friend and student of Schleiermacher, gave the following judgment in the *Heidelberger Jahrbücher der Literatur I* (1808): "Let us frankly admit what we think. No one has so completely understood Plato himself and taught others to understand him as this man." In his book *The Philosophy of the Greeks in its Historical Development*, Eduard Zeller praises Schleiermacher's achievement in interpretation. "In Schleiermacher's works the idea of arranging the writings of this philosopher according to their internal organization was for the first time fruitfully applied and consistently executed."[4]

---

2. *Platons ausgewählte Werke*, vol. 1, trans. F. Schleiermacher (Munich, 1918), p. 34.

3. Ibid., p. 35.

4. E. Zeller, *Philosophie der Griechen in ihrer geschichtlichen Entwicklung*, vol. II/1, 3rd ed. (Leipzig, 1875), p. 429.

Schleiermacher's image of Plato, which became classic in the nineteenth century, has not been accepted in its full scope by scholarship with regard to the particulars of his chronological arrangement. Even Dilthey, having expressed in his biography of Schleiermacher the highest praise for his work on Plato, also remarked that Schleiermacher conceived the internal structure of Plato's writings too inclusively and too inflexibly. This eventually led to Karl Friedrich Herrmann's successful demand, in his *The History and System of Platonic Philosophy*,[5] that the historical and biographical development of Plato's life must be considered in a broader and different way for the determination of the authenticity of the dialogues and their chronological arrangement than Schleiermacher had done. Further Plato research has supplemented this particular criticism. In his work, *Paideia*, Werner Jaeger has given a lucid and detailed account of the course of this further examination of the dialogues as to their authenticity and relation to the life of Plato.[6] But even in this definitive survey by Jaeger, Schleiermacher's contribution remains undisputed; he revealed the true Plato for the first time since the Neoplatonic reinterpretation of the Greek philosopher, especially because he was able to recognize the outlines of the metaphysical content of the Greek system. This contribution has stood up through the antimetaphysical Neo-Kantian criticism and despite the additional emendations by Werner Jaeger. Indeed his translation has been judged by critics not as unsurpassable but as still unsurpassed.[7]

We are also interested in knowing what the work on Plato meant for Schleiermacher's own philosophical and intellectual development and what implications Plato's objective idealism had on Schleiermacher's own world of thought. Under the influence of Plato, Schleiermacher overcame romanticism, i.e., romantic reflection, clever playfulness, the aphoristic, and its somewhat individualistic subjectivism. Not confession but receptive objective knowledge now determined Schleiermacher's work. He did not want to talk *about* Plato but wanted to allow Plato *himself* to speak. His hermeneutics surpassed the limits of his romantic period and he attained the objectivity of understanding. The basic principles of

5. K. F. Herrmann, *Geschichte und System der platonischen Philosophie* (Heidelberg, 1839).
6. W. Jaeger, *Paideia*, vol. II, 2d ed. (Leipzig, 1954), p. 131. English translation: *Paideia: the Ideals of Greek Culture*, vol. II, trans. Gilbert Highet (New York, 1943), pp. 80 ff.
7. W. Schmidt in Christ, *Griechische Literaturgeschichte*, 6th ed. (1912), p. 718.

his hermeneutics led him to this objectivity; these principles involved, first, the consideration of the whole and the inner systematics of the work to be interpreted, and, second, the research into the fundamental intention of the author and the "germinal decision" based on his individuality and manifested in the real content of his intellectual work.

B. MEMBER AND ORGANIZER OF THE BERLIN ACADEMY OF SCIENCES

Schleiermacher belonged to the Philosophical Division of the Berlin Academy of Sciences from the Spring of 1810. In his inaugural address of May 10, 1810, he described the task of philosophy as the "immersion of the Spirit into the innermost depths of itself and of things in order to fathom the relations of their [spirit and nature] being-together."[8]   In 1814 he was made the permanent secretary of the Philosophical Division. Adolf von Harnack acknowledged the extent of Schleiermacher's activity in the Academy, and in his history of the Prussian Academy of Science arrived at the conclusion: "Only Schleiermacher was a true representative of philosophy, but at the same time it can also be asserted that from 1815 to 1834 he impressed the stamp of his own spirit on the Philological Division of the Academy."[9]

"It was Schleiermacher who really led beyond Kant, stripping Kantianism of the residues of the eighteenth century and profoundly transforming it, without thereby losing himself in Fichte's subjectivism or in Schelling's pansophism."[10]   Beyond this he belongs to the founders of modern cultural-historical studies. For example, the new study of antiquity as a combination of philosophy with the history of philosophy, law, and art developed in the Academy with Schleiermacher's support. He also participated in the Academy's important new undertaking of collecting in an extensive corpus all Greek and Latin inscriptions from antiquity. At his recommendation the Academy prepared a critical edition of the works of Aristotle.

He contributed to the organization of the Academy through a series of searching memoranda. His many papers for the Academy made valuable contributions to the areas of classical philology and philosophical ethics. To recognize their importance one has only

---

8. *S. W.*, III/3, p. 6.
9. Adolf von Harnack, *Geschichte der königliche preussischen Akademie der Wissenschaft zu Berlin*, vol. I, part II (Berlin, 1900), p. 848.
10. Ibid., p. 626.

to look at his lecture on the distinction between natural and moral law (1823) which contains the foundations of his philosophical system. He did not deal with the area of theology at all in the Academy.

Hegel, who during the 1820s ascended to near unlimited dominance in philosophy, held himself aloof in proud isolation, recognizing only Goethe other than himself. Although Schleiermacher had urged the appointment of Hegel to Berlin he enjoyed no personal relationship with him. Hence Hegel was not elected to the Academy until shortly before his death, and he did not live to participate in his formal admission to the Academy.

In 1826 Schleiermacher resigned as Secretary of the Philosophical Division and asked to belong only to the Historical-Philological Division, which in turn elected him as its secretary. Schleiermacher's work with the Academy clearly shows how strongly he influenced not only theology but also the development of modern cultural and historical studies. In his history of the Academy Harnack arrived at the following judgment:

> Schleiermacher was the second great philosopher to lead the Academy, and his intellectual influence is more discernible in it than that of Leibnitz. . . . Schleiermacher sought to take the conception of the world beyond the opposition of 'revealed' and 'natural' systems and into a historical and yet ideal point of view which would allow many various views and make room for internally related but externally different world views. This undertaking by its very nature is constantly a newly posed and never finished task. That is the way it was alive in Schleiermacher, the great hermeneutical thinker. . . . Only to superficial people did he appear vacillating and changeable; fundamentally he was a steady man of forceful candor.[11]

---

11. Ibid., p. 627.

V.

HIS SERVICE IN THE EVANGELICAL CHURCH

A. ECCLESIASTICAL ADMINISTRATOR

In the opinion of experienced churchmen, ecclesiastical politics may be even more difficult and disagreeable than secular politics. In this respect Schleiermacher had to endure several unpleasant disputes in the period from 1814 to 1829. Three problems of Prussian church politics were at issue in these struggles: (1) the union of both Protestant confessional churches; (2) a new liturgy for the Prussian church which the sovereign as the highest bishop wished to institute; (3) the constitution desired by many members of the Evangelical church but only reluctantly conceded by the Prussian government.

It is only Schleiermacher's position and attitude that are interesting for our inquiry. He was a most impassioned participant in these debates, and came into serious conflicts with the Prussian king and his ministers. We can understand Schleiermacher's attitude only by analyzing his motives. The main motive for his action was his completely new understanding of the nature of the church and therefore also of its structure. Schleiermacher's new understanding of the church stood in opposition to that of older Protestantism and even more so to that of the Enlightenment. In older Protestantism the church was the supernatural institution of grace and salvation whose commission was the true proclamation of the word of God according to the understanding of Reformation theology. Thus the church was essentially defined by the word-event of the gospel. Its sociological structure was taken to be a supernatural institution of salvation, whose function in its relation to state and society was defined by Luther's doctrine of the two kingdoms. Over against the church, older Protestantism placed the sect. The sect was a religious community of pious individuals. It understood itself as a free association of true Christians, hence rejecting infant baptism, and it understood the Christianity of the church or of the religious community as consisting not in the commission it had as an institution,

but as being manifest in the religious and moral achievements of
its members in the process of salvation.

The Enlightenment had no understanding whatsoever of the
theological conceptions of older Protestantism. For it, the church
was only an association. This concept of association was a juridical
and sociological category which could also be applied in exactly the
same manner to the state and family. Its essential mark was the
function of the association. Accordingly the church was an association
for the purpose of nurturing piety, for instruction and moral education.
Its statutes were the creeds which at that time claimed a secular,
juridical status similar to the statutes of other associations. In
Schleiermacher's view the sociological and juridical category of
associations is as inapplicable to the church as was old Protestantism's
theologico-sociological category of an institution of grace and salvation.
The church is above all a community of faith and life.

He interpreted the concept of community according to its meaning
in his ethics and philosophy of history. Community is a whole,
prior to the single individual, but including the individual as a free
individual. The tension between the identical-universal and the
individual-particular which is distinctive in his philosophy of history
and sociology applies in a special way to the church. The origin
and content of this community is christocentrically-pneumatologically
defined. Hence the church is a living historical process founded by
Christ and effective in the history of Christianity through the
continuing activity of Christ. The church is in no way a mere loose
union of individuals sharing a religious life. No subjective-pietistic
emotionalism is to be found in this doctrine of the church. But
neither is it a mere abstract vision of an ideal invisible church remaining in a transcendent other world; rather it is the activity of
Christ through his Spirit among the faithful, and the union, founded
by Christ, of the total life of the faithful in community with their
Redeemer. It is therefore as invisible-visible as the *congregatio
sanctorum* of older Protestantism in which the word of God is preached
and the sacraments administered. But its origin and its substance
are Christ, his Spirit, and the communal life founded by him.
Proclamation through the word, the word-event in the sacraments,
the portrayal of the Christian life in the common worship service,
in the confessions, and also in theology are secondary in comparison
with Christ and his Spirit. They are the founded elements, Christ
and his Spirit the founders.

Schleiermacher's distinct position on the service of public worship,
the liturgy, the validity of the creeds, and the constitution should

be interpreted in terms of this understanding of the church. We can no longer easily understand the originality of Schleiermacher's views on the church because the ecclesiastical-political thinking of nineteenth century liberalism misunderstood this completely new interpretation of the church in terms of its own liberal views, i.e., in terms of the freedom of conscience of each individual, the definition of the community as the creation of free individuals, and total detachment from dogma. On the other hand, reawakened nineteenth century confessionalism falsely claimed that the church is constituted not solely through the gospel but also through the creeds, interpreting the creeds ultimately as the binding statutes of the association and as a juridical obligation for the members of the association. Confessionalism missed both the reformers' and Schleiermacher's new organic concept of the church.

Consequently we must take a new intensive look at that which is essential in Schleiermacher's original conception, particularly in trying to understand the debates and battles of church politics from 1814 until the end of his life. Schleiermacher suffered considerably from these battles and conflicts. The most painful conflict for him was no doubt the heated dispute with the Prussian king.

Ever since his youth Friedrich Wilhelm III had wished to carry out the unification of the Lutheran and Reformed churches. As a member of the Reformed church he would have liked to celebrate the Lord's Supper together with his Lutheran wife. On September 27, 1817, he informed the ecclesiastical authorities that he wished to partake of the Lord's Supper together with his family on Reformation Sunday, 1817, according to the order of worship of the United Evangelical churches. He appealed to the goodwill and understanding of his subjects, particularly the clergy, requesting that they find the correct form for this union which he desired as the highest sovereign and also as the highest bishop of the church. Schleiermacher agreed with the wish of his king. He had just been elected presiding officer of the first united Berlin synod and made known the will of this synod and its accords by publishing a most constructive work, *Official Declaration of the Synod of Berlin Concerning Its Celebration of the Lord's Supper on October 30, 1817.*[1]

By this declaration the synod demonstrated its desire for union of worship without it being necessary to establish any dogmatic or liturgical uniformity.

---

1. *Amtliche Erklärung der Berlinischen Synode über die am 30. Oktober von ihr zu haltende Abendmahlsfeier* 1817, *S. W.*, I/5, pp. 295 ff.

We want only to establish the fact that Christians of both per-
suasions can harmoniously and devoutly enjoy together the Lord's
Supper.   This essential can be achieved if the liturgy of communion
as a whole emphasizes the main points commonly acknowledged
by all and overlooks the disputed incidentals, and if the distribution
of the Lord's Supper, rather than reminding us polemically of
differences between both parties contents itself with the words
of Christ himself.   The different interpretation of these words
led to the different understandings of the Lutheran and Reformed
beliefs.   And it is in terms of these [words of Christ] that every
individual can become aware of his full conception.[2]

On October 30, sixty-three Berlin clergymen, all professors of
theology at the University of Berlin, and many high state officials
gathered for communion in Berlin's Nicolai Church.   The Reformed
Schleiermacher and Marheineke the Lutheran shook hands before
the altar.   The sixty-three dignitaries represented the overwhelming
majority of Berlin's officiating clergymen.   It was also Schleiermacher
who continued to support this union of worship in various types
of publications during the ensuing years.

He argued theologically for the spiritual right of union against
the newly strengthened advocacy of confessionalism in the church
as well as against Enlightenment theology.   Claus Harms, the
confessional Lutheran who as a student of theology had been decisively
influenced by Schleiermacher's *Speeches*, attacked the union as an
aberration and confusion in his "Ninety-five Theses" of 1817,
describing modern systematic theology generally as "apostasy against
the Christian faith."   In Thesis 75 he warned: "Like a poor maiden
the Lutheran Church is now to be made rich through nuptials.   Do
not consummate the act over Luther's grave.   If you do he will
awaken from the dead — and then woe to you!"   During this argument
Schleiermacher treated Claus Harms with respect.   He honored
him "as a well-meaning, devout, and truly Christian man filled with
righteous zeal."   Despite this personal regard he did not have a
very high opinion of Claus Harms's theses with their "oracular
half-truths in pursuit of glitter and glory."   For Schleiermacher
these theses were not fiery flashes, but artificial, malfunctioning
rockets — some of which did not rise and others which burst too
soon.

Schleiermacher opposed Ammon, the Prelate of Dresden, quite
differently.   Ammon, an ally of Claus Harms, entered the dispute

---

2. *Ibid.*, pp. 302 ff.

in a work entitled *Bitter Medicine for Today's Weaknesses of Faith* (*Bittere Arznei für die Glaubensschwäche der Zeit*). Schleiermacher demonstrated that Ammon was superficial in his theologicial work, unable even to state clearly the theological difference between Lutheran and Reformed churches, and that in his advocacy of confessional Lutheranism he was guilty of duplicity and equivocation; having been a former Enlightenment theologian, Ammon now wanted to play the role of confessional supernaturalist. This response to Prelate Ammon for his examination of Harms's theses may well be one of Schleiermacher's sharpest polemical writings, attacking not only Ammon's position but his person as well.[3] In this writing the anger of the Reformed Schleiermacher over the many offensive attacks on his friends of the Reformed tradition was expressed. As far as Schleiermacher was concerned Ammon was now finished as a theologian and scholar.

Schleiermacher expressed his views on the question of the union in the second edition of *The Christian Faith*.[4] Two other essays are full of very heated and vigorous polemics: "On the Peculiar Value and Binding Character of Symbolical Books"[5] and his "Open Letter" to Dr. von Cölln and Dr. Schulz.[6] He objected as much to the doctrinal absolutism that wanted to impose binding symbols on the church as to the Enlightenment suspension of the validity of church confessions.

It should be noted that Schleiermacher did not actually want to set up a new union. In particular, he considered it impossible to produce such a union through liturgical or dogmatic regulations. Uniformity of liturgy and literal uniformity in dogmatic rules of faith and doctrine do not create the spiritual community in Christ which constitutes the essence of the church. This spiritual whole of the organic undivided Christian community is for him already a reality experienced by the faithful Christian. It does not need to become organized for it is already present. This spiritual reality manifests itself in the empirical church, including the National Church of Prussia.

The Christian faith is precisely not an affirmation of literally prescribed dogmatic propositions even if they are about God and Christ; rather it is being grasped spiritually by God and his revelation

---

3. *S. W.*, I/5, pp. 327 ff.
4. *Der Christliche Glaube*, 2d ed., Preface, p. vi; § 26.
5. *Über den eigentümlichen Wert und das bindende Ansehen symbolischer Bücher, S. W.*, I/5, pp. 423 ff.
6. *S. W.*, I/5, pp. 667 ff.

in Christ. Therefore the church is not a union of individual believing Christians and is not sustained by the desire of these believing Christians to come together; it is rather the result of the genesis of the organism created and preserved through Christ and his spiritual presence. The same holds true for the right relationship to the confessions of the Fathers and their writings. The confessional writings are theology, and the witness of proclamation and theology belongs to the essential functions of the church as a spiritual community. Thus the symbols and confessions of faith are not regulations for faith and doctrine. They are not commandments about the *Credendum* [that which must be believed] but confessions about the *Creditum* [that which has been believed]. The Protestant principle of the radical distinction between the revelation of God and the word of man is also applied to the theological statements in preaching and in the confessional writings. Thus, the unity of the church is not established on the confessions, no matter how well formulated.

The Protestant symbols have their value and validity in the fact that they were the first declarations of the Protestant church. Like all human words, however, they are subject to historical development and change. They must be understood in terms of their own times; moreover, their value and validity must be recaptured through a new understanding of their doctrinal intent and their spirit; this cannot be accomplished by literalism. Within the Protestant church and its theology there can be no absolute formulation that is valid and obligatory for all times. Hence there must always be differing formulations; whether in fact there can still be heresy in the Protestant church is another question. Christians should be cautious with the charge of heresy in theological disputes. Sincere and vigorous discussion striving for the truth has the promise of finding it. The Holy Scripture is norm and guide for proclamation and theology. Critical questioning after truth in research and theology is required for the interpretation of Holy Scripture. Therefore, Schleiermacher constantly fought against finding a new confessional formulation for the union church because he feared, first of all, that a kind of third confession would arise in addition to the Lutheran and Reformed, and, second, because he adhered to his belief that the character of the union could not be laid down literally in binding doctrinal formulations.

Schleiermacher has in no way dismissed the confessional writings. They are for him the valuable testimony of the past and everyone who works with theology must recover these testimonies for himself by discovering the doctrinal intention of these confessional writers.

But only those freely convinced can grasp the intrinsic meaning of these confessional writings. He rejected all coercion in matters of faith and doctrine since it would only evoke hypocrisy which would deaden every sort of life. It is completely misleading to attribute to him the demand for an undogmatic Christianity. Schleiermacher wanted the witness of faith in proclamation and in theology to conform to the norm of Holy Scripture. When Schleiermacher was asked later in his life why he had opposed binding obligation to the confessions or had such critical reservations inasmuch as he himself had once subscribed to them, he answered that at his ordination he had in fact subscribed to the *Confessio Sigismundi*. He stated:

> What actually has astonished me is that neither of the two open letters has accused me of bearing false witness since surely the two gentlemen could know that at my ordination as a Reformed preacher I subscribed to the confession of the Elector Sigismund. But certainly they also knew that this subscription includes the qualifier, 'insofar as it corresponds with Holy Scripture,' — whereby every restrictive obligation again is set aside.[7]

Schleiermacher generally did not have much influence on the particular ecclesiastical policy for implementing the union. But he did do something to support the union in his own congregation. On December 6, 1820, with the agreement of Marheineke and Schleiermacher, the ratification of a union was proposed to the pastors and the church council, and on Palm Sunday, 1822, the celebration of the unification could take place. With Schleiermacher's cooperation a united hymnal for Berlin was produced.[8] Among the many confirmands who after the ensuing union found their way to Schleiermacher's congregation the most famous was young Bismarck in 1830.

1.   Schleiermacher and the Liturgical Dispute

The disputes about ecclesiastical polity in which Schleiermacher had become involved from 1814 until the end of his life did not focus on the questions of the union and the validity of the confessions alone; remarkably enough their real emotional center was found in the area of the liturgy. It is difficult for theologians and Protestant Christians of a later time to understand initially why the issue of

---

7. *S. W.*, I/5, p. 708.
8. *Über des Berliner Gesangbuch 1830*, *S. W.*, I/5, pp. 629 ff.

restructuring public worship could be carried on with such passion and with such appeals to the freedom of conscience. After all, the Augsburg Confession had already pointed out in Article 7 that the true unity of the church — i.e., faithful obedience in response to conscience — requires only the true proclamation of the gospel and the correct administration of the sacraments. The unity, uniformity, and solidarity of Christians in faith and in the Spirit of Christ do not require ceremonial and liturgical uniformity. Therefore, the differences in orders of worship cannot abolish religious community.

Nevertheless, divisions on the question of the liturgy were sharp in the first half of the nineteenth century. One would not really expect Schleiermacher to "go to the barricades" over the issue of the order for divine worship. Could the restructuring of public worship really lead to ruptures in theology and faith? Here some understanding must still be possible among Christians. Schleiermacher also would have been the last to oppose restructuring the order of worship. He was not a man of the Enlightenment who could regard the liturgy as unimportant and could dispense with all liturgical form. He came from the Moravian community. He loved the liturgical richness of the Moravians. The spiritual community of the Moravian Brethren in which the Spirit created living forms was constantly before him as the ideal for worship. That Schleiermacher did get involved in the quarrel was due to Schleiermacher's conception of the union as well as to the Prussian king's conception of his liturgical prerogative as sovereign.

At first the king had a quite liberal understanding of the matter. Court Chaplain Eylert, whose reports on the life of Friedrich Wilhelm III and his *Kulturpolitik* are surely not always reliable and are colored by the theology of the court, has probably accurately reported the original attitude of Friedrich Wilhelm III on the question of the sovereign's liturgical prerogative. In his work, *Portrait of Friedrich Wilhelm III*, he wrote that the king expressly forbade him to recommend a new liturgy to the common people on the grounds that the sovereign wanted it. Friedrich Wilhelm III wanted to issue no orders as sovereign in these matters and stated as a reason for his restraint that faith is the finest act of the soul. Above all, as an act of the individual, it cannot be commanded. "I have no right to give orders in this matter, and I am not Lord of the Church."[9]

---

9. R. E. Eylert, *Characterzüge Friedrich Wilhelms III*, vol. III, part I (Magedeburg, 1843–46), pp. 332–33.

Nevertheless there developed a literary quarrel that lasted for decades and a small war on ecclesiastical polity over the introduction of a new liturgy and over the question whether the sovereign could order a word-for-word, indeed, a letter-for-letter, adherence to a liturgy and a liturgical uniformity for the Evangelical church. The issue of the internal structure of the liturgy also played a role, but it was secondary compared to this fundamental problem. For Schleiermacher the question about the liturgy was bound up with the question about the consitution of the church. Schleiermacher insisted upon the independence of the church from the state. Time and again he appealed to Luther's doctrine of the two kingdoms and in the name of this basic Lutheran doctrine he called for an ecclesiastical constitution. For him only the presbyterial-synodal constitution was appropriate since that was the form of polity which best corresponded to his conception of the church and a free spiritual community. The polity of the church cannot be deduced from the Bible and the gospel but must correspond to the nature of the church.

This ecclesiastical community has, according to Schleiermacher, the right to determine freely its own liturgical order and form. It is a community of the Spirit. The Spirit must be able to fill the forms of the liturgy and the order of worship with life. This freedom of spiritual efficacy also includes the possibility that there may be many orders. The diversity of liturgical practices cannot negate the unity of the church.

On the other hand, Schleiermacher did not want arbitrariness and chaos. But it is not the state that can give form to the living organism of the church. This form must be determined by the church itself. Therefore Schleiermacher was dismayed that the sovereign and his advisors who had planned a presbyterial and synodal order, even if hesitatingly, put all these plans on ice after 1819. This decision was connected with the fact that after this time the struggle for a constitution aroused suspicions in the political realm and was persecuted outright as democratic demagoguery. Schleiermacher first wanted to have the ecclesiastical constitution so that the church could provide its own liturgical order. After 1819, however, the king no longer wanted to grant this to the church, and in 1822 the king ordered that the liturgy which he and his advisors had proposed should now be introduced. The king at first appealed to the clergy and their congregations to accept the order voluntarily. But he suffered a disappointment. Only a sixth of the Prussian clergy declared themselves ready to accept the king's liturgy. With that the king resolved to put an end to the liturgical chaos. Court Chaplain

Eylert reports verbatim one of the king's comments on this point: "Inasmuch as the reverend clergy are unable and unwilling, and since it is impossible to satisfy everybody, and since this divergence cannot continue to exist in one and the same Church, I will therefore exercise the liturgical rights granted to me just as did my forefathers."[10]

In contrast to his earlier convictions the king was now persuaded of the sovereign's liturgical prerogative. He was supported in this view by opportunistic professors and theologians. Professors Augusti and Delbrück presented the Roman Emperor Constantine and Charlemagne as historical proofs of this right. They earned by this only the scorn and ridicule of the knowledgeable Protestant theologians, including Schleiermacher. Schleiermacher was more impressed by the argument that the congregation had the right to set the liturgy. Some argued that after the removal of the Roman hierarchy during the Reformation period, the congregation, which actually had the authority to determine its order of worship, transferred the authority of church government to the prince as the *praecipuum membrum ecclesiae*. Schleiermacher, in turn, answered that the princes and lords did not thereby become bishops but at most guardians of the church. Such a guardian does not have the duty to make decisions about church government in a bishop's capacity; rather he has to guarantee and vouchsafe the freedom of the church to have its own independent government, helping it to perceive and find its own rights.

In contrast to other southern German princes, the Prussian king resolved immediately to impose a new liturgy upon the congregations through an official sovereign decree. At first he sought to secure the acceptance of the liturgy by the churches through moral influence and persuasion. But already political measures were taken so that in some places one could observe the phenomenon of "voluntary coercion." At first Schleiermacher ridiculed this development. Legend has it that it was Schleiermacher who coined the phrase that the new liturgy was introduced to the congregations on the wings of eagles — i.e., on the wings of the Red Order of the Eagles which were awarded to clergymen. Corresponding to this legend is the word which circulated among the common people: the award of the Prussian Order of the Eagle was not bestowed *propter acta*, but *propter agenda*.[11]

---

10. Ibid., p. 351.
11. Translator's note. *Agenda* in this pun was also the German word for liturgy.

Marheineke, Schleiermacher's colleague at the University of Berlin and Trinity Church, defended his sovereign's assumption of episcopal authority and liturgical prerogative, arguing that during the period of the Reformation the miraculous work of divine providence was active, indissolubly binding state and church together. Prelate Ammon of Dresden also stood up for the strict state-church principles of old Saxony. The Prussian king himself was most dignified. He himself took up the pen and in 1827 published "Luther in Relation to the Prussian Church Liturgy." This work subjected Schleiermacher to a cutting and harsh theological criticism.

At the same time Schleiermacher joined eleven other well-known Berlin clergymen in protesting to the consistory against the introduction of the liturgy in the churches. A heated dispute followed. The advisors of the king, even Minister Altenstein, were resolved to proceed against Schleiermacher and his friends with disciplinary action. Disciplinary proceedings were initiated against the "twelve apostles of Berlin." Nevertheless, the Prussian king was ultimately convinced that he could not carry out the suspension of Schleiermacher which was recommended by his ministers. The counsel of two men played an important role in the decision: that of his son Friedrich Wilhelm IV, who was then crown prince and later king, and also that of Minister of Commerce Matz who was much more moderate and understanding than the minister responsible for this area, von Altenstein.

Why did Schleiermacher so passionately contest the king's liturgical prerogative? It was not only dislike for the rather dilettantish way in which the king and his advisors put together a liturgy on the basis of the old Lutheran orders of worship, intending to make it appear as archaic as possible. The king was of the opinion that Luther was the highest authority and that even in liturgical matters every Christian would have to acknowledge Luther's authority. Schleiermacher objected that this new liturgy was more Catholic than what Luther actually wanted and that it even antedated him. It is not Lutheran for the court to govern the church, for the clergy to be commanded like lower bureaucrats and to be threatened with fines, and to ask of the congregations that they change their order of worship by supreme command. In his polemical writings he posed the question: "Luther I know, but who are you?"[12] And he saw the moment coming nearer when it would be a duty of conscience to leave the

---

12. Translator's note. See Acts 19:15 for the source of this pun.

church and attempt a new reformation on the basis of the freedom of doctrine, conscience, and worship.

Schleiermacher did not want to grant the ruler the authority to determine liturgical matters. He indicated that if his judgment departed from that of the ruler and authorities he would still have to claim that he was more capable of judging and had more thoroughly researched and investigated what could best serve to edify public worship. The minister found Schleiermacher's remarks so improper that he wanted to initiate legal proceedings against him. He hoped to disarm this resisting clergyman, and he became convinced that more than ever the Evangelical church needed to be firmly controlled. In his writing Schleiermacher answered with the later often quoted assertion: "The Reformation still goes on!" He meant that the true spirit of the Reformation does not live in the strict uniformity of liturgical prescriptions; a new reformation is required to reform the hidden Catholicism still prevailing in the Evangelical church. This expression — "The Reformation still goes on" — is found in Schleiermacher's adroit and witty critique of 1827, *A Dialogue Between Two Thoughtful Evangelical Christians Concerning the Essay "Luther in Relation to the New Prussian Liturgy": A Last or Maybe Only a First Word*.[13]

The dispute was finally concluded in 1829. The government decided to allow, through liturgical commissions, certain peculiarities of previous orders of worship among congregations in individual Prussian provinces. Schleiermacher was assured that he could utilize an extract of the liturgy prescribed by the king and that he was not bound to it word for word. The consistory ordered its introduction on April 12, 1829, and the king decreed the introduction of the liturgy by an order of the cabinet on April 19. Schleiermacher gave an explanation for the record with which the official minister, von Altenstein, generally agreed in a letter to the superintendents. Schleiermacher took the liberty of employing an abbreviated liturgy and expressed the hope that after an administration as long as his own the authorities would not fear that he would misuse such freedom and introduce something alien into public worship. He then demanded to be freed from making the sign of the cross prescribed in the liturgy. He did not recite the Apostles' Creed. He also declined to offer prayers with his back to the congregation and facing the altar because his conscience would thus bind him. What Schleiermacher

---

13. *Gespräch zweier selbstüberlegender evangelischer Christen über die Schrift "Luther in Bezug auf die neue preussische Agende," ein letztes Wort oder ein erstes*, 1827, *S. W.*, I/5, p. 625.

presumably meant by this was that he was not a priestly mediator between God and the congregation, but a servant of the congregation and a member of the church as a community of the Spirit and hence he must turn to the congregation when praying. He wanted to avoid everything reminiscent of priestly conduct in the Roman mass. Thus Schleiermacher had saved a certain degree of liturgical freedom for himself personally and also for his congregation. But in the long run he still had yielded to the will of the king.

Jonas later came to the following conclusion:

> The Berlin opposition — and specifically Schleiermacher — was very harshly criticized by some for having begun the battle and by others for not having pursued it faithfully. I, too, wish that Schleiermacher had gone farther. But I challenge those who would deny him the purest motives. He considered the issue of the liturgy important enough to battle for it and he led the battle with courage and intelligence; he did not regard it important enough to leave the national church on account of it when the principle he advocated did not win, but was also not defeated. Whoever considers this last an important result for the then existing relations must thank Schleiermacher if he wants at all to be just.[14]

B. THE PREACHER

In evaluating Schleiermacher's lifework his accomplishment as a preacher and the contribution of his preaching within his total lifework is often overlooked. In purely quantitative terms the scope of his published sermons accounts for approximately a third of the collected edition of his works.

He felt himself called to be a preacher and happily committed himself to this vocation in all periods of his life. His friends even spoke of his engaging enthusiasm for the pulpit.[15] With great seriousness and inner joy he acknowledged in 1808, as the chaplain of Berlin's Charité: "I rather consider the position of the preacher as one of the most noble, capable of being worthily filled only by a truly religious, virtuous, and serious nature; never of my own will would I exchange it for another."[16] In the later period of his life, at the grave of his son Nathanael, he declared: "I always wanted nothing but to be a servant of the divine word with a joyful spirit

---

14. *Monatsschrift für die unierte evangelische Kirche*, vol. 3 (1848), p. 481.
15. *Briefe*, III, p. 376.
16. Ibid., p. 284.

and heart."[17]   A great many of his friends regarded Schleiermacher's preaching as his best work.   This was Friedrich Schlegel's judgment about the first volume of sermons published in 1801: "Did you know that I am very much inclined to regard them as your best work? . . .   They are filled with such peace and are free of every appearance of affectation."[18]

For over forty years — from 1790 to 1834 — Schleiermacher occupied the pulpit nearly every Sunday; at Landesberg, the Charité in Berlin, Stolp, the academic services at Halle, and Trinity Cathedral in Berlin.   The already greatly overworked Berlin professor also preached from 1809 to 1834 almost every Sunday at Trinity Cathedral either at the main service at 9:00 or at the 8:00 early service.

His preaching did not only affect his listeners directly; it also influenced the readers of his collected sermons, which were at that time a popular form of literature.   During his life Schleiermacher himself published seven collections of his sermons between 1801 and 1833.   They were brought together in the first two volumes of sermons in his *Collected Works*.   In addition some copies of his sermons, which he himself could only edit superficially, were published between the years 1831 and 1833.   They are found in Volume III of the collected edition.   Also, individual sermons are included in Volume IV of the collected edition.   Most of the sermons in Volumes I to IV are thematic sermons delivered at the main service of worship.   In the early service during his time at Berlin, Schleiermacher preferred an interpretation of Holy Scripture, which some have imprecisely described as homilies. Actually they are not homilies. Rather, Schleiermacher treated continuous larger sections of single biblical books from a specific viewpoint.   Volumes V to X contain copies of such exegetical studies of the Gospel of Mark, the Letter to the Colossians, the Acts, the Letter to the Philippians, and an exposition of the Gospel of John, Schleiermacher's favorite. Despite this large bulk of ten volumes not all of Schleiermacher's sermons are included — e.g., neither the confirmation sermon which he delivered in 1830 for his confirmands that included Bismarck, nor Schleiermacher's last sermon before his death is included. Schleiermacher research should long have seen its task in preserving these remains from dispersion by including them in an eleventh volume.   It is regrettable that this has not yet been done.

---

17. *S. W.*, II/4, p. 838.
18. *Briefe*, III, p. 292.

Most of the sermons were not published in the same form in which they were delivered. According to his own admission (in the Preface to the first volume of sermons in 1801), Schleiermacher was accustomed since the time at Schlobitten not to write out his sermons in advance except for notes on a few pieces of paper. He wrote down many sermons only after he had preached them. His preparation consisted of a thorough study of the basic ideas, structure, and organization down to the smallest detail which he memorized. Schleiermacher defended himself against the charge that such preparation was negligent. On the other hand, he was careful not to make it into a rule for others. For publication purposes he further reconstructed and expanded the orally given sermon, since a sermon that is read can and may be more detailed than the delivered one.

What, then, was characteristic and specifically new and original about Schleiermacher as a preacher? His sermons signify as much a new start in the history of preaching as his theology did within the history of theology. However, what is "new" is difficult to discern because his sermons underwent development and the originality of his manner of preaching only appeared gradually.

The first volume of sermons of 1801 unmistakably bears the traces of his Enlightenment past, i.e., of his passage through Enlightenment theology and thought. Thus they are, in the sense of the Enlightenment, moral sermons. The higher life they proclaim is the moral life, such as, for instance, Kantian ethics demands in opposition to eudaemonism and the utilitarian philosophy of the Enlightenment. The young preacher spoke in the name of religion and conscience. Both of these were for him identical with the demands of understanding and prudence. Nonetheless there was a deeper tone in these moral tractates. Morality does not live out of itself but has a religious soul. The sermons are not, as Brunner and other critics have charged, mere religious adornments of philosophical treatises. Trillhaas is entirely right in saying that a man as serious as Schleiermacher was conscious of the difficult situation of being in the pulpit. That is why he gladly made himself available for this service. Hence his sermons should be understood on their own terms and examined as to their theological intention and especially as to their concern with proclamation.

What, then, was the particular theological concern which led beyond the Enlightenment? Very early the young preacher opposed the eudaemonism, the anthropocentrism, the self-satisfaction, and smugness of Enlightenment piety. Unbelief was for him irreverence toward God; it was the defiance of the self-righteous "enlightener" who disregarded God's holy law. Faith leads to self-knowledge and humility, and this humility grants inner peace and serenity. But especially he relates the activity of God to one's own daily life. The history of God with man should become the history of each man's heart.

Of all Schleiermacher scholars it was Wehrung who particularly attempted to compare the *Speeches* and the sermons. He believed one could detect in the *Speeches* more of the Moravian heritage and in the sermons more of the passage through the Enlightenment. The *Speeches* are more advanced in theological understanding than the sermons. The breakthrough to the Christian doctrine of redemption comes in the Fifth Speech. The separation of the finite from the infinite is understood as sin, and there develops a readiness for redemption through Christ. All of this is not yet present in the sermons in the same fashion.

The sermons emphasize much more strongly the moral content of the Christian faith than do the *Speeches* which ask for a piety free from metaphysics and ethics. It is nevertheless clear how the preacher was also about to overcome the Enlightenment and Kant's morality. The world, sensuous finitude, is not eternal. Even the laws of nature are not eternal. "God did not make even the worlds for eternity."[19] Man is filled with the question of God, for his life stands under the threat posed by the transitoriness of the finite. The sermons arrive at the submissive tone of humility before God, the deepening self-judgment, the peace and serenity which spring from trust in God.

The patriotic and political sermons comprise another stage of development. Schleiermacher himself attributed a very definite meaning to them and considered this form of preaching a special calling and challenge during the Wars of Liberation. Unfortunately the greater part of these sermons from 1813 was not published. Dilthey, Schleiermacher's biographer, gave his patriotic sermons a special place in the history of the Protestant sermon. He considered Schleiermacher "the first political preacher in the grand style produced by German Christianity."[20] Furthermore, Dilthey as well as Holstein, the political philosopher, viewed not only Schleiermacher's political sermons but also his political ethics as a new stage in the development of Protestant political thinking.

Schleiermacher overcame the restrictions of the older Protestant social ethics with its reliance on the idea of state authority and the

---

19. *S. W.*, II/1, p. 66.
20. Dilthey, *Leben Schleiermachers*, vol. I, 2d ed., p. 829.

private morality of its subjects, and placed social and political life under the claim of a new form of Protestant piety. Certainly Schleiermacher had a new conception of the state which differed from the older Protestant conceptions of authority. For him the state was a community of law and culture in the sense understood by transcendental ethical philosophy. That which is new in his political sermons, however, does not lie in his view of the state, but in the new religious and theological foundation that he laid for political ethics. It was Dilthey's view that another religious motif, originating in Reformed Protestantism, came to expression here in Schleiermacher. It is an active and dynamic motif directed toward political action, whereas the older Protestant Lutheranism was still too exclusively oriented toward personal edification of the individual in God's redemptive will, toward the experience of grace, and toward justification and the continuance of sanctification; in social ethics Lutheranism left the leadership up to the state authority, and required of the citizen submission to God's redemptive will and passivity in political affairs. Schleiermacher carried the development present in his own Reformed church even farther. "In his ethics are found the resources for bringing the aggressive spirit of Reformed religion into the right relationship with the other motifs of Christianity."[21]

The basic religious mood of his political preaching was not the passivity of absolute dependence, but a profound faith in providence that conveys the impulse toward political activity on behalf of the nation. Political activity, like all cultural activity, is according to Schleiermacher's philosophy of culture essentially and most profoundly moral activity; it is in political activity that the responsibility of man to become lord of the earth and to form life in accordance with moral principles, is manifested. This faith in providence is "the apprehension that the law, which rules in devout men, and the power, which guides the whole range of human concern, are one and the same."[22]

God, the Lord of history, opens the eyes of the religious man to his responsibility of cooperating in actualizing the dominion of God and the moral order willed by him. God is not the infinite. He is not an abstract absolute totality; rather, God is the bearer of the values of history. In God both the law to which nations are subjected and the single individual, both fate and character, are one. Only he is eternally secured who lives a life obedient to the will and law of God. For whoever lives according to the will of God is liberated

21. Ibid., p. 830.
22. Ibid., p. 821.

from the fear of men and death; no longer does he cling to earthly
goods. He has renounced temporal goods that he might commit
himself to eternal goods. It would be wrong to see in this belief
in providence only a variant of the objective idealist's conception
of moral order. The religious content of the political sermons in
this historically critical hour is deeper and more vital than that
previously found in the sermons from the first period of Schleiermacher's youth.

This belief in providence is theologically and christologically
grounded and is not simply ethical optimism. In his *The Christian
Faith* Schleiermacher subsequently thought through this problem
much more thoroughly and theoretically. His opponent is the effete
eudaemonism of a spiritless age; it is despair and human anxiety.
The man who loves the world and not God is characterized with
Reformed sternness as a sinner. The order of the world has its
ground in God the Creator. This order of the world rests upon
the religious idea of the dominion of the Spirit over the finite, over
flesh. However, this moral idea of the Lordship of God, which man
as its organ must serve, does not stand simply by itself but is bound
up with its christological foundation; God, the Lord of history, is
the Father of Jesus Christ. He has given Christ power over the
hearts of men, ordaining him for his great work of redemption. Hence
the manifestation of the divine Spirit in Christ and in the living
community created through him is the "ultimate world-forming
power"; this is the way that Schleiermacher subsequently formulated
it in § 169 of *The Christian Faith*.

The patriotic sermons already show signs of this dual foundation
of the belief in the Lordship of God in history, which resulted from
belief in the Creator and Providence, and above all the belief in
redemption. The political sermons were not meant to promote
politics but rather to interpret the historical fate of the people and
its politics in relation to God. According to the lectures in practical
theology, the preacher should not promote politics from the pulpit,
although he should "make politics religious," i.e., the political life
also stands under the law of God.[23]

Because of his understanding of history and his faith in redemption
and perfection Schleiermacher had to proclaim not only the judgment
and the law of God, but also the promise of God to his own as well
as other nations. His call for repentance was directed to the people
in order to depict for them the disguised blessing of Prussia's defeat

---

23. *S. W.*, I/13, pp. 209 ff.

in 1806. It is God's judgment on cowardice. The grievous errors of Prussian politics, including among other things the unjust division of Poland, are therein chastised. Only when the people submit to the holy God and his law will they again be able to overcome national calamity. The reconstruction of the state is only possible through such ultimate moral and religious power.

In these powerful sermons of 1806 to 1814 the theme of faithful renunciation of temporal goods and surrender to the eternal emerges; the fear of God overcomes fear of death and fear of man. Through Schleiermacher this idea generally became a fundamental motif for the political ethics of liberal Protestantism. For this idea Schleiermacher chose the formulation: "We — we who are Christians — fear God and nothing else in the world." In his lectures on aesthetics he referred to the fact that he had taken over this formulation from Voltaire, who first developed it in his tragedy, *Calas*.[24] This view was expressed also in the sermon Schleiermacher gave for his confirmand Bismarck; Bismarck in turn — perhaps without actually recalling his confirmation but still emphatically influenced by this motif of Protestant political ethics — reaffirmed it in the well-known declaration before the *Reichstag* in the 1880s: "We Germans fear God and nothing else in the world."

In 1933, in his incisive and comprehensive analysis of Schleiermacher's sermons, Trillhaas rightly called attention to the fact that these sermons by Schleiermacher are stamped by their particular historical time. It is doubtless a rule for political preaching that it find its specific but also limited application within its own historical hour. For those of us who come later the decisions of that earlier time appear relatively simple. The fronts were unambiguous. According to the Christians of that time war was morally justified as liberation from national subjugation by the dictator Napoleon. The battle for the freedom of the nation is a moral duty and a service to the divine ordering of the world. Schleiermacher later posed the critical question of whether the revival of Christian piety had been genuine during the wars of liberation or whether the national enthusiasm did not also contain a strong element of desire for retaliation and other such worldly motives.

During the period of the Restoration and persecution of the demagogues he held fast to the ideals of the period of reform in Prussia and stood up fearlessly for the basic views of his political

---

24. *Aesthetik*, S. W., III/7, p. 247: *"Je crains Dieu, mais hors je n'ai point d'autre crainte."*

ethics.   The religious basis of his political ethics was made even
more profound and comprehensive because faith in God the Creator
and Lord of history and the faith in God who through Christ redeems
mankind from sin and death were united in a close union in Schleiermacher's preaching and theology.

The earthly love of creation theology was transformed and completed
by the glorious new structure of love in Christ.   Objective idealism's
conception of life is contained in these ideas, but it is transposed
into a Christian context.   The Christian and the human mutually
illumine and vivify each other.   The Christian element becomes
increasingly strong in the course of his life.   But even as Christ
is the firstborn of many brothers in Schleiermacher's Christology,
so too the ethos which arises from the good news of what God has
done in Christ is bound to the historical faith of the doctrine of
creation.

On the basis of this inquiry into the development of Schleiermacher's
sermons, which stand in close analogy to the development of his
total theological conception, it is also easier to recognize that which
is typically original in Schleiermacher's sermons.   This uniqueness
grows out of the underlying assumption of his sermons.   The
preacher turns to the church as the community of Jesus Christ which
continually lives in communion with the Redeemer.   It is not the
empirical church but the church of faith and the Spirit which is
active in the empirical church.   Thus Schleiermacher's sermon is
no orthodox moral sermon.   It is also no moral rearmament or
fortification.   It is the confession and witness of the Christian community which enjoys a living relationship with Christ and which,
through the preacher, brings this relationship to expression in
"representative   communication."   Schleiermacher   had   already
formulated this meaning of the sermon in his new conception of
the task of the sermon in § 280 of *Brief Outline of Theological Study*.
It states: "Edification in Christian worship emphatically rests upon
the communication of pious self-consciousness which has developed
into thought."

For contemporary understanding this formulation stands in need
of interpretation.   We take offense at his basic concepts.   The
content of the sermon should be the gospel and the word of God,
not religous self-consciousness.   The sermon should not merely be
communication, but proclamation.   But Schleiermacher must be
understood from within his own time and in the context of his own
particular language.   What he meant by religious self-consciousness
cannot be understood in psychological categories.   It is wrong to

see in this religious self-consciousness only a psychological phenomenon. Moreover, religious self-consciousness, even when it has been conceptualized, is not logical thought. In any case, logical-conceptual formation is not the decisive thing. Even less can one grasp it with sociological categories and regard it as an ideology, which as ideology would support the human intuition of life. Religious self-consciousness is the becoming aware of the divine Spirit in human life; it is the manifestation of the divine Will and the divine Spirit in the process of the Spirit's growing dominion over the flesh as the ungodly element.

The second original aspect in Schleiermacher's sermons is related to the fact that he introduced a new hermeneutic. Every motif of religious self-consciousness should be thought through theologically. However, this reflection should present the Christian kerygma in its totality. Every particular idea is to be integrated into the whole of Christian proclamation. It is this context that Schleiermacher sought to express conceptually and that he tried to raise to the knowledge and certainty of faith through progressive dialectical discourse. Hence it is understandable that those who heard his sermons were so profoundly affected by them. He dispensed with the sensational and sentimental, with edifying stories and illustrative tales. All rhetorical effects that usually play a major role in devotional and revival sermons are missing. Nonetheless he elevated the single ideas within the sermon to the level of the full context of the Christian gospel.

The third characteristic of Schleiermacher's originality is the manner in which he bound together the Christian and the human, the gospel and the concrete life. The way to God and the gospel is not alongside the daily human life but leads through it and into it. One should not too quickly defame this as a cultural Protestantism. Whatever is derived from Christ is Christian for Schleiermacher; however, the intensification and fulfillment of the human also belongs to that which is Christian. Without a doubt the strength as well as the weakness of his preaching lies in the way he connects the gospel with concrete life. The question should be raised: Did Schleiermacher not prematurely transfigure life into something Christian, and, above all, did he not too quickly accept a Christianizing of the daily life of culture?

The fourth typical aspect is his molding of the sermon into a work of art. We are not referring here to the aesthetic beauty of the sermon, but rather to the shaping of the sermon according to the rules of content and style in rhetoric. The rules of classical rhetoric, as described by Plato and Aristotle, were carried over to the modern world and filled with new life. For both Plato and Schleiermacher all rhetoric is guidance of the soul. The major requirements of rhetoric which must be fulfilled are the following: (1) The sermon should give knowledge of the true nature of the subject, i.e., the essence and truth of Christian proclamation; (2) It should give knowledge of the nature of the human soul. The soul should not be pressured and coerced; rather the soul should be filled with the impulse to strive for the appointed goal and should be accompanied on the way to this goal;   (3) The proper outward order should be found in the mode of speaking.

Diverse ideas should be held together within a self-contained movement of ideas, which progresses on the basis of its own inner dynamic and which is directed to a specific goal. The sermon is a self-contained act that invites the hearer spiritually to follow as well as to think through its meaning, and by means of this living experience of participation it communicates to the hearer the feeling of an inward advance and elevation. For Schleiermacher the highest form of preaching was a sermon for the educated congregation of Trinity Church. But even ordinary listeners received some benefit from his sermons. J. Konrad has held, in an analysis of Schleiermacher's sermons on marriage, that Schleiermacher preached on "two levels."[25] He could do this because his sermons contained a *cantus firmus* which gripped not only the educated but also the common hearers. In Schleiermacher's sermons this *cantus firmus* was the concentration on the centrality of the living Christian community with the Redeemer within his congregation.

25. J. Konrad, *Die evangelische Predigt* (Bremen, 1963), p. 179.

VI.

HOME AND FAMILY, PERSONAL LIFE
AND DEATH

If — according to Fichte's aphorism — a philosopher's philosophy depends upon what kind of a man he is, the analogy also holds for Schleiermacher's theology and philosophy. The Berlin professor was no erudite eccentric, system builder, and book writer. He was above all a virtuoso of friendship and sociability, a genius of understanding, someone open to the world who enjoyed traveling and who annually took trips, in his later years with his family, to Rügen, in the Riesengebirge, to the Rhein, Salzburg and Tyrol, to England, Sweden, and Denmark.

A cynical aphorism maintains that for the valet there are no heroes. Schleiermacher had nothing to fear from examinations of his private life. Through the correspondence he left behind, the intimacy of his private life lies more open to us than that of many other renowned people. Of course, the greater part of his correspondence with Eleonore Grunow and Henriette Herz and his letters to Friedrich Schlegel (who apparently lost them during his restless life) is missing. It is unfortunate that his extensive correspondence was not published with more precision and unity. The four volumes of letters published by Jonas and Dilthey between 1858 and 1863 are too inexact and too incomplete for today's needs. The correspondence with J. Christian Gass and Count Dohna as well as with A. W. Schlegel was also subsequently published. A valuable supplement is found in the three volumes published by Heinrich Meisner, for many years the director of the German literary archives in Berlin. These volumes contain Schleiermacher's correspondence with his fiancée and other letters to family and friends and carry the title *Schleiermacher the Man*.[1]

From his youth Schleiermacher had been in poor health. He was nearsighted and also bothered by stomach disorders. His family

---

1. Heinrich Meisner, ed., *Schleiermacher als Mensch: Familien- und Freundes-briefe*, (Gotha, 1922, 1923).

physician, Dr. Meier, attempted to cure him through natural remedies. He was afforded considerable relief by magnetopathic treatments by the physician, Dr. Wolfart. This then modern therapy had an unfortunate influence on Schleiermacher inasmuch as he became tolerant of parapsychology — which he ordinarily critically opposed — and permitted Professor Fischer, a female spiritualist, in his home as a friend of his wife, although for years he sought to demonstrate to her that her prophecy and consultation with spirits were wrong.

In addition to the correspondence between the engaged and later married couple and various biographical contributions by friends, we gain insight into Schleiermacher's family life from the autobiography of his stepson, Ehrenfried von Willich.[2] He greatly admired his stepfather and was critical of his mother and her weaknesses; he praised his father particularly because he sincerely cherished and supported his wife even with her weaknesses and faults out of respect for the individuality of the marriage partner.

In May, 1809, Schleiermacher married the widow of his friend, Army Chaplain von Willich, who died in a typhoid epidemic during the siege of Stralsund in 1807. The young widow, née von Mühlenfels, was the daughter of Lieutenant Colonel von Mühlenfels and Pauline von Campagne, a descendant of a French Huguenot family. Henriette von Mühlenfels was betrothed at the age of fifteen, became a mother at seventeen, and a widow at nineteen. Through his friendship with von Willich, Schleiermacher developed a very close attachment to both him and his wife, and the young wife who had lost both parents very early in life respected Schleiermacher like a father. Henriette Herz and Charlotte von Kathen, good friends themselves and both acquainted with Schleiermacher as well as with the von Willichs — they were even related to them — apparently arranged with feminine ingenuity that Schleiermacher would meet Henriette von Mühlenfels at Sargard in 1808 during a journey to Rügen which he had undertaken on behalf of political friends; they subsequently became engaged.

The difference in their ages, approximately twenty years, was considerable. Finally in May, 1809, when Schleiermacher was appointed to the post of preacher at Trinity Cathedral, the wedding took place. The couple moved into the living quarters for the preacher of Trinity Cathedral at 4 *Kanonierstrasse* at the corner of *Taubenstrasse*, where the young bride found an already well-organized

---

2. E. von Willich, *Aus Schleiermachers Hause. Jugenderinnerungen seines Stiefsohnes* (Berlin, 1909).

household directed with great efficiency by Schleiermacher's half-sister, Nanny, who remained with them until she left her brother's home to become the wife of Ernst Moritz Arndt. During the summer Schleiermacher's family moved to a dwelling in the *Tiergarten* in the vicinity of today's *Bendlerstrasse*, which at that time was a quite undeveloped rural area.

Each was very devoted to the other in his or her own distinct way. Not only was the difference in age noticeable but also the spiritual and religious attitude of the young wife differed greatly from Schleiermacher's. In accordance with her narrower pietistic religion she preferred to attend the sermons of Gossner rather than her husband's since she was apparently not always able to follow his ideas. In later years it was particularly disturbing that she came completely and uncritically under the influence of her friend Madame Fischer. She considered the parapsychological appearances in the life of Mrs. Fischer, her visions and prophecies, as something sacred, as a special form of revelation. She even took Mrs. Fischer and her children into her household. Schleiermacher bore all this because he loved his wife and because he respected the independent development of individuality in his wife as well as his children.

Both parents were filled with deep sorrow when they lost their nine-year-old son, Nathanael, after being stricken with diphtheria. The burial sermon, which Schleiermacher himself delivered and subsequently wrote down in his distinctive handwriting (it is still available in Schleiermacher's literary remains), affords us deep insight into his inner life. He disdained all human and superficial consolations at the graveside of his son in whom he had placed so much hope. "Thus I depend for my consolation and my hope solely on the modest and yet so very rich word of Scripture: 'It does not yet appear what we shall be; but we know that when he appears we shall be like him, for we shall see him as he is,'[3] and upon the powerful prayer of the Lord: 'Father, I will that they also, whom thou hast given me, be with me where I am'."[4]

The author of the *Soliloquies* at one time pledged himself to eternal youth. Of course this eternal youth was for him not a biological phenomenon but the consciousness of inner freedom. He resolved that the pulse of his inner life would remain vital until death. "I pledge myself to eternal youth" is the wish that the inner freedom and joy of life and action would, through the dominion of spirit

---

3. 1 John 3:2.
4. John 17:24.

over flesh, permit him to overcome the finitude and sensuousness of life. This wish was fulfilled for Schleiermacher. While still in the midst of his creative work death came to him February 12, 1834. He delivered his last sermon Sunday, February 2, 1834, and his last lecture Thursday, February 6. On that same Thursday he appeared for the last time at a session of the Academy hoarse and with a terrible cold, so that von Raumer reprimanded him for having come at all. Thursday night a severe case of pneumonia developed from which he died Wednesday, February 12, 1834. Under his picture by A. Hüssener, Schleiermacher's own words stand as motto: "I have always wished to die while in full possession of my faculties, seeing death surely and irrevocably approach, without surprise or deception."

As the pneumonia developed Schleiermacher recognized the seriousness of the hour and expected his death. He went into this final hour with the courage and determination of faithful acceptance and firm hope. For him death was the fulfillment of life because communion with Christ and its completion was the fulfillment of his own life. His wife described the hour of his death: he had his wife read some spiritual songs by the friend of his youth, Albertini, and as he felt his end coming he called his household to him to celebrate the Lord's Supper together. He gave the bread and wine to his wife, her friend Mrs. Fischer, his stepson Lommatzsch, using the biblical words of institution from 1 Corinthians 11 and then added: "To these words of Scripture I hold fast. They are the foundation of my faith." After the blessing he again looked steadily at each one there and affirmed: "In this love and communion we will remain one." With this, death overtook him. His children were brought in, and the Holy Communion was brought to a close by distributing the already consecrated elements to the children kneeling at the bedside of the dead man.

In his eulogy Steffens reported still another form of Schleiermacher's words introducing the Lord's Supper: "Whoever like myself seeks salvation, believing in Christ's redeeming death, will enjoy the Holy Supper with me."[5]

His death moved the entire population of Berlin. The outpouring of sympathy was a kind of spontaneous public mourning. As the long funeral procession made up of professors and students, administrators and friends, moved for several hours through the city

5. F. Strauss, F. A. Pischon, H. Steffens, *Drei Reden am Tage der Bestattung des weiland Professors der Theologie und Predigers Herrn Dr. Schleiermacher* (Berlin, 1834), p. 35.

from the house of mourning to the cemetery on *Bergmannstrasse* thousands of Berliners filled the streets. The enthusiastic and exultant Bettina von Arnim spoke of hundreds of thousands expressing their sympathy. The sober historian von Ranke estimated the number of mourners to be twenty to thirty thousand Berliners. Pischon, Schleiermacher's student and former assistant minister, spoke at the grave; Schleiermacher had himself designated Pischon for this service. The eulogy in the academic service at the university was given by Heinrich Steffens, the old friend from the years at Halle, who only two years earlier had renewed his friendship with Schleiermacher when he was recalled to Berlin as a professor. His colleague Marheineke preached the memorial service at Trinity Cathedral the following Sunday. In his reminiscences Steffens reported: "Never has a funeral similar to his taken place. It was not something arranged but a completely unconscious, natural outpouring of mourning love, an inner boundless feeling which gripped the entire city and gathered about his grave; these were hours of inward unity such as have never been seen in a metropolis of modern times."

It is noteworthy — and for many of Schleiermacher's critics incomprehensible — that according to his wife's account he offered wine in the chalice to his household but water to himself. This might be explained by the fact that his physician had forbidden him the use of wine and Schleiermacher strictly followed his instructions. But then Schleiermacher was also of the opinion that according to their custom the Jews would mix wine with water during meals and for this reason he held that Christ had offered his disciples wine to which water had been added. From this he deduced the right to celebrate the Lord's Supper with water and wine.

BIBLIOGRAPHY

1. Collections:

   Friedrich Schleiermachers sämmtliche Werke. Edited by Ludwig Jonas, Alexander Schweitzer, Friedrich Lücke et al. Berlin: Reimer, 1835–1864.

   Three divisions:
   I. Theological subjects, vols. 1–13 (9 and 10 lacking)
   II. Sermons, vols. 1–10
   III. Philosophical subjects, vols. 1–9.

   Schleiermachers Werke: Auswahl in vier Bänden. Edited by O. Braun and D. J. Bauer. Leipzig: Meiner, 1911.

2. Letters:

   Aus Schleiermachers Leben in Briefen. Edited by Wilhelm Dilthey and Ludwig Jonas. Berlin: Reimer, vols. I–II (1860), vols. III–IV (1861–63).

   The Life of Schleiermacher as Unfolded in His Autobiography and Letters. Translated by Frederica Rowan. London: Smith, Elder and Co., 1860.

   Schleiermacher als Mensch. Sein Werden und Wirken. Edited by Heinrich Meisner. Gotha, 1922–23.

   Briefe Schleiermachers. Edited by Hermann Mulert. Berlin, 1923.

3. Selected Critical Editions and Translations:

   Dialektik, aus Schleiermachers handschriftlichen Nachlasse. Edited by Ludwig Jonas. In *Friedrich Schleiermachers sämmtliche Werke,* III/4, 2. Berlin: Reimer, 1839.

   Friedrich Schleiermachers Dialektik. Edited by Rudolf Odebrecht. Leipzig: J. C. Hinrichs, 1942.

   Über die Religion: Reden an die Gebildeten unter ihren Verächtern. Critical edition by G. C. B. Pünjer. Braunschweig: C. A. Schwetschke & Son, 1879.

   On Religion: Speeches to Its Cultured Despisers. Translated by John Oman. London, 1893. Harper Torchbook edition, New York: Harper & Row, 1958.

On Religion. Translated by Terrence Tice. Research in Theology, Ser. No. 1. Richmond, Va.: John Knox Press, 1969.

Schleiermachers Weihnachtsfeier: Ein Gespräch. Edited by Hermann Mulert. Philosophische Bibliothek, Vol. 117. Leipzig, 1908.

Christmas Eve: Dialogue on the Incarnation. Translated by Terrence Tice. Richmond, Va.: John Knox Press, 1967.

Friedrich Schleiermacher: Monologen nebst den Vorarbeiten. Critical edition by Friedrich Michael Schiele. Leipzig: Dürr'sche Buchhandlung, 1902. Expanded by Hermann Mulert. Leipzig: Meiner, 1914.

Schleiermacher's Soliloquies. Translated by H. L. Friess. Chicago: Open Court, 1926.

F. D. E. Schleiermacher, Hermeneutik: Nach den Handschriften. Critical edition by Heinz Kimmerle. Heidelberg: Carl Winter-Universitätsverlag, 1959. Original edition by F. Lücke. *Friedrich Schleiermachers sämmtliche Werke*, I/7. Berlin: Reimer, 1838.

Schleiermachers Kurze Darstellung des theologischen Studiums. Critical edition by Heinrich Scholz. Leipzig: A. Deichert, 1910; Hildesheim: G. Olms, 1961.

Brief Outline of the Study of Theology. Translated by W. Farrer. Edinburgh, 1850.

Brief Outline on the Study of Theology. Translated by Terrence Tice. Richmond, Va.: John Knox Press, 1966.

Der Christliche Glaube nach den Grundsätzen der evangelischen Kirche im Zusammenhange dargestellt. Critical edition by Martin Redeker. Berlin: Walter de Gruyter, 1960.

The Christian Faith. Translation of second edition by H. R. Mackintosh and J. S. Stewart. Edinburgh: T. & T. Clark, 1928, 1948. Harper Torchbook edition, New York: Harper & Row, 1963.

Schleiermachers Sendschreiben über seine Glaubenslehre an Lücke. Edited by Hermann Mulert. Giessen: Alfred Töpelmann, 1908.

Friedrich Schleiermachers Grundriss der philosophischen Ethik. Edited by A. Twesten. Berlin, 1841.

Entwurf eines Systems der Sittenlehre. Edited by A. Schweizer. *Friedrich Schleiermachers sämmtliche Werke*, III/5. Berlin: Reimer, 1835.

Ungedruckte Predigten Schleiermachers. Edited by Johannes Bauer. Leipzig, 1909.

4. Biographies:

Dilthey, Wilhelm. *Leben Schleiermachers*, Vol. I. Berlin, 1870. Second edition edited by Hermann Mulert. Berlin: Vereinigung wissenschaftlicher Verleger, 1922. Vol. II, *Schleiermachers Philosophie und Theologie*. Edited by Martin Redeker. Berlin, 1966.

——————. "Denkmale der inneren Entwicklung Schleiermachers erläutert durch kritische Untersuchungen." Appendix to Dilthey's *Leben Schleiermachers*. Berlin: Reimer, 1870.

——————. "Schleiermacher." *Gesammelte Schriften*, IV. Stuttgart: Tübner, 1921.

Kantzenbach, Friedrich W. *Friedrich Daniel Ernst Schleiermacher in Selbstzeugnissen*. Rowohlts Bildmonographien. Hamburg, 1967.

Meisner, Heinrich. *Schleiermachers Lehrjahre*. Edited by Hermann Mulert. Berlin and Leipzig, 1934.

Meyer, E. R. *Schleiermachers und C. G. von Brinkmanns Gang durch die Brüdergemeinde*. Leipzig, 1908.

Mulert, Hermann. *Schleiermacher*. Religionsgeschichtliche Volksbücher. Tübingen, 1918.

Schenkel, Daniel. *Friedrich Schleiermacher*. Elberfeld, 1868.

5. Selected Secondary Studies:

Bartelheimer, Wilhelm. *Schleiermacher und die gegenwärtige Schleiermacherkritik: eine Untersuchung über den Subjectivismus*. Leipzig: J. C. Hinrichs, 1931.

Barth, Karl. *Protestant Thought*. New York: Harper & Row, 1959.

——————. *Die Theologie und die Kirche*. Munich: Chr. Kaiser, 1928.

Bender, Wilhelm. *Schleiermachers Theologie*. Nördlingen: C. H. Beck'sche Buchhandlung, 1876.

Brandt, Richard. *The Philosophy of Schleiermacher*. New York: Harper & Row, 1941.

Brunner, Emil. *Die Mystik und das Wort*. Tübingen: J. C. B. Mohr, 1924.

Eck, Samuel. *Über die Herkunft des Individualitätsgedanken bei Schleiermacher*. Giessen, 1908.

Flückiger, Felix. *Philosophie und Theologie bei Schleiermacher*. Zollikon-Zurich: Evangelischer Verlag, 1947.

Funk, Robert W., ed. *Schleiermacher as Contemporary*. New York: Herder and Herder, 1970.

Gundolf, Friedrich. "Schleiermachers Romantik." *Deutsche Vierteljahresschrift für Literaturwissenschaft und Geistesgeschichte* 3 (1924): 418 ff.

Hertel, Friedrich. *Das theologische Denken Schleiermachers untersucht an der 1. Aufl. der Reden*. Zurich, 1965.

Hirsch, Emmanuel. *Geschichte der neuern evangelischen Theologie*. Gütersloh: C. Bertelsmann, 1952–66.

Johnson, William A. *On Religion: A Study of Theological Method in Schleiermacher and Nygren*. Leiden: E. J. Brill, 1964.

Jörgensen, Paul. *Die Ethik Schleiermachers*. Munich: Chr. Kaiser, 1959.

Kappstein, Theodor. *Schleiermachers Weltbild und Lebensanschauung*. Munich, 1921.

Kluckhohn, Paul. *Das Ideengut der deutschen Romantik*. Halle, 1941.

Mackintosh, Hugh Ross. *Types of Modern Theology*. New York: Charles Scribner's Sons, 1937.

Mann, Gustav. *Das Verhältnis der Schleiermacherschen Dialektik zu Schellingschen Philosophie*. Stuttgart: Stuttgarter Vereins-Buchdruckerei, 1914.

Martin, Alfred von. "Das Wesen der romantischen Religiosität." *Deutsche Vierteljahresschrift für Literaturwissenschaft und Geistesgeschichte* 3 (1924): 367 ff.

Mulert, Hermann. *Schleiermachers geschichtsphilosophische Ansichten in ihrer Bedeutung für seine Theologie*. Giessen: Alfred Töpelmann, 1917.

——————. *Schleiermacher und die Gegenwart*. Frankfurt, 1934.

Naumann, Friedrich, ed. *Schleiermacher der Philosoph des Glaubens*. (Essays by E. Troeltsch, A. Titus, P. Natrop, P. Hensel, S. Eck, M. Rade.) Berlin, 1910.

Niebuhr, Richard R. *Schleiermacher on Christ and Religion: A New Introduction*. New York: Charles Scribner's Sons, 1964.

Reble, Albert. *Schleiermachers Kulturphilosophie*. Erfurt: Kurt Stenger, 1935.

Samson, Holger. *Die Kirche als Grundbegriff der theologischen Ethik Schleiermachers*. Zollikon: Evangelischer Verlag, 1958.

Scholz, Heinrich. *Christentum und Wissenschaft in Schleiermachers Glaubenslehre*. Berlin: Verlag Duncker, 1911.

Schultz, Franz. "Romantik und Romantisch." *Deutsche Vierteljahresschrift für Literaturwissenschaft und Geistesgeschichte* 3 (1924): 349 ff.

Schultz, Werner. *Das Verhältnis von Ich und Wirklichkeit in der religiösen Anthropologie Schleiermachers.* Göttingen: Vandenhoeck & Ruprecht, 1935.

——————. *Die Grundprinzipien der Religionsphilosophie Hegels und der Theologie Schleiermachers, ein Vergleich.* Berlin: Junker and Dünnhaupt, 1937.

——————. *Schleiermacher und der Protestantismus.* Hamburg-Bergstedt: Evangelischer Verlag, 1957.

Seifert, Paul. *Die Theologie des jungen Schleiermachers.* Gütersloh: Bertelsmann, 1960.

Senft, Christoph. *Wahrhaftigkeit und Wahrheit, die Theologie des 19. Jahrhunderts zwischen Orthodoxie und Aufklärung.* Tübingen: J. C. B. Mohr, 1956.

Spiegler, Gerhard. *The Eternal Covenant: Schleiermacher's Experiment in Cultural Theology.* New York: Harper & Row, 1967.

Süsskind, Hermann. *Christentum und Geschichte bei Schleiermacher.* Tübingen: J. C. B. Mohr, 1909.

——————. *Der Einfluss Schellings auf die Entwicklung von Schleiermachers System.* Tübingen: J. C. B. Mohr, 1909.

Tice, Terrence. *Schleiermacher Bibliography.* Princeton: Princeton Theological Seminary (pamphlet no. 12), 1966.

Trillhaas, Wolfgang. *Schleiermachers Predigt und das homiletische Problem.* Leipzig, 1933.

Ungern-Sternberg, Arthur von. *Freiheit und Wirklichkeit, Schleiermachers philosophische Reifeweg durch den deutschen Idealismus.* Gotha: Leopold Klotz, 1931.

Wehrung, Georg. *Der geschichtsphilosophische Standpunkt Schleiermachers zur Zeit seiner Freundshaft mit den Romantikern.* Strassburg: C. Müh & Co., 1907.

——————. *Die philosophisch-theologische Methode Schleiermachers.* Göttingen: E. A. Huth, 1915.

——————. *Schleiermacher in der Zeit seines Werdens.* Gütersloh: Bertelsmann, 1927.

Wendland, Johannes. *Die religiöse Entwicklung Schleiermachers.* Tübingen: J. C. B. Mohr. 1915.

Willich, Ehrenfried von. *Aus Schleiermachers Hause. Jugenderinnerungen seines Stiefsohnes.* Berlin, 1909.

INDEX OF PERSONS

Index of Persons

221

Schlegel, August
Wilhelm, 31 f., 46,
61, 64, 181, 209

Schlegel, Friedrich, 22,
27, 29 ff., 36, 42,
46, 61, 64 ff., 69,
181, 200, 209

Schleiermacher, Daniel
(Grandfather), 6,
7

Schleiermacher, Gottlieb
(Father), 7, 8, 10,
14, 19, 23

- -, Katharina, née
Stubenrauch
(Mother), 7, 10

- -, Charlotte (Sister
"Lotte"), 7, 11,
29, 30, 73

- -, Carl (Brother), 7

- -, Nanny (Half-sister),
11, 211

- -, Nathanael (Son),
199, 211

Schmalz, 93, 95

Schmidt, W., 184 n. 7

Scholz, Heinrich, 104 n.
59, 121 n. 101

Schuckmann, 92

Schultz, Franz, 31

Schulz, Dr., 191

Schweizer, Alexander, 99

Seifert, P., 22 n. 19

Semler, 12, 15, 76

Shaftesbury, 36

Shakespeare, 181

Sigismund, 193

Socrates, 79

Sophocles, 11

Spalding, 26, 74

Spener, 53

Spinoza, 8, 22, 23, 43,
44, 55, 74, 154

Steffens, Henrich, 76, 77,
79, 86, 91, 98, 212,
213

Stein, 91 f., 93, 95, 165

Steinthal, 176

Stewart, J. S., 42 n. 27,
84 n. 27

Stolberg, 13

Strauss, David Friedrich,
135, 149

Strauss, F., 212 n. 5

Stubenrauch, Judith,
née Chabanon, 16

Stubenrauch, Samuel
Ernst Timotheus,
7, 14 ff., 20, 23, 82

Süvern, 95

Tacitus, 11

Tertullian, 107

Theophrastus, 11

Tholuck, 124

Tice, Terrence, 104 n.
59

Tieck, 31, 61, 69

Tillich, Paul, 132

Trillhaas, 201, 205

Troeltsch, 154

Twesten, A., 34, 79 n.
11, 102 f., 111

Uhden, 95

Varnhagen, Karl August,
86 n. 37

Varnhagen, Rachel, 27

Vater, 77

Veit, Dorothea, 65

Virgil, 11

Voltaire, 205

Voss, Johann Heinrich,
181

Wackenroder, 31

Wehrung, George, 116,
153, 154, 202

Weiss, Bruno, 152

Wichern, 124

Wieland, 12, 66

Wilhelmina, Princess, 91

Willich, Ehrenfried von,
(Stepson of
Schleiermacher),
47 n. 46, 210

Willich, Ernst von, 68,
210

- -, Henriette von, née
von Mühlenfels,
210 ff.

Wolf, Friedrich August,
15 f., 77, 78, 95,
178

Wolfart, Dr., 210

Wolff, Christian, 15, 76,
77

Wolff, Pastor, 28

Zeller, Eduard, 183

Zinzendorf, 10, 103, 130